Only the Names Have Been Changed

Only the Names Have Been Changed

Dragnet, the Police Procedural, and Postwar Culture

Claudia Calhoun

University of Texas Press *Austin*

Printed in the United States of America
First edition, 2022
First paperback printing, 2026

♾ The paper used in this book meets the minimum requirements of ANSI/NISO Z39.48-1992 (R1997) (Permanence of Paper).

Library of Congress Cataloging-in-Publication Data

Names: Calhoun, Claudia, author.
Title: Only the names have been changed : Dragnet, the police procedural, and postwar culture / Claudia Calhoun.
Description: First edition. | Austin : University of Texas Press, 2022. | Includes bibliographical references and index.
Identifiers:
LCCN 2022001419
ISBN 978-1-4773-2539-1 (paperback)
ISBN 978-1-4773-2540-7 (pdf)
ISBN 9781477325414 (ePub)
Subjects: LCSH: Los Angeles (Calif.). Police Department—In mass media. | Dragnet (Radio program) | Dragnet (Radio program)—Influence. | Dragnet (Television program : 1951–1959) | Dragnet (Television program : 1951–1959)—Influence. | Television cop shows—History and criticism. | Television cop shows—Social aspects.
Classification: LCC PN1992.77.D736 C35 2022 | DDC 791.45/72—dc23/eng/20220519
LC record available at https://lccn.loc.gov/2022001419

doi:10.7560/325384

Contents

ACKNOWLEDGMENTS

A LONG PROJECT ACCRUES MANY debts of gratitude. Thanks go first to my dissertation advisors, Joanne Meyerowitz and Charles Musser, who helped this project take shape. Thanks also Jean-Christophe Agnew and Ronald Gregg for their careful reading and thoughtful comments in the dissertation stage. Thank you to manuscript reviewers Jason Mittell, Kathy Battles, and Neil Verma, who made later drafts so much better. Thank you to Jim Burr at the University of Texas Press, who shepherded this project through unprecedented times.

I am grateful for so many scholars and friends. Josh Glick, obviously. Annie Berke. A New York–based television crew made up of Brandy Monk-Payton, Melissa Phruksachart, Linde Murugan, and Feng-Mei Heberer. The Ladies Dissertation Roundtable (Emily Johnson, Jadzia Biskupska, Caitlin Verboon, and Mattie Fitch) was as great as it sounds. Yale's Graduate Writing Center provided much support, including the star writing group led by Laurie Lomask and including Yan Yang and Shari Rabin. I benefitted greatly from "Rough Cut," the works-in-progress series of the Film and Media Studies Program, organized by Misha Mihailova and Katherine Germano, at which I received guidance from John MacKay, Francesco Cassetti, Brigitte Peucker, and Dudley Andrew. Tim Retzloff, Leigh Ann Wheeler, Deborah Jaramillo, and Catherine Martin sent me valuable sources. J. D. Connor influenced this project by offering me new ways of thinking about media. I am grateful to Josh Alvizu for research assistance. To Anila Gill, copy editor and inspiration. To Miriam Posner, who, in just living her life, has served as a model scholar-teacher-human being. And to so many others: Megan Asaka, Alex Beasley, Jordan Brower, Marie-Amelie George, Carolee Klimchock, Najwa Mayer, Devin McGeehan-Muchmore, Raisa Sidenova, Chloe Taft, and Lauren Tilton.

Thank you to colleagues at New York University, especially Anna McCarthy, Dana Polan, Antonia Lant, and Toby Lee. The faculty of the Department of Visual and Performing Arts at Fairfield University has created a wonderfully supportive environment, and I am so grateful for that. Special thanks to my chairs, Marice Rose and Kathy Schwab; longtime program director Laura Nash; and film folks Patrick Brooks, Meryl O'Connor, and Dennis Donovan.

I received research support in the form of a John F. Enders Research Grant from Yale University, allowing me to visit key archives without restriction. I also thank the College of Arts and Sciences Publication Fund at Fairfield University for its help with publication.

This project was immeasurably improved by the generosity of Michael Hayde, who bought me lunch, gave me hard-to-find materials, and donated his research on *Dragnet* to the Library of American Broadcasting at the University of Maryland. Thanks to Michael Henry and the UMD staff for making those materials available to me before they were catalogued. Mark Quigley at the UCLA Film and Television Archive guided me through their enormous and invaluable collection. I also thank the librarians and the archivists at the Margaret Herrick Library of the Academy of Motion Picture Arts and Sciences, UCLA Special Collections, the Warner Bros. Archive at USC, and the Mason Library at Keene State College.

I could not have done this project without the hundreds of independent collectors of "old time radio" and early television who have made their personal archives available online. I wish I could thank them all by name.

I am deeply indebted to the developers of Scrivener, Zotero, and OpenOffice/LibreOffice. Microsoft has more of my money, but y'all have more of my heart.

More personally: Ashley Mathis, Kim Baker, Rebecca Mauldin, and Karuna Bunk were and are great friends and have supported me in writing and in so many other things. I could always hear the cheers of the JHJ Girls—Maggie Jennings Nudelman, Charlisa Daniels, and Saralyn McMorris—from the sidelines. My family—Karen and Warren Calhoun, Alzay Calhoun and Tonya Howard Calhoun, and Martina Calhoun—offered not only the comforts of family but also, at different points, the comforts of rent-free living; cold, hard cash; and copyediting services. My grandparents, Virgie and Theo Gipson, supported me every day of my life, and their memories are a blessing. In more recent times, the Teversons, the Rainses, and the Gore-Booths have very politely inquired into how the book was going and then allowed me to dodge the question, which is how I knew I was loved.

Finally, I would like to express gratitude for Richard Teverson and Ella Patricia Calhoun Teverson. Richard arrived midway through this project, bringing patience and kindness and intelligence, and he always, always, always helped. Ella came late and didn't help at all, to be honest—but I love her very much anyway.

Only the Names Have Been Changed

INTRODUCTION

Dragnet and the Police Procedural

DURING THE LATTER HALF OF the twentieth century, Sergeant Joe Friday of the Los Angeles Police Department was the best-known police officer in the United States. He was, of course, a fictional character, one of the lead detectives on the radio and television series *Dragnet*, which appeared on broadcast schedules across the United States for decades. Americans knew Sergeant Friday by name, by face, by voice, and by badge number (714). They even knew him by staff notes, according to one telling anecdote from the height of *Dragnet*'s popularity: One day in or around 1954, a Hollywood post office received an envelope with musical notes scrawled across the front. Rather than sending the letter to dead mail, a postal worker who could read music hummed the notes aloud—"DUM-DE-DUM-DUM." The post office forwarded the letter to Jack Webb, the creator, director, and star of *Dragnet*, a show so distinctly recognizable that the opening four notes of its theme music could stand in for a street address.[1]

Best known as a television series, *Dragnet* appeared across media and across culture from its creation in 1949. It ran first on radio (1949–1957), then moved to television (1951–1959), and was made into a feature film in 1954.[2] Inescapable in the 1950s, *Dragnet* remained a cultural touchstone in later decades. It was one of the first shows to be brought back to television, when it was rebooted for a second run from 1967 to 1970. And it was rebooted again, for shorter runs, from 1989 to 1991 and again from 2003 to 2004. During the network and cable eras, the 1950s and 1960s series were widely syndicated in markets across the United States. In the streaming era, terrestrial viewers can still watch episodes of *Dragnet* on nostalgia channels such as MeTV, while cord-cutters can watch on Pluto TV, YouTube, and other streaming sites. Modern viewers can regularly see the show's impact in the genre that it redefined, and that became one of the medium's enduring genres: the police procedural. Today, even as television has changed, the police procedural

FIGURE 0.1. On the cover of *Time*, Jack Webb appears alongside imagery from his show. Notice the notes of *Dragnet*'s iconic theme music wafting behind Webb's right shoulder. Cover illustration by Boris Chaliapin. From TIME, https://time.com/. © 1954 TIME USA LLC. All rights reserved. Used under license.

persists, whether encountered on network television in shows such as NBC's *Law and Order: SVU* (1999–present) or on streaming services in shows such as Amazon Prime's *Bosch* (2014–2021).

When it premiered at the tail end of the 1940s, *Dragnet* felt new and fresh to radio audiences, who were used to more sensational stories of crime and policing. Instead of focusing on crime and criminals with storytelling dependent on chases and gunfire, *Dragnet* told its story entirely from the police perspective, and it preferred minor crimes to major ones. Each episode was narrated by the calm, serious Detective Sergeant Joe Friday, who, alongside his police partner, interviewed victims and witnesses, tracked down leads, discussed the case with their captain, visited the police laboratory, researched in the records office, and eventually, usually, captured the culprit. But in *Dragnet*, the process—the procedure—was as critical as the outcome.

Dragnet also became part of American policing, as Jack Webb's Sergeant Friday came to stand in for police officers everywhere. With his laconic delivery, emotional detachment, and unapologetic commitment to the job, he was the ideal officer within a "professionalized" police department. The LAPD, which undertook reforms in the 1940s and 1950s that turned it into an internationally recognized model of professional policing, embodied the tenets of the philosophy: the management of crime through an organized, hierarchical structure; the use of advanced scientific and technological tools; and the necessity of independence from political pressures. The reforming LAPD wholly embraced *Dragnet*: in return for lending the show its authority, its iconography, and its cases, the department received a radio and television show, with a regular audience of many millions, as a publicity vehicle.

In addition to its place within the history of American policing, *Dragnet* must also be understood more broadly, as an artifact of the postwar period. The immediate postwar era brought new possibilities and pressures in all areas of American life, and the police procedural genre was an expression of that transition. *Dragnet* and other procedurals provided to Americans an education in their responsibilities as postwar citizens: to be informed about the law and cooperative with the police. *Dragnet* emerged as the most compelling example of the genre. Its creators brought a new realism to the police story, an aesthetic that imbued the show with an explicitly pedagogical purpose. By listening on radio and watching on television and film, audiences could learn how the police actually worked at the same time that they learned how, as citizens, they could support the work of the officers who were committed to keeping them safe.

To illuminate the show as both media history and cultural history, I situate *Dragnet* within distinct but overlapping frames, each of which constitutes a chapter in the book: as a reflection of postwar confidence in institutional efficacy, a program of distinctive aesthetic influence, a cultural site that built prestige and significance as it crossed mediums, and a document of postwar policing. Looking back at *Dragnet*, we can see how popular media participated centrally in the elaboration of dominant culture in the years after World War II, defining and modeling appropriate forms of civic participation. While versions of *Dragnet* were produced in nearly every decade of the second half of the twentieth century, I concentrate on the years between 1945 and 1960, during which the show defined itself and redefined the police procedural genre. Looking forward from *Dragnet*, we can see how the police procedural remains a cultural space that presents to audiences dominant—and restricted—understandings of the police and their relationship to communities in the United States.

The Pedagogy of the Police Procedural

Although the police procedural has been a popular genre across media for many decades, it has attracted surprisingly little scholarly interest.[3] The topic of crime and media, especially crime shows on television, has attracted considerably more attention.[4] But the police procedural is a distinct genre with specific characteristics, worthy of its own attention. A police procedural narrative is distinct from investigative stories that focus on the inductive reasoning of a brilliant mind, and distinct from narratives that prioritize spectacular encounters between cops and criminals. Police procedurals present to listeners and viewers what appears to be the full investigation of a crime. A procedural drama usually begins with a crime (most often a murder), introduces the police investigators early in the narrative, and then follows their progress through to the final confrontation with the criminal. Though the narrative might also follow, in parallel, the actions of the criminal, the police investigation drives the story.

As Haden Guest summarizes, the main interest of the procedural is "the very police system itself," including "the routine tasks, or procedures, that together comprise the collective labor of law enforcement agencies and their officers."[5] The commission of the crime is not only a means by which to tell an entertaining story but also a prompt to display to the audience the inner workings of law enforcement. The procedural narrative includes regular discussions of the steps of the investigation—explanations of what the police know about the crime, what the perpetrators are likely to do, what the investigators need to do next. Procedurals almost always include scenes that display specialized spaces, personnel, and equipment: medical examiners' offices, forensics laboratories, and expansive file rooms. The audience is brought into the process of the investigation via privileged access to both the logical reasoning and the practical tools of professional investigators.

A defining element of the police procedural genre is realism, which is connoted through narrative choices—including the focus on the *work* of policework—as well as through aesthetic choices. The aesthetic choices that connote "realism" have changed over time and have depended on the expectations of each medium. In 1940s police procedurals films, shooting on location was key to connoting realism for audiences accustomed to films made entirely on sound stages. On radio, procedurals restrained their sound effects in order to mark their difference from more sensational crime stories. Later, television procedurals used handheld cameras to simulate documentary realism. The look and sound of the genre has varied across time and mediums, but what remains constant is the necessity to convince audiences that the world presented to them is contiguous with the world they inhabit.

Through this realistic display, the police procedural has functioned not only as a means of audience entertainment but also as a means of civic education—a means of public pedagogy. The concept of public pedagogy has been most closely associated with Henry Giroux, who has explored the ways in which learning happens outside of institutions specifically dedicated to the purpose. Building on the work of Stuart Hall, Giroux argues that popular culture, and especially media culture, shapes individual and group identity, as powerfully as institutions like schools and churches do. Writes Giroux, "It is through the pedagogical force of culture that identities are constructed, citizenship rights are enacted, and possibilities are developed for translating acts of interpretation into forms of intervention."[6] For Giroux, the impact of a single text is not as important as the *saturation*. In his work on Disney, for example, Giroux is as deeply concerned about the power and reach of the Disney Corporation as he is about the way its smothering discourse of "innocence" discourages critical engagement. Giroux recognizes that texts are polysemous (contain many possible readings), but he also argues that we cannot ignore the unevenness of power. As Giroux insists, we must give critical attention to these texts that "saturate everyday life."[7] The police procedural is not a corporate behemoth, but a genre can saturate culture as surely as a brand can, and the police procedural genre has saturated everyday life since World War II, when *Dragnet* and its procedural brethren began spreading these specific narratives across film, radio, and television. By offering realistic, detailed, *repeated* narratives of the police, the genre offers a shared curriculum in citizenship.

Citizenship, a term with many meanings, has been the topic of a broad and ongoing conversation in media studies. Strands of this conversation look at the ways in which nonfiction media has shaped citizens through the delivery of news and public affairs programming, modes that often explicitly understand themselves as part of a democratic project.[8] Other scholarship looks at the relationship between media and cultural citizenship, particularly in the context of the "consumer's republic" of the post–World War II era when, as Sarah Banet-Weiser writes, "the very definition of citizenship shifts to include the commercial realm."[9] The police procedural sits in an unusual place in this conversation, as a genre of fictional, commercial media that nevertheless engages explicitly with the real-life politics of contemporary civic life. The genre's understanding of citizenship is the traditional, political definition of liberal democracies—citizenship as a set of rights and responsibilities. So that citizens might receive the benefits of individual liberty, the state promises public safety. In exchange, the citizen owes compliance with the state's rules and regulations. The genre seldom concerns itself with the complexities of legal citizenship; the procedural understands the rights as universally due and the responsibilities as universally owed. In the police procedural, to be a citizen is to behave like one.

Across the genre, police procedurals teach audiences that the police are competent, well-trained officers who follow the clear guidelines of a professionalized system of policing. Audiences learn that the police work tirelessly on behalf of the citizens they serve, that individual officers know the law thoroughly and apply it in an unbiased way, and that competent police are essential for public safety. Audiences also learn how the behavior of ordinary citizens either helps or hinders the police as they do their jobs. In procedurals, audiences see the clear public benefit of respectful cooperation with law enforcement as well as the community harm caused by unhelpful citizens, including the bad actors of the criminal class.

Procedural elements can be found in films and radio programs before World War II, but after the war the police procedural evolved into its current position as an integral part of the media landscape. Close study of the procedurals in this period shows us that the pedagogy of the procedural as we have inherited it was not oriented toward exploring universal truths but toward teaching specifically postwar lessons.

The Police Procedural and the Postwar World

Although police stories have been present in media since the earliest days of film, it wasn't until the 1930s that an interest in telling "realistic" stories of police investigations, in films such as *G-Men* (1935) and radio programs such as *Calling All Cars* (1933–1939), emerged. And it wasn't until the 1940s (with the help of *Dragnet*) that the police procedural genre truly came into its own. Between 1945 and 1960, police procedurals exploded across film and broadcasting. A nonexhaustive list includes *This Is Your FBI* (radio, 1945–1953), *The Naked City* (film, 1948; television, 1958–1963), *The Street with No Name* (film, 1948), *Port of New York* (film, 1949), *Panic in the Streets* (film, 1950), *Bunco Squad* (radio, 1950; television, 1950), *Between Midnight and Dawn* (film, 1950), *Southside 1-1000* (film, 1950), *The Silent Men* (radio, 1951–1952), *The Lineup* (radio, 1950–1953; television, 1954–1960; film, 1958), *The Man behind the Badge* (television, 1953–1955), *21st Precinct* (radio, 1953–1956), *Highway Patrol* (television, 1955–1959), *M Squad* (television, 1957–1960), and *The Case against Brooklyn* (film, 1958). *Dragnet*, on radio, television, and film, was foremost among these in the breadth of its success, the depth of its cultural resonance, and the length of its influence. But it is important to place *Dragnet* within its cohort to understand the cultural concerns with which the show engaged.

The explosion of police procedurals in the postwar period raises compelling questions about the era. What prompted this transmedia preoccupation with the procedures of law enforcement in this period? One strand of scholarship encourages us to look toward the Cold War context for answers. Cultural histories of the period are often concerned with the ways in which Cold War concerns are expressed through media. Highly influential has been the work of Elaine Tyler May, who saw the anti-Communist political and military strategy of "containment" deployed metaphorically throughout culture, including media.[10] Other important work discusses the atomic fears expressed through the postwar renewal of science fiction and describes the uses of television as a Cold War weapon.[11]

A parallel strand of scholarship in postwar cultural history de-emphasizes Cold War frameworks. As Peter Kuznick and James Gilbert have argued, many aspects of domestic life seemed to be "remarkably untouched" by the Cold War, including areas of gender, family, sexuality, and class.[12] As Kristin Matthews writes, Americans were not only fighting Cold War battles in this era "but also engaging in a complicated internal battle to frame the terms of citizenship and nationhood amid a changing set of political, social, and economic realities."[13] As these scholars argue, historical processes apart from, or alongside, the major Cold War debates determined many areas of culture.

It is reasonable to try to understand police procedurals within the context of "Cold War culture." Indeed, the scattered scholarship on these films and series has tended to discuss them in the context of film noir, which is itself most often read as a space for the expression of progressive politics within the context of Cold War anti-Communism. Most recently, Dennis Broe has written about postwar procedural films as an attempt to "contain" the more radical expressions of film noir. Broe writes that while transgressive noir films featured "the criminal cop, the vigilante cop, or the psychotic fugitive," police procedural films "were snapped back into conformity by the lead character of the lawman or woman, by the validation of government agencies, and by the fetishization of surveillance modes."[14] Readings like Broe's are supported by the industrial context in which these films were produced. The HUAC investigations, the prosecution of the Hollywood Ten, and the creation of the blacklist deeply impacted postwar filmmaking, including curtailing the careers of personnel involved in procedurals, most prominently *The Naked City* writer Albert Maltz and director Jules Dassin.

But the development of the procedural genre cannot be fully explained by the context of Cold War politics. The films and series themselves directly engage with other issues, such as nonatomic advancements in science and technology, and domestic economic crimes like racketeering. Haden Guest, whose work represents the most complete study of the police procedural genre, argues that postwar police procedurals reflect a concern with "the general state of government . . . embodying both the postwar administration's overriding concern for the nation's economy and the dramatic expansion of government agencies."[15] Of the procedurals in the semi-documentary style, Guest sees a focus on the policing of a peacetime "homefront" that "suggest[s] a deeper connection and continuity between the war and post-war periods."[16]

Indeed, the postwar procedural is most profitably understood as a genre that responded to a key question of the transition from war to postwar: What happened to the buildup of training, technology, intelligence, institutional capacity, and bureaucratic knowledge required to fight and win a half-decade-long global conflict? The arc of the police procedural genre suggests that these competencies were translated into the workings of the managerial state, and particularly into structures of law enforcement. The successes of war mobilization in the United States led to increased confidence in the efficacy of government and other large-scale institutions. The police procedural expressed this new, distinctive confidence through its understanding of the efficacy and necessity of law enforcement agents. The police procedural, then, is not a Cold War genre but a demobilization genre—or, rather, a remobilization genre. In the explosion of police procedurals across mediums, we see the emergence of an ideology in which American democracy is possible only through the management of individuals, communities, and cities by an organized police force.

Perhaps ironically for a crime genre, key lessons of the genre are found not in the representation of crime and criminals but in the representation of average citizens. Procedurals' attention to the larger social world, the people who inhabit it, and the relationship between police and citizens was a particularly postwar development. Reflecting the ideals of wartime cooperation, police procedurals stressed interconnectedness between Americans, de-emphasized distinctions among citizens, and intentionally included groups who had been subject to exclusions by these same kinds of narratives in previous decades. At the same time, these films and series reinforced familiar racial and gender divisions. Film, radio, and television procedurals—each in their own medium, and also influenced by one another—presented both an expanded circle of citizenship *and* a hierarchy of citizenship in which a demilitarized organization man was at the top. These films and series seldom, if ever, directly acknowledged histories of exclusion or discrimination; as noted in the previous section, the procedural understands citizenship rights as universally awarded and citizenship responsibilities as universally owed. But the shift in patterns of representation nevertheless reveals an awareness of histories that are never addressed.

The representations of everyday citizens in the genre was more remarkable than the representations of police officers: postwar police procedurals intentionally broadened the boundaries of citizenship to include more kinds of people more equally, and to emphasize the ways in which citizens of different backgrounds were bound to one another. We can see this by looking at the maneuvering of genre conventions within each medium and how each sought to include communities that would have gone unrepresented in similar stories before the war. Films tended to make this argument visually, seeking to capture onscreen populations marked by visual differences. Radio and television programs had scope to represent a range of backgrounds over the duration of a season or a series, building new conventions and presentations of difference.

Panic in the Streets (Elia Kazan, 1950) is the best example of film's use of visual space to expand the boundaries of representation. In the film, the city of New Orleans is threatened by an outbreak of pneumonic plague. The disease is discovered in a corpse that had been dumped on the docks, and the film follows the authorities who are desperately trying to track the killers, likely infected, who threaten to spread the epidemic throughout the city. The search is a joint effort by federal and local authorities, led by Lieutenant Commander Clint Reed, a doctor from the United States Public Health Service (Richard Widmark), and Captain Tom Warren of the New Orleans Police Department (Paul Douglas). Narratively as well as visually, the film emphasizes the interdependence of the communities it presents.

Director Elia Kazan brought his personal fascination with New Orleans and its people to *Panic in the Streets*. The director explained, "I used to wander around that city night and day, so I knew it well."[17] His film, too, wanders around the city. The audience sees segments of the city that seldom appear in Hollywood films as the film tracks the movements of the investigators and the criminals through New Orleans. Casting nonprofessional and local actors in all but the leading roles highlights the average faces and distinctive accents of New Orleans residents. The film pays unusual attention to racially integrated—and racially stratified—spaces. One scene brings the audience into the integrated brotherhood of dock workers in the National Maritime Union hiring hall, where we see dozens of workers crowded into the same waiting room, mingling without distinction. Later in the film, the investigators board a ship called the *Nile Queen*, and the film displays for the audience the variety of people who work on the New Orleans docks, including white officers and the Black, white, and Asian ship workers.

The film's relentless framing reinforces the interconnectedness of the residents and transients of New Orleans. The frame is always packed with people: in Joe MacDonald's deep-focus photography, it is filled from back to front as well as from side to side. There are clearly lead actors, but they are seldom picked out by close-ups or special lighting. Kazan's camera stays at a distance, keeping these men in the context of their work and the people around them. As the officers wind their way through New Orleans, they reinforce lessons learned from war mobilization: how necessary everyone's participation is in protecting the social body from harm. In *Panic in the Streets*, all residents are included as constituent parts of the synergetic workings of this urban space managed by white, male officers.

As film lent conciseness to procedural narratives, radio and television brought expansion through seriality, opening up their neighborhoods and cities week after week. To present more diverse worlds through sound, radio producers had to contend with the conventions of aural characterization. In the decades before World War II, radio had created a catalog of ethnic types signaled by accents and dialects with varying degrees of sympathy and care. Across the dial, radio programs of all kinds exploited the quick characterizations of Irish cops and housemaids, African American train porters and domestic workers, and Jewish tinkerers and shopkeepers. Shortcuts to setting were provided by accents—a stereotyped Chinese accent signaled San Francisco, and the stern, halting English of caricatures of American Indians indicated a Western frontier space.

Seeking to avoid these conventions, procedural radio shows like CBS's *21st Precinct* (1953–1956) experimented with different means of aural inclusion. In some radio shows, including *Dragnet*, expansion of the citizenry was achieved through the removal of vocal differentiation, signaling difference instead through contextual cues such as descriptions of the neighborhood. *21st Precinct*, written and directed by crime radio veteran Stanley Niss, sought to connote difference while avoiding stereotypes. In "The Dollar" (May 12, 1954), the racial and ethnic diversity of the setting is made audible as the officers of New York's Twenty-First Precinct respond to an emergency call in "lower Harlem." The officers, led by Captain Frank Kennelly, find that a woman has been stabbed to death by her husband. The officers interview the victim's mother, who speaks only Spanish. For several minutes, the captain and the mother speak to each other in Spanish. The captain stops every few lines to translate for his fellow officer, and for the English-speaking audience:

> MOTHER: Yo estaba aquí.
> KENNELLY [*to another officer*]: She was here in the kitchen.
> MOTHER: Traté de ayudarla. . . . Tenía mucho miedo.
> KENNELLY: She tried to help her.
> MOTHER: [*Speaks quickly in Spanish about how drunk the husband was.*]
> KENNELLY: Bueno, bueno, espere un momento. [*To officer*] She said she was very frightened, she was in the kitchen, heard her daughter scream, she ran in and tried to help her, but she was afraid he'd kill her too. [*To mother*] Bueno, adónde fue cuando cayó?
> MOTHER: Afuera . . . corriendo.
> KENNELLY: Por la puerta? [*To officer*] She says he just ran out, Mac. Out the door. . . .
> MOTHER: Dijo que me mataría que no me fuera.
> KENNELLY: Él dijo eso?
> MOTHER: Sí, él dijo eso.
> KENNELLY: She says he threatened to kill her, too, if she didn't get out of the room.
> MOTHER: Tenía miedo, mucho miedo.[18]

Strikingly unusual for a fictional show, this exchange requires listeners to sit and listen to dialogue they are not expected to understand and attempts to force sympathy across a linguistic divide. This episode explicitly includes a Latinx family in a contemporary (rather than historical) context and treats native Spanish speakers in a respectful way, breaking from precedent in radio characterization.

Other characterizations were more awkward but still provide evidence of an attempt to include more people in the circle of citizenship. The same episode of *21st Precinct* also characterizes an African American New Yorker, though the show has more difficulty creating a characterization that avoids elements of caricature. With no language difference to utilize, the show employs other markers to signal racial difference: through his name, "Leroy Purford"; through his job as a fry cook; and through a slight accent and the use of vernacular English. The most problematic signifier is Purford's performance of deference: he refers to each of the officers as "sir," while the officers call him "Leroy." However, although Leroy is awkwardly characterized, he is not stereotyped, and the information he gives the police leads them straight to the criminal, who is hiding out in a restaurant. When the Black Purford and the white ethnic police officers arrive to find Latino Bernardo (the suspect), the scene of the arrest in the restaurant marks one of the most ethnically integrated scenes in postwar radio drama.

As the *21st Precinct* example shows, efforts at aural inclusion did not erase distinctions between citizens. These distinctions are legible in both the procedurals and their reception. In *Panic in the Streets*, for example, reviewers marked the realism of Elia Kazan's New Orleans by noting the presence of "local plain people, drifters and trollops," or by the "extraordinary rogues' gallery of types . . . plus the citizens, plain and fancy, of New Orleans."[19] These reviewers noticed the unexpectedly wide range of citizens included in the film while also making judgments on their deviation from the presumed norm, thus indicating the contingency of their inclusion.

On the broadcasting side, while radio dramas evolved their characterizations of citizens, early television procedurals attempted neither the kinds of experimentation that had been made on radio nor the visual inclusion of films like *Panic in the Streets*. Television procedurals of the early 1950s—even those adapted directly from radio series—presented all-white worlds of cops, criminals, and citizens. However, in the late 1950s, procedurals reintroduced intentional investigations of race and ethnicity. Most prominently, the landmark series *Naked City* (1958–1963) brought new energy to the genre through its interest in emotional and psychological realism as well as its earnest attempts to broaden the view of television procedurals. The premiere episode, "Meridian" (Sept. 9, 1958), which opened with a scene in the apartment of an impoverished Puerto Rican family, made clear that *Naked City* was invested, as the original film was, in showing citizens on screen who looked a little more like audiences at home.

All citizens in procedurals, regardless of background and irrespective of medium, were subject to the authority of white male police officers, who comfortably inhabited their place at the top of the hierarchy of citizenship. The procedural genre presented responsible, compliant masculinity as essential for peacetime civil society, and the officers in charge fulfilled their responsibilities without chafing. The officers in postwar police procedurals tended to be conspicuously unremarkable both demographically (neither old nor young, often from nowhere in particular) and dispositionally (bland, emotionally muted). Some scholars of the postwar United States have described a crisis in masculinity in the period, focusing on cultural expressions of male anxiety. However, as James Gilbert argues, "it is just as plausible to argue that these same public figures were reacting with hostility to the changes that other men in society were quite happy to accept."[20] The ordinariness of the officers and the evident ease with which they performed their duties highlights the genre as a cultural space that reaffirmed, rather than questioned or challenged, stubborn hierarchies of citizenship in the United States.

Within that hierarchy, gender divisions often were reinforced but also sometimes were challenged. The procedural's presentation of comfortable male authority tends to reproduce the traditional divide between men's and women's spheres, as was also common in postwar media more broadly. *Panic in the Streets* includes sensitive domestic scenes between an officer and his wife and child as a contrast to the harried work of investigation and discovery. The world of women, children, and the home is portrayed as essential, as that which balances and gives meaning to the men's work.

At the same time, women at work are surprisingly visible in the procedural. While the genre does seem to prefer that women stay in the domestic sphere, it also reflects the changed status of women in the workplace after the war, when, as Laura McEnaney writes, "many women used their wartime leverage to push the door of opportunity open for good."[21] Especially in radio and television procedurals, white women hold jobs in law enforcement, the privileged site of the genre, though more often as helpers than as managers. Sometimes women appear in small roles as police officers, called in to interrogate female suspects or to oversee the care of children. Most often, women perform less prestigious yet equally necessary support work: as file clerks in records offices, telephone operators at the central switchboard, stenographers taking down confessions, and secretaries typing reports.

Women are also visible in other spaces outside the middle-class home, in the larger world into which the male officers go. Women own and manage stores, rent apartments and rooms in boarding houses, work at diners and in offices, and work as actresses, models, and sex workers. Women work to support their families when men are not around, and sometimes even when they are. Women are victims. They are robbed; they go missing; they are beaten; they are raped; they are murdered. Women commit crimes. They neglect their families, abuse drugs, steal cars, forge checks, and murder boyfriends. In the professional realm, women are helpers rather than leaders, but in the wider community, women are included—and therefore addressed—as citizens.

Across film and broadcasting, the postwar police procedural was markedly different from crime storytelling before the war. In these films and series, we see genuine attempts to paint a more diverse social world. Not everyone is fully included, or included in an equal way, but in the attempt we see the lesson of the developing genre: all citizens share in the responsibility to make and keep a peaceful postwar world, a responsibility that is fulfilled by generous cooperation with systems of law enforcement.

The Police Procedural in 2020

Among the many police procedurals produced in the 1940s and 1950s, *Dragnet* emerged as the paradigmatic example of the genre. *Dragnet* exemplified the genre's central tenets: a focus on the work of the police, as done by white male officers who competently manage a diverse body of citizens. More than any other example of the genre, *Dragnet* became, in its moment, a teaching tool recognized for its pedagogical intentions and effectiveness as well as for its popularity and influence. The show's careful, deliberate representation of the relationship between police and citizens over the decade of its original run earned *Dragnet* a privileged site among media artifacts in the 1950s and a reputation that has extended through syndication, reboots, and continuing cultural relevance.

In the following pages, I emphasize how *Dragnet*'s pedagogy was historically situated: reflective of particularly postwar ideologies, formed by aesthetic expectations of older and newer mediums, and shaped by postwar police reform movements. In looking back, I also recognize *Dragnet*'s persistence. Contemporary police procedurals, while reflecting many social and cultural changes between the 1950s and the 2020s, have retained the genre's core elements in different proportions: focus on professional work, restriction to the police perspective, use of realist aesthetics, and incorporation of investigative technologies. The genre continues to teach viewers that the way to ensure public safety is through cooperation between professionalized police and responsible citizens, the same relationship that *Dragnet* represented so effectively.

The underlying ideological structures of the police procedural, and of crime shows more generally, have been challenged in important ways by the racial justice uprisings of the 2010s and 2020s. In 2014 and again in 2020, protests erupted across the United States and the world, inspired by the deaths of Mike Brown, Eric Garner, Sandra Bland, Rekia Boyd, George Floyd, Breonna Taylor, and too many others killed by police officers or while in police custody. The Movement for Black Lives has forced many Americans to confront racism in the criminal justice system as well as to deepen their understandings of the ways in which anti-Black racism has structured all aspects of American society. While activists and members of targeted communities have been actively protesting police brutality for as long as there have been police, many Americans in the first decades of the twenty-first century began to see for the first time that the presence of the police makes some communities less safe rather than more safe.

Among those engaged more deeply in critical reflection in the summer of 2020 were creators and consumers of cop shows. Many reflected publicly on their complicity through social media and other media outlets. Actor Griffin Newman, who had a small role on the police drama *Blue Bloods* (2010–present), donated $11,000—a reflection of his salary from that role—to a bail fund for protestors who had been arrested. On Twitter, he posted his donation receipt and challenged other actors who had made money from playing police officers to "do the math."[22] Many actors followed his example, donating to bail funds and tweeting their receipts.

Writers and producers also took to public forums. Tom Scharpling, who worked on *Monk* (2002–2009) in both capacities, tweeted, "If you—as I have—worked on a TV show or movie in which police are portrayed as lovable goofballs you have contributed to the larger acceptance that cops are implicitly the good guys."[23] Showrunner Warren Leight, who for years has overseen *Law and Order: SVU* (1999–present), the longest-running police procedural in television history, was unusually publicly reflective. In an interview on a *Hollywood Reporter* podcast, Leight was asked whether the police were represented "too positively" by police shows. Leight responded that he was not sure whether, as one person, he was "miscontributing to society," but he was sure about the impact of his genre: "Collectively, are we? *Yeah*."[24]

Television critics also stopped to reflect on the cumulative impact of a mountain of series that privilege the perspective of the police. Alyssa Rosenberg argued in the *Washington Post* that Hollywood should stop making police shows until they can reform their storytelling. As Rosenberg writes, Hollywood is "addict[ed] to stories that portray police departments as more effective than they actually are; crime as more prevalent than it actually is; and police use of force as consistently justified. . . . Given what policing in America has too often become, Hollywood's version of it looks less like fantasy and more like complicity.[25] For *Vulture* readers, the critic Kathryn VanArendonk curated a list of twenty-one procedural series without police protagonists. VanArendonk's list includes narratives that center nondominant perspectives, such as the black female private investigators of *The No. 1 Ladies Detective Agency* (2008–2009), as well as series that push the limits of the form, such as the science-fiction period piece *Quantum Leap* (1989–1993), in which the protagonist is "forced, again and again, to see through other people's eyes."[26] Without meaning to, VanArendonk's list spoke directly to Rosenberg's appeal, in fact demonstrating that Hollywood already has models for procedural storytelling that look less like complicity.

All of these actors, writers, producers, and critics share a belief that fictional police stories—including, and perhaps primarily, the police procedural—have been key spaces through which Americans' understandings of policing have been reflected and taught. In the 1940s and 1950s, the creators of *Dragnet* presented to mid-century listeners and viewers police stories that aligned with a postwar faith in institutions that suffused the larger culture. They struck at the right time, making an aesthetic intervention in a transitioning medium (radio) that allowed the show to gain a foothold in an ascendant medium (television). Within both media history and cultural history, *Dragnet* was an artifact of and for its time.

The next generation of police stories will emerge from the technological and cultural ruptures of today, and will respond to the challenges, beliefs, and aspirations of our own time. In the summer of 2020 the most resonant police story on television was not a contemporary police procedural but the dystopic superhero series *Watchmen* (2019), which won critical acclaim from the moment of its winter premiere and was awarded eleven Emmy Awards the following fall. The creators of *Watchmen* adapted the 1980s graphic novel for the contemporary moment, using the Tulsa Race Massacre of 1921 to frame an alternate future in which vigilante police fight white supremacy. *Watchmen* takes its name from a well-known Latin quotation attributed to Juvenal: "Quis custodiet ipsos custodes?" The query is sometimes translated as, "Who will guard the guards themselves?" Other translations posit, "Who watches the watchmen?" In this era, no American, including and perhaps especially the producers of police procedurals, can escape asking themselves this question, as we are all forced to look deeply at the workings of systems of law enforcement and criminal justice that neglect to protect those they claim to serve.

THE *DRAGNET* EFFECT

The following four chapters explain how *Dragnet* came to sound the way it did, look the way it did, feel the way it did, and take up the space in US culture that it came to occupy. Chapter 1 focuses on the semi-documentary film cycle of the mid- to late 1940s. *Dragnet* was directly inspired by the film *He Walked by Night* (1948), which was one of a number of films exploring a new kind of realism in the postwar period. The majority of the semi-documentary films were dramas of crime and policing; they borrowed techniques from contemporary documentary filmmaking to explore the structures of civic life.

Looking closely at significant films in the cycle—*The House on 92nd Street* (1945), *Call Northside 777* (1948), and *The Wrong Man* (1956)—we can see how these films were documents of a short but significant period of aesthetic experimentation in Hollywood, as well as documents of a longer cultural moment that saw the construction of the ideology of consensus liberalism.

Although *Dragnet* might first come to mind as a television series, it was on radio that it established itself as a police show of unusual authenticity and authority. Chapter 2 analyzes *Dragnet*'s aural aesthetic, explaining how Jack Webb and his team created a compelling narrative through a muted—and deceptively simple—soundscape. The show's aural strategies aligned with its pedagogical orientation: in constructing active listeners, and placing them within the fictional world of the police in the story, *Dragnet* encouraged listeners to sympathize with actual, hardworking officers and to see themselves as active participants in civic life.

Chapter 3 tracks *Dragnet*'s movement from radio into other mediums. *Dragnet* traveled across culture in the 1950s, most significantly through its successful translation from a well-regarded radio program to an important early example of a high-quality television series. The success of its television adaptation allowed *Dragnet* to further saturate postwar culture: in addition to the concurrent radio and television broadcasts, postwar audiences engaged with *Dragnet* through a feature film, a comic strip, radio hits, and licensed merchandise.

Chapter 4 considers the consequences of *Dragnet*'s cultural saturation, exploring the relationship between the fictional police show and the real-life Los Angeles Police Department. *Dragnet* was formed, from the very beginning, through cooperation with the LAPD: its officers volunteered cases to be dramatized for the show, reviewed scripts for accuracy, and served as on-set technical advisors. The relationship benefited both parties. The imprimatur of the LAPD bolstered the show's realist claims, and *Dragnet* helped to rehabilitate the image of the LAPD, offering free publicity that also served to obscure major problems that accompanied the department's postwar reforms.

Through extensive research in industry and newspaper archives, and through close analysis of film, radio, and television texts, I trace *Dragnet*'s importance as a media text and a cultural text, arguing that both histories have depended on the other. By taking *Dragnet* seriously, I suggest that we should take seriously the idea that media artifacts not only reflect historical change but work as agents of change. I hope to show how looking across media and across disciplines leads to new discoveries about the ways in which our culture, and therefore our lives, are shaped by media.

CHAPTER 1

"Our Neo-realism"

The Hollywood Semi-documentary Cycle

Had this story been told in the traditional Hollywood manner, no one would feel tempted to inquire into its implications. But the documentary style in which the film is actually developed changes everything. . . . A story originally intended to feature an exceptional individual turns, by sheer dint of documentary treatment, into a vivid comment on our present mores.

Siegfried Kracauer on *Boomerang!*, "Those Movies with a Message," *Harper's Magazine*, June 1948

"In order to obtain the maximum of realism and authenticity," the final card of the title sequence of the 1947 film *13 Rue Madeleine* tells audiences, "all of the exterior and interior settings in this Motion Picture were photographed in the field—and, wherever possible, at the actual locations." A fade-out then fades into a shot that affirms the statement, with cars, streetcars, and pedestrians passing in front of the camera, a view of the US Capitol that could have been taken only from the National Mall. *The Naked City* does not employ a title card, but any viewer can tell that it, too, was filmed "in the field": the streets of New York are too unpretty, its sidewalks scarred by wide grates and its uneven curbs decorated with litter. In *Phenix City Story*, the newspaperman Clete Roberts and broadcast journalist Ed Strickland stand "in the field" before even the credits begin; on the wide concrete steps of a government building in Alabama, they discuss the recent murder of an attorney general, the story told in the film to come. In these and other films of the 1940s and 1950s, audiences were introduced to a new look and feel within studio-based fiction films as filmmakers borrowed elements from nonfiction filmmaking to create more "realistic" storytelling. Producers and critics described the cycle of films in this style as "documentary," "in the documentary style," or—most often—"semi-documentary."[1]

Media scholars have long noticed that in the years after World War II, Hollywood began producing films that approached real-world topics with new seriousness. Historians of American cinema have discussed these as "social problem films," noting the range of topics covered by these films: the reintegration of veterans (*The Best Years of Our Lives* [1946], *Till the End of Time* [1946]), anti-Semitism and racism (*Gentleman's Agreement* [1947], *Home of the Brave* [1949]), alcohol abuse (*The Lost Weekend* [1945]), and mental illness (*The Snake Pit* [1948]).[2] Scholars have seldom looked in depth at one of the more prominent forms of civic interrogation in postwar Hollywood, the semi-documentary film cycle.[3] Semi-documentary films not only highlighted the concerns of contemporary life but also developed a new aesthetic with which to do so, integrating techniques from newsreel and documentary filmmaking into their fictional storytelling.

Inaugurated in 1945 with 20th Century-Fox's *The House on 92nd Street*, the semi-documentary film cycle comprised well-known films and obscure ones, including *13 Rue Madeleine* (1947), *T-Men* (1947), *Boomerang!* (1947), *He Walked by Night* (1948), *The Iron Curtain* (1948), *Call Northside 777* (1948), *The Naked City* (1948), *Lost Boundaries* (1949), *Border Incident* (1949), *State Department—File 649* (1949), *Port of New York* (1949), *Appointment with Danger* (1950), *Southside 1-1000* (1950), *The Big Lift* (1950), *Women from Headquarters* (1950), *Walk East on Beacon* (1952), *Dragnet* (1954), *The Phenix City Story* (1955), and *The Wrong Man* (1956).

Semi-documentary films were distinguished by several or all of the following characteristics:

- a narrative based on a true story, roughly contemporary rather than historical;
- an investigatory orientation, in which the investigatory body is on the side of justice;
- a prologue, often featuring a voice-of-God narrator, attesting to the film's adherence to fact;
- a credit announcing the filmmakers' gratitude to participating agencies/institutions that authorize the story (the FBI, the Department of the Treasury, etc.);
- location shooting in the actual setting of the story (interiors and exteriors);
- integration of newsreel and/or documentary footage into the narrative;
- a cast of low-wattage stars and nonprofessional actors;

- narrative integration of sequences that explicate a legal, judicial, scientific, or technical procedure or process;
- a linear narrative, often within a flashback structure;
- an emphasis on groups over individuals as the subjects of the story (e.g., multiple protagonists; continual interaction between varied participants in the story, such as police, politicians, and public; and inclusion of a cross-section of society as characters);
- a sense of extended narrative time (conspicuous pauses, deliberate pacing, inclusion of extraneous material); and
- an atypical soundscape, punctuated by silences and using a sparse musical score.

Like all film cycles, this one was relatively short: it petered out in the mid-1950s as it became clear that filmmakers were less committed to the documentary project and critics were less pleased with the attempts.[4]

Though there has been little scholarly work on this cycle, several semi-documentary films have been studied individually, usually within the context of the critical behemoth film noir. Many films in the semi-documentary style are marked by elements common to canonical noir films: they are crime stories, they are set in cities, and they feature low-key lighting. Several have become canonical films noir themselves: *The Naked City*, *T-Men*, *He Walked by Night*. It is common to find these and other semi-documentaries grouped in the "film noir" sections on streaming platforms or bundled within anthologies of film noir. Though film noir has been a productive category for film and media scholars, it is also a notoriously slippery term with permeable boundaries. Steve Neale argues that the "category" of film noir is "incoherent," observing that the films referenced by different authors shifted with the priorities of the authors.[5] It is also a term that was not available to the audiences who first saw these films.

Neither would postwar audiences have recognized these films as "police procedurals," another retrospective genre category into which many semi-documentaries fit. Although crime films in the procedural style can be traced back at least to the 1930s, the term *police procedural* did not come into film discourse until decades later. The earliest references to "police procedurals" in the popular press appear in book reviews in the 1960s in discussions of the police-detective novels by Ed McBain, Elizabeth Linington, Dell Shannon, and others; in the 1970s, film and television critics imported the term. Scholars came later to the conversation: the earliest book-length scholarly study of the police procedural was an analysis of the literary genre—George

N. Dove's *The Police Procedural*, which appeared in 1982—though media was part of the definition even when it was not the subject. In introducing the term, Dove leaned on the best-known example of the genre, which was not a novel at all. "The easiest way to define the police procedural," Dove explained, "is to call it the *Dragnet* kind of story."[6] Dove's use of *Dragnet* as his best example illustrates the contributions of postwar documentary-style media to the development of the police procedural, even before the genre had a name. Although the postwar period was the critical period of genre development, "police procedural" was not an available genre category for audiences of the 1940s and 1950s.

What *was* available to audiences was the term *semi-documentary*, and understanding that term helps us to see the extent to which producers, critics, and audiences saw transformative potential in these films. As Rick Altman has argued, "Genres are not inert categories shared by all . . . but discursive claims made by real speakers for particular purposes in specific situations."[7] The discursive claiming of *semi-documentary* tells us that, for an important moment in those postwar years, filmmakers and audiences believed that Hollywood was pioneering a new, meaningful kind of cinema.

Elia Kazan, the director of *Boomerang!*, later told the film critic Michel Ciment, "It was our neo-realism, exactly at the same time as *Paisà*, but of course in no way as good as *Paisà*."[8] Kazan's comparison to the celebrated film movement is illuminating. Though the meanings of Italian neorealism have been hotly debated for decades, shared aesthetic strategies are evident in films such as *Rome, Open City* (Rossellini, 1945) and *Bicycle Thieves* (De Sica, 1948), including the choices to shoot on location and to cast nonprofessional actors. These same strategies were used in Hollywood, where different conditions led filmmakers to similar aesthetic innovations. Semi-documentary directors filmed far away from Hollywood sound stages (Stamford, Connecticut, in the case of *Boomerang!*) and cast nonprofessionals alongside more established performers.

Though they shared certain aesthetic elements, these two movements highlighted very different social problems, or rather, they displayed very different understandings about what the social problems were. Italian neorealist films tended to highlight the problems of ordinary people, especially those living in poverty and navigating the destruction of the recent war. "American neorealist" films tended to be narratives of crime and investigation, exploring social reality through civic institutions. While Italian neorealist films tended to end in ambivalence or tragedy, American semi-documentary films were basically optimistic. Even as the films focused on stories of wrongdoing,

Kazan remembered that they expressed "the belief that the good in American society will finally win out."[9]

This ideological confidence in American institutions was expressed through an approach to realism that served as an aesthetic and ideological link between the war and postwar eras. Though the polarities of the Red Scare have often led scholars to look for binary views in postwar artifacts, Will Straw has acknowledged the political complexity within these films:

> At the heart of the semi-documentary was the tension between its restricted institutional frame and the rich possibilities offered by narrative worlds outside the studio backlot. This tension does not map easily onto that between right and left, as if the semi-documentary film enacted the struggle between an ascendant security state and a populist, neorealist opening onto social life. The incoherence of the semi-documentary resides in the ways in which, at least initially, it set two sorts of progressive inquiry against each other.[10]

Straw is right to see semi-documentary films as neither progressive nor reactionary, but they are not incoherent in their politics when we see them as reflective of the emergent liberal consensus, rather than as failed leftist projects.

American political historians have argued that a liberal consensus emerged and became dominant in many areas of American society after World War II. Historian Gary Gerstle succinctly summarizes this ideological accord: "Everyone agreed that the productivity of American capitalism and its capacity to spread affluence throughout the social order had made questions of class inequality meaningless."[11] In this period of American ascendency, as Godfrey Hodgson writes, it was "assumed . . . that social problems in America were residual and could be 'cured' by the action of government and nongovernmental organizations, informed by the new and essentially American social science."[12] This "nonideological" ideology structures the semi-documentary films. The films take a sociological approach to the problem of crime in the United States, using the realism effect of documentary to present fictional narratives that also feel like a study of the inner workings of government agencies. Although the films sometimes explore the possibility of institutional failures, they largely present an argument for the necessity of these institutions to protect individual freedoms, public safety, and American democracy.

Like other sources that constructed the new liberal consensus, semi-documentary films developed in direct response to the recent wartime experience. These films show us that in the unsettled years after the war, filmmakers and audiences were looking for stories and forms that would help them grapple with the increased state presence and power that had been built up during the war, to imagine how this power would be deployed in peacetime, and to better understand Americans' responsibilities as citizens within these more powerful structures. In ways that both construct and exceed their narratives, semi-documentary films explore the architecture of institutions, the kind of work done within them, the skills and technologies used by their experts, and the quality of the involvement of average citizens. The semi-documentary film cycle lasted only through the 1950s, but these ideological concerns, and the aesthetic that communicated them, persisted in the form of the police procedural, which applied the documentary form to a narrower piece of civic architecture and led to the development of a more robust genre that spanned film, radio, and television for decades after.

From Documentary to Semi-documentary: *The House on 92nd Street*

> But it is the method of telling the exciting espionage yarn that is especially good and unusual. . . . Film opens as though it were a factual, or documentary revelation of the workings of the Federal Bureau of Investigation. There are authentic newsreel shots of the roundup of leading Nazi agents. You get a look behind the elaborate fingerprinting processes of the FBI and the patient and persistent detail that goes into its filing systems. And then, barely noticing the switch from fact to fiction, you are whipped into the story of "the Christopher case"—or the German attempt to get at the atomic bomb.
>
> Dorothy Manners, review of *The House on 92nd Street*, *Los Angeles Examiner*, Oct. 19, 1945

When Dorothy Manners breathlessly described the attractions of *The House on 92nd Street*, she was one of the many film critics who, exhausted by the mediocre films produced by Hollywood during the war, welcomed the possibility that Hollywood was finally turning an aesthetic corner—one marked by a new and urgently needed form of realism. Produced by Louis de Rochemont and directed by Henry Hathaway for 20th Century-Fox, *The House on 92nd Street* fictionalized the story of a wartime spy ring and the American double agent who helped to break it up. As Manners and others wrote, though the story was exciting, the documentary style made the strongest impression. *House*'s success—in pioneering this new aesthetic as well as in its performance at the box office—kicked off the decade-long semi-documentary cycle.

The House on 92nd Street not only told a story from the war but also extended wartime experiences in other ways. Its use of documentary realism built on the expanded role that nonfiction filmmaking had taken on during World War II, when documentary became a key means through which Americans learned about the war as well as about government expectations for their participation. While nonfiction filmmaking had been an important part of American cinema from its earliest years, it had always been decidedly overshadowed by fiction filmmaking in the American cultural landscape. The war increased the production of, and popular interest in, nonfiction film of all types: newsreels, training films, propaganda films, shorts, and features. As Jack Ellis puts it succinctly, during the war "more filmmakers made more nonfiction films for larger audiences than ever before."[13]

The war also broke down barriers between fiction and nonfiction filmmaking. Hollywood personnel served in the military and were deeply enmeshed in propaganda filmmaking, including enlisted directors John Ford, John Huston, George Stevens, William Wyler, and Frank Capra, all of whom made notable documentary short films or features.[14] Additionally, above- and below-line personnel were used to produce training films and educational shorts for the military and government agencies; they returned to Hollywood with experience and training in documentary techniques. Documentary also became a more visible part of the industry landscape, as marked by the addition of the Best Documentary category of the Academy Awards in 1942, which signaled rising, broad interest in the form as well as affirmed new industrial investment.

The semi-documentary film cycle was an extension of these cultural changes and collapsed barriers. Most practically, the integration of personnel from nonfiction filmmaking led to the integration of documentary aesthetics into fiction filmmaking. Indeed, the cycle can be traced to the influence of one nonfiction filmmaker: Louis de Rochemont. In the 1930s, de Rochemont had cofounded *The March of Time*, creating the distinctive style of what became the leading American newsreel. *The March of Time* made its reputation with its lively, dramatic, visual presentation of newsworthy events, combining captured footage, reenactments, fast editing, and a colorful voice-over provided by Westbrook Van Voorhis.[15] De Rochemont expanded his documentary work during the war, when he brought his style of storytelling to feature-length documentary production. *The Fighting Lady* (1944), a coproduction between 20th Century-Fox and the US Navy, told the story of the aircraft carrier USS *Yorktown* and its crew. That film led to a longer relationship between the documentary producer and the movie studio: following the success of *The Fighting Lady*, which won the 1945 Academy Award for Best Documentary, de Rochemont stayed with Fox and began producing films that straddled the boundary between nonfiction and fiction.

Out of the big studios, Fox was the best match for the kind of serious-minded movies that de Rochemont wanted to make.[16] The studio was headed by Darryl F. Zanuck, a studio executive long associated with films that explored contemporary social issues. Zanuck had brought a brutal form of social realism to Warner Bros. in the 1930s with *Little Caesar* (1930) and *The Public Enemy* (1931) before becoming the head of 20th Century-Fox. After the war, Zanuck's liberal bent led to productions that pushed Fox to the edges of mainstream political respectability, with the anti-Semitism exposé *Gentleman's Agreement* (1947) and the anti-racism film *Pinky* (1949). Zanuck's support of de Rochemont's experiments with realistic fiction filmmaking led the studio to contribute more films—and most of the best films—to the semi-documentary cycle, including *The House on 92nd Street*, *13 Rue Madeleine*, *Boomerang!*, and *Call Northside 777*.[17]

The House on 92nd Street was explicit in its realist intentions: within the narrative, through a variety of formal choices within the film, and in the press and marketing materials. These together created for audiences an approach to realism that straddled the inside and outside of the film. One key to the film's "authenticity" was its relationship with the Federal Bureau of Investigation. As Hayden Guest points out, the strategic alliances between studios and police agencies had mutually reinforced one another since the 1930s, when *Beast of the City* (1932) and *G-Men* (1935) glamorized federal agents in the same ways that *Scarface* (1932) and *The Public Enemy* (1931) glamorized gangsters.[18] None of those early films were as closely tied to the FBI as *The House on 92nd Street*, nor did they take their responsibilities to their authorizing agencies as seriously. The FBI's role in *House* was elemental: by cooperating with the FBI, de Rochemont was able to tell a story that only the police agency could give permission to tell, and to get as close as Hollywood could get to "breaking news." According to the film's narrator, "The Bureau went to war with Germany long before hostilities began. No word or picture could then make public the crucial war service of the FBI. But now it can be told." By cooperating with de Rochemont, the FBI got a wartime story in which the police agency (rather than any military branch) was the hero.

Press around the film emphasized that *House* was a true story, constructed

FIGURE 1.1. In *The House on 92nd Street*, the studio shares its producers' credit with the FBI, a visual declaration of the collaboration between the filmmakers and the policing agency.

out of documents provided directly to the filmmakers by the FBI. In the *New York Times*, Thomas M. Pryor reported that the screenwriter "listens to FBI recordings of conversations by enemy agents to guide him in putting the right words into the mouths of the right characters."[19] The screenwriter was not the only one with privileged access to heretofore-confidential materials. When audiences saw the film, they, too, saw documents provided by the FBI. Integrated into the film's explanatory prologue are actual surveillance films taken by the FBI outside the German embassy in Washington, DC. In the film, we see grainy footage of figures coming in and out of the building, greeting one another with casual "heils." As we watch, the narrator informs us that these people, protected by diplomatic agreements until the start of the war, were quietly recruiting American Nazis. The integration of FBI footage is a particularly spectacular addition and adds immeasurably to the film's realism: there is no doubt that this is a true story.

And it is an amazing story; the film would be gripping if it only showed how the FBI broke up a domestic spy ring. But the producers also got lucky. When de Rochemont began examining the FBI's materials, he did not know what secret was being sought by the spy network he was reconstructing. Three months before *House* premiered, details on the development of the atom bomb were finally released, and de Rochemont learned that "Process 97" had been part of that secret.[20] Unexpectedly, the film became an important document of the recent war, in addition to being an exciting experiment in filmmaking.[21]

To integrate the documentary material seamlessly, the film's visual aesthetic was built around the preexisting material, rather than strictly fitting Hollywood conventions. As *Los Angeles Times* writer Philip Scheuer noticed, Henry Hathaway adjusted his camera to match the style of newsreels and the documentary footage they used. Hathaway eschewed medium shots, resisted mobile framing to better match the immobile FBI shots, and even "permitted his cameraman to photograph people who were partly but not 'full in' the frame—a cardinal sin in orthodox Hollywood."[22]

The major formal intervention was the heavy use of location shooting. For audiences accustomed to films shot entirely on Hollywood sound stages, *House*—in which less than thirty seconds of the film was filmed on sound stages—looked much more authentic.[23] Location shooting soon became identified with the documentary style that de Rochemont pioneered in this film. As Eugene Lyons wrote a few years later in *Reader's Digest*, "During recent months every major studio in Hollywood has released what *Time* calls 'the Louis de Rochemont type of realism, shot on location.'"[24] More than any other attribute, location shooting became the largest part of what made a film semi-documentary.

While location shooting in *House* functioned as a kind of spectacle, it was, in Hollywood style, also fully integrated into the narrative. Narratively, location itself is critically important; the film is intentionally precise about where events take place. Locales are explicitly announced and displayed: FBI headquarters in Washington, DC; a spy training center in Hamburg, Germany; the Nazi spy ring run out of the house on the Upper East Side (at Ninety-Second Street and Madison Avenue); the Bowling Green subway station in lower Manhattan. These places lay out the geopolitical centers through which the undercover part of the war was conducted, as well as allowing the film to display how untethered it is from the studio backlot.

The occasional visual flourish showed off the fact of being on location without drawing attention away from the narrative. One-third of the way through the film, there is a brief fade out–fade in from an urban location to a rural location. The camera pans slowly from left to right, taking in the scenery—brush and small trees against the water. The pan then reveals a doorframe, then a row of windows, and then an American agent sending out a radio signal. A pan, not a cut, indicates that they are shooting from inside the actual "secluded cabin less than one hundred miles from Manhattan" that the narrator describes. Such well-integrated flourishes were meant to add to, not detract from, the film's "feeling of realism."[25]

Location was also useful extratextually: filmmakers encountered problems while working away from the studio that provided great press material.

FIGURES 1.2 AND 1.3. In *The House on 92nd Street*, location shooting is shown off in exterior shots (top), such as when a character leaves the Bowling Green subway station in New York City, and interiors (bottom), as when the lead investigators play their scene against a window overlooking a view that is neither painted nor projected.

The studio publicity machine emphasized the problems location filming incurred and emphasized the creativity of the filmmakers and crew in overcoming obstacles. Location shooting on *The House on 92nd Street* "was a problem of major proportions," according to studio publicity. Mobile production required ingenuity and resourcefulness, and filmmakers got help in unexpected ways and from surprising places. The release explained: "Since some of the action took place on the streets, in parks and public buildings, a means had to be devised whereby these sequences could be filmed without causing crowds to gather. This problem was solved by the F.B.I., when they loaned the company one of their special surveillance vehicles which they use for secret photography. Inside, the camera crew could point their lenses in any direction without being seen by people passing by."[26] Sound on location was also an issue for filmmakers. Long before cordless mics made mobile recording easy, "another problem that confronted the company was sound equipment light enough to be carried wherever their sets happened to be. The lightest unit capable of recording feature picture quality weighed a ton. 20th Century-Fox engineers ingeniously built it into fourteen metal suitcases which could be taken anywhere."[27] Studio materials are filled with anecdotes that emphasize the challenges of overcoming technical difficulties, gaining the trust and cooperation of the locals, and other problems met and solved in the pursuit of filmic realism.[28]

While an audience today might see *House*'s version of filmic realism as a minor variation on classical Hollywood style, contemporary reviews help us see that this film looked and felt very different to postwar American audiences.[29] Critics who wrote about the film always emphasized its distinctive style. Bosley Crowther of the *New York Times* described the film as "a fresh form of screen expression," while the *Hollywood Reporter* described its "revolutionary technique."[30] The *New York Herald-Tribune* reviewer wrote that the film opened up untold possibilities for the entire medium: "A fascinating spy film has come to the Roxy to remind one that the screen is an extraordinarily flexible medium[,] . . . a blend of fact film and fancy which is as right as it is radical."[31] Lowell E. Redelings proposed in the *Hollywood Citizen News*, "There's no reason why more films of the same excellent quality as this FBI thriller can't be produced with similar results."[32] As it turned out, similar results *were* produced, perhaps not all of "the same excellent quality" but all engaging with the same core cultural questions.

Faith and Doubt in the Semi-documentary Cycle: *Call Northside 777* and *The Wrong Man*

The incorporation of documentary techniques into fiction filmmaking allowed *The House on 92nd Street*, and the films that followed it, to show Americans a plausible representation of the workings of state agencies. This new kind of cinema developed after the war in response to the issue of increased governmental power. As a rule, the films expressed a belief that a powerful centralized government is the best means through which to address pressing social issues. The semi-documentary presentation of efficacious, centralized, bureaucratized state agencies was an argument for consensus thinking that was offered as a fact of American life.

Scholars who have revisited the idea of liberal consensus in the years since its seminal articulation by Godfrey Hodgson in the 1970s have made clear that the ideology is not applicable to every aspect of American society. A history of the postwar period that insists on the ideological dominance of consensus liberalism would not capture well the challenges of civil rights, changes in the realms of gender and sexuality, or even the direct opposition of political conservatives.[33] As Gary Gerstle writes, reflecting on the limitations of the paradigm, "There are reasons aplenty . . . to think about discarding the concept of liberal consensus." But Gerstle insists that it has value. He writes, "I would like to suggest a different strategy for going forward: identifying the areas in which a liberal consensus ruled and the areas where it had little or no jurisdiction."[34] The semi-documentary cycle is well within its jurisdiction. The cycle was made up almost entirely of stories that addressed the social problem of crime and highlighted the successful response of government agencies, usually focusing on the work of federal or local police.

Rarely, the semi-documentary aesthetic was applied to other kinds of stories. After leaving Fox, de Rochemont independently produced *Lost Boundaries* (1949), which told the story of a Black doctor and his family who chose to pass as white. Fox also produced, without de Rochemont, *The Big Lift* (1950), which told the story of the Berlin Airlift through the experiences of two Air Force pilots. Both films are singularly fascinating documents, but they are exceptions that prove the rule: the body of films in the cycle indicate that postwar Hollywood filmmakers found that the best matches for documentary form were stories of investigation that stayed on the side of the authorizing agency.

The driving question of these films is *how* the authorizing agency will address the problems presented. Nearly all of the films in the cycle are linear accounts of successful investigations, portraits of effective bureaucracies at work. Moreover, most were based on real-life crimes that had been successfully solved, so audiences knew, even before the film started, that the system worked. The outcome of the war is not in question in the films set during the war (such as *The House on 92nd Street* and *13 Rue Madeleine*). When semi-documentary narratives evolved into the tales of civilian crime, the films' association with a sponsoring police or state agency assured audiences that the government men (or, rarely, women) would prevail in the end. Even the most noir films in the series, which contemporary viewers might expect to tell labyrinthine tales of societal failure, are more tonally distinctive than narratively so. The shadowy, hard-nosed *T-Men* and the ironic, sardonic *The Naked City* are, at the narrative level, straightforward police stories.

Though semi-documentary films tended to tell successful stories of the pursuit of criminal justice, the form did have some capacity to carry ambivalence about the system. *Call Northside 777* serves as an example of a semi-documentary film that raises questions about the criminal justice system at the same time that it maintains its faith in it. *The Wrong Man*, released at the tail end of the cycle, stretches the form to recount an institutional wrongdoing and, in doing so, demonstrates that the postwar semi-documentary cycle could tolerate ambivalence but not pessimism. The success of *Call Northside 777* and the failure of *The Wrong Man* evince that while semi-documentary filmmakers might raise doubt, they needed, at the same time, to believe.

Call Northside 777 was among a small subset of semi-documentaries that raised significant questions about the procedures of the criminal justice system.[35] Like most films in the cycle, it was based on a true story, one that was familiar to many viewers from the *Reader's Digest* story that inspired the film.[36] In the film, Chicago reporter P. J. McNeal (James Stewart) reluctantly accepts an assignment from his editor: to discover why a cleaning woman has placed an advertisement offering $5,000 for information about the murder of a police officer twenty years before. McNeal learns that the woman, Tillie Wiecek, is the mother of one of the two men convicted for the crime, Frank Wiecek, and she has saved her wages for years to offer the reward. Although McNeal is skeptical of her story and her son's innocence, he continues his reporting at the urging of his editor. As McNeal becomes more convinced of Wiecek's innocence, the journalist changes tack and begins to investigate the crime itself. It is a tough slog—the police are uncooperative, city officials are skittish, and the key witness cannot be found. McNeal's relentless legwork eventually results in sufficient evidence to convince the state pardon board to authorize Wiecek's release from prison.

Call Northside 777 is markedly ambivalent about the workings of the criminal justice system. As McNeal moves from skepticism to certainty on the question of Wiecek's innocence, he plants in the audience seeds of uncertainty about the inviolability of the justice system. Through McNeal's investigation, we see that police are not wholly trustworthy. Not only is there corruption (Wiecek complains of the police "taking [him] around the horn"), but we also see a police cover-up as it happens (McNeal asks for the original arrest records and is told that they are not available). The intertwined relationships between media, police, court officers, and politicians is represented on-screen, and we see these groups reflect different interests at different times: publicity, self-protection, and, only sometimes, justice.

FIGURE 1.4. Semi-documentary realism: in *Call Northside 777*, James Stewart (as P. J. McNeal) plays a scene inside the Illinois State Penitentiary.

Most critically, the film does not address the other miscarriage of justice: the conviction of Wiecek's friend. In one scene, the warden says to McNeal, "You know, up here, every man claims to be innocent. But the prisoners are the harshest judges of themselves. And they believe we have only two men who don't belong here: Tomek Zaleska and Frank Wiecek." The film does not spend much time with Zaleska, whose real-life counterpart was still in prison at the time of the film's release.[37] Reviewers noticed the discrepancy but attributed different significance to it. *Newsweek* graciously—and perhaps disingenuously—offered, "You can overlook the fact that the script forgets to mention what happened to Frank's equally innocent companion."[38] Virginia Wright of the *Los Angeles Daily News* was more genuinely disappointed: "The ending of the picture is somewhat less than satisfactory for while Wiecek gets his release the other boy goes unmentioned."[39]

Audiences might have been more likely to overlook the question of "the other boy" if the film's publicity did not continually call attention to the congruence between the real and fictional stories. A two-page spread in *Life* on March 1, 1948, featured a picture of a gigantic movie poster—dwarfing the two figures next to it—advertising *Call Northside 777*, which the poster blares is "Chicago's own strange and startling story! Every biting word, Every Sensational Scene Is True!"[40] Attesting to that is the caption beneath the poster, which tells the reader that the two figures peering at the advertisement are Joe Majczek and Tillie Majczek, real-life son and mother. Stories like these shored up the film's claims to authenticity, but they also implicitly pointed audiences toward the other miscarriage of justice and the innocent man who remained in prison.

Call Northside 777 thus opened up space for audiences to critique the workings of government, and particularly to question the motives and competence of the police. At the same time, the film's narrative framework and elements of its documentary style circumscribed this space for critique. While the film uncovers corruption in the past, it also asks audiences to trust in the tools in the present. *Call Northside 777* emphasizes that the railroading of Frank Wiecek was a result of the specific conditions of an earlier era. The film's opening starts with a capsule history of Chicago, noting that "no period in Chicago's history was more violent than that of Prohibition." Most other semi-documentaries use their prologues to emphasize how contemporary their stories are; *Northside* instead places the murder and the subsequent bad arrests firmly in the past. McNeal emphasizes this historical distance throughout. He tells his editor when given the assignment, "1932 was open season for cops." "Back during Prohibition, the police department was pretty tough when a cop got killed," McNeal says to a police officer who resentfully assists the reporter in accessing arrest records. "Back in 1932, a steady stream of convictions made good publicity," McNeal explains to a room of politicians concerned about the impact of his reporting. Though the events of the story took place only sixteen years before the film was released, the earlier period is presented as a distinctly different time. The film does not fully explain what changed in the meantime, only suggesting that the end of Prohibition and an unspecified change in city leadership led to the elimination of corruption in policing and politics.

The semi-documentary form was often used to highlight the capabilities of new technologies, aligning with postwar liberalism's investment in the liberatory potential of scientific advances, including developments in the social sciences. This tenet of the belief system has particular importance in *Northside*, in which the certainties of science and technology can correct past wrongs and, by extension, prevent future wrongs. As also happens in other semi-documentaries, *Northside* pauses the narrative to explicate a specific piece of technology. Almost halfway through the film, the narrative effectively stops to allow the audience to observe a lie detector exam, which McNeal offers to Wiecek to support his claim of innocence. In the eight-minute scene, the audience watches the patient administration of the exam. First, the technician, Leonarde Keeler (a real-life developer of the polygraph), describes the machine and its parts to the reporter. Keeler then conducts the test, complete with control questions and a false start. Following the

FIGURE 1.5. The real Leonarde Keeler administers a lie detector test to the character Frank Wiecek (played by Richard Conte).

FIGURE 1.6. The film cuts to close-up during the last stage of the film enlargement process, as McNeal (and the audience) wait for the crucial date to appear.

examination, the technician explains how he will read the scribbled lines on the graph paper that the machine has printed out.[41] The film then cuts to a close-up of McNeal's typewriter pressing the following headline onto paper: "FRANK WIECEK PASSES LIE TEST." This scene could have been done much more economically—through, say, a montage of questions and answers. In fact, the film could have cut directly between existing scenes, from McNeal asking Wiecek to take the test to the typewriter shot. But the film is interested less in narrative economy and more in showing the audience how scientific knowledge can be applied to the pursuit of legal justice.

While McNeal often encounters resistance from other people, scientific tools never let him down; technology is important throughout the film as a corrective to human frailty. The lie detector report is inadmissible in court, but the availability of a different new technology is more consequential. The final twist in the plot—the last piece of evidence needed to clear Wiecek—is revealed through a photo enlargement, which is presented in the film as a cutting-edge tool. McNeal discovers the possibilities of this technology only after the film spends ten minutes following his pursuit of a key witness, who refuses to provide the testimony that would free Wiecek. Following that disappointment, McNeal pursues one final lead—not a person, but the newspaper photo. McNeal visits a special laboratory to have the picture enlarged so that it can provide the critical information that discredits the recalcitrant witness and secures Wiecek's release.

The ending of *Call Northside* 777 explicitly tells the audience that although the journalist has revealed significant problems in the workings of government, the system can and does have the capacity to correct itself. "It's a big thing when a sovereign state admits an error," McNeal tells Wiecek as he walks the newly freed man out of the prison. "Remember this: there aren't many governments in the world that would do it." The film's faith in the government, shaken by its own discoveries along the way, is restored in the end.

The Wrong Man, on the other hand, cannot restore what it never had. Directed by Alfred Hitchcock, *The Wrong Man* was the last major feature film to employ the techniques that de Rochemont and Hathaway pioneered at Fox. The film tells the story of Manny Balestrero (Henry Fonda), who was arrested for committing a string of burglaries in New York City. Misidentified by witnesses, harassed and intimidated by the police, and wrongly imprisoned, Balestrero is cleared of the charges only by accident, when the real burglar robs a grocery store and is detained by the proprietors. The film, which flopped with critics and audiences, both unintentionally exposed the ideological limits of postwar semi-documentary and marked the end of the film cycle.

With its opening, *The Wrong Man* associated itself with other semi-documentaries while signaling its difference. The film opens with a prologue that announces that it is based on real events, as do most of the other films in the cycle. But this prologue is not in the voice of an objective off-screen narrator; it is delivered by the director himself, mimicking the prologue that

FIGURE 1.7. In the opening of *The Wrong Man*, Alfred Hitchcock appears in menacing shadow.

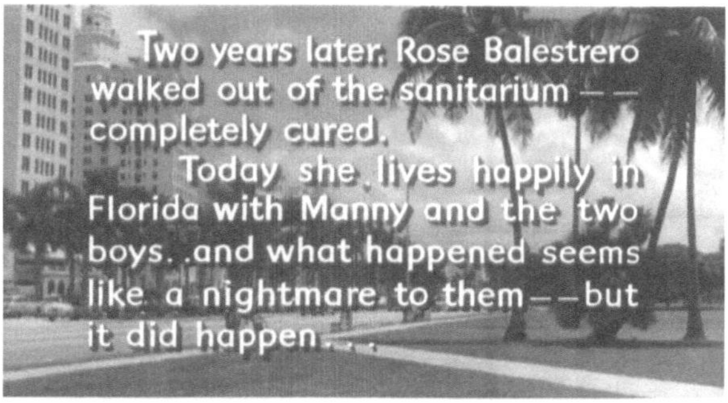

FIGURE 1.8. *The Wrong Man*'s tacked-on "happy" ending cannot make up for all the pessimism of the preceding 105 minutes.

made his anthology television series *Alfred Hitchcock Presents* (1955–1962) so distinctive. Hitchcock stands in a long shot, his full-body profile partly lit by a triangle of light emitting from behind him. He announces, "This is Alfred Hitchcock speaking. In the past, I have given you many kinds of suspense pictures. But this time, I would like you to see a different one. The difference lies in the fact that this is a true story, every word of it. And yet it contains elements that are stranger than all of the fictions that I've made before." The shadowy prologue is less assuredly authoritative than those of other semi-documentary films and more intentionally unsettling.

The film starts as it goes on, every aspect shadowy and bleak. Because the film takes the side of the wrongly accused, the persistence of the police in their investigation is threatening rather than reassuring. The officers' stone-faced countenances as they question the wrong man are dispassionate rather than objective. The intense pressure on the family breaks the spirit of Manny's wife, Rose (Vera Miles), and she enters a mental hospital. The events that lead to Manny's release occur only ten minutes before the end of the film, and the reprieve of the last few minutes is not sufficient to outweigh what has come before. The form that had been used for more than ten years to tell stories of investigation is employed here for a story of persecution and poses a direct challenge to the consensus ideology that the semi-documentary had encoded.

Critics nearly universally panned *The Wrong Man*, generally agreeing that the film just did not work. The reviewer for *Cue* wrote, "For all that the film is realistic, grim and harrowing, oddly enough it has little dramatic impact, other than to picture the mental anguish which the innocent man and his bewildered wife undergo."[42] "Lifelike but Plodding" read the headline of the *Los Angeles Times* review.[43] *Time* concurred: "Turning the story into fiction without fictionalizing, [Hitchcock] stripped it of its emotional impact; by sticking to the facts, he missed the truth."[44] Looking at *The Wrong Man* alongside the others in the cycle, it is clear that the film did not work because its pessimism and the semi-documentary format were basically incompatible. The semi-documentary cycle could and did accommodate films that were less earnest and straightforward than *The House on 92nd Street*, the first in the cycle. *The Naked City* upholds its raised eyebrow throughout, but it applies its irony to its characters and its environment, not to the systems of policing. The form could accommodate some critique of the criminal justice system, but as in *Call Northside 777*, the system must also have the capacity to correct past wrongs. Films could be as brutal as *T-Men*, but the brutality must be perpetrated by the criminals, not by the system itself. *The Wrong Man*, all doubt and no faith, showed audiences that the semi-documentary cycle had run out of road.

Audiences were probably fine to see it go, having endured a fair number of mediocre films alongside the exceptional ones. Within just a few years after *House* premiered, critics began to notice that some films were less committed than others to the semi-documentary form, even as they used its elements to add "realism" to their stories. Rather than reinvigorating the Hollywood cinema, as the most optimistic critics had hoped it would, the experimentations of the semi-documentary form—especially the use of location shooting—were integrated into other kinds of films while the semi-documentary film cycle itself petered out. By the mid-1950s, the best place for audiences to find storytelling like that of *The House on 92nd Street* and *Call Northside 777* was not in movie theaters but in their own homes, where police stories on radio and television sounded and looked a lot like semi-documentary films.

The man who carried forward the torch of this style of realism, Jack Webb, was trained on the set of the 1948 semi-documentary police procedural

FIGURE 1.9. Jack Webb plays a police lab technician in *He Walked by Night*, the film that led directly to the creation of *Dragnet* and significantly influenced its form and style.

He Walked by Night. Within film scholarship, *He Walked by Night* is best known for its climactic chase through the Los Angeles sewers, a sequence that displays the chiaroscuro cinematography of film noir favorite John Alton and prefigures the lauded chase through the sewers in Carol Reed's *The Third Man* (1949). For the scholar with an eye toward larger cultural questions, however, the key sequence of the film is not the sewer chase but an earlier scene in which the police gather the victims of a recent spate of robberies. The police and the citizens sit together in a room with a projector operated by a lab technician. As the victims describe the criminal's face, the technician shifts the slides in the projector, adding and adjusting characteristics—wavier hair, smaller eyes, a thinner mouth. For five minutes, they carefully and collectively create a composite photograph of the criminal. At the close of the scene, one of the witnesses says to the lead officer, "It's positively *amazing* that you found out what he looked like." But, of course, it is not so amazing; the film has just shown us how: through a combination of painstaking work, rational procedures, modern technology, trustworthy public servants, and alert citizens. The aesthetic and ideology represented in this scene made a strong impression on the actor behind the projector. Soon after, Jack Webb decided to create a show that would translate this visual aesthetic into an aural one, a show he would produce and direct and in which he would star: *Dragnet.*

CHAPTER 2

SILENCE, NOT SIRENS

Dragnet's Aural Realism

JACK WEBB COULD NOT HAVE known when he showed up for his first day of work on the semi-documentary film *He Walked by Night* (1948) that the film would change the course of his life. On set, he met the Los Angeles Police Department officer Marty Wynn, who was assigned to the production as the technical advisor and tasked with guiding the cast and crew toward creating a realistic police procedural drama. Between scenes, Wynn complained to Webb about the ways that police usually appeared in film and on radio, representations that in no way reflected the job as he knew it. The film that the two men were working on was an exception, but even these filmmakers were as interested in the criminal as they were in the cops who chased him down. When, Wynn wanted to know, would Hollywood give the proper respect to real cops by showing their actual job?

On set, Marty Wynn offered Webb access to LAPD case files. Webb demurred. Webb remembered telling Wynn that the market was pretty crowded: "There are already a lot of similar shows—*True Detective Mysteries*, *Gangbusters*, and so on." Wynn responded, "Sure there are. . . . And they're all jazzed up and the detectives are all supermen, and they do it with mirrors. Real cops don't work like that." Webb remembered replying, "That's why the fiction shows have such high ratings."[1] Several months after wrapping the film, however, Webb began to reconsider. He began to think that he could, actually, make a hit out of a radio series without smoke and without mirrors, one that had the documentary feel of *He Walked by Night*. Within a year Marty Wynn—who had not expected much from a casual conversation between temporary coworkers—was a technical advisor on the kind of show he had imagined.

When Wynn and Webb met, Jack Webb had no producing or directing credits; he was solely a working actor, taking whatever radio and film jobs he could get. Born and raised in the Los Angeles area, Webb left Los Angeles to serve in the Army Air Corps during the war. After the war, Webb relocated to the Bay Area and found local success as a radio performer. In San Francisco, he hosted his own comedy show (*The Jack Webb Show* [1946]) and starred in the short-lived but well-loved private detective series *Pat Novak for Hire* (1946–1947).[2] When Webb returned to his hometown, he worked in small parts in the movies, but he struggled to find steady work.

Working only intermittently, the ambitious Webb was frustrated. He eventually decided to make his own work, to create a radio show that, inspired by Wynn and the film on which they had both worked, had "realism" as its watchword. Though Webb was the driving force, a number of collaborators contributed to the development of the show, including Marty Wynn, who allowed Webb to shadow him at work; William Rousseau, who directed the first several episodes of the new show; and the actor (and friend) Herb Ellis, who helped Webb come up with the title—*Dragnet*. Webb began by conceiving of the lead detective. He later wrote, "I wanted him to be an honest, decent, home-loving guy—the image of 50,000 real peace officers who do their work without the help of beautiful, mysterious blondes, hefty swigs from an ever-present bottle and handy automatics thrust into their belts or hidden in their socks."[3] Wanting a name with no background, biases, or baggage, Webb called his man *Joe Friday*.

From this beginning, Webb and his team ensured that listeners understood their commitment to making *Dragnet* as real as possible. In the publicity around the show, this was always Webb's major point. Webb insisted, "We're trying to play fact and not fiction. . . . We try to make cops human beings, guys doing a job for low pay, but we're trying to get away from the 'dumb-cop' idea. They aren't dumb; they're pretty smart. The average law officer has a handful of law books in the back of his car."[4] Webb claimed that his show was an accurate reflection of the tone of the Los Angeles Police Department as he had observed it firsthand. Webb remembered noticing that at the station, "There was always something going on, like robbery, a hot detail. . . . But they're very calm; they don't shriek and yell. It's a business. That's what we try to do in *Dragnet*."[5]

In trying to accurately recreate the atmosphere Webb described, he and other members of the production team believed that they were pioneering a necessary aesthetic move forward in the medium. In an interview with *True Detective* magazine, producer William Rousseau said, "In producing *Dragnet*, I feel that we are trailblazing in a technique that has been neglected in dramatic radio. . . . That is the terse, documentary-type presentation of actual true-to-life stories. . . . I believe that a more realistic approach is the coming thing in radio, as well as in other types of dramatic narration."[6] Although

FIGURE 2.1. Jack Webb (second from left) with his first technical advisors, Los Angeles Police Department officers Vance Brasher, Marty Wynn, and Jack Donohoe. © Sid Avery/mptvimages.com.

Rousseau left the show after the first several episodes, he was correct in his prediction: *Dragnet*'s realism would be deeply influential.

Webb's decision to break with the conventions of radio crime and detective shows meant that he had some trouble getting it on the air. He first brought the idea to his agent, who was wary of the concept and wary of the idea of using real cases. Webb remembered that his agent insisted, "You need a Sam Spade character," and also warned him, "You'd get sued for libel on every program."[7] Webb also ran into roadblocks at CBS, which was willing to entertain the idea but would not finance a pilot. Eventually, Webb and his partners convinced NBC to sponsor a limited run during the summer. *Dragnet* began under a four-week contract as a sustaining program, which meant that the show was to be underwritten by NBC until the network could attract the interest of an outside sponsor. As part of the preproduction negotiations, Webb also sought out the cooperation of the Los Angeles Police Department. The LAPD resisted at first, but Chief Clemence B. Horrall agreed to cooperate after he heard a sample program. The LAPD gave permission to three police officers, including Marty Wynn, to serve as technical advisors on the show.[8] The show was finally able to move forward, even without a fast-talking detective at the center, while retaining the use of real cases.

Although the show had some trouble getting on the air, when it finally did—on June 3, 1949—the summer program quickly gained popularity among radio listeners, critics, and station affiliates.[9] *Dragnet* had the highest Hooper rating of any NBC program at the end of the summer; 6.2 percent of total homes were listening in.[10] Even more important to the producers and the network, *Dragnet* attracted a sponsor. After several weeks of successful episodes, Liggett and Myers picked up the show, and for the next several years, its Fatima and Chesterfield cigarette brands brought *Dragnet* to listeners.

Radio critics appreciated the new approach of the show, which they saw as distinctly different from the police dramas, crime shows, and mystery programs that populated the nighttime schedule. John Crosby wrote in the *New York Herald Tribune*:

> "Dragnet" . . . is an astonishing cops-and-robbers job simply because nothing very astonishing happens on it. . . . The show rings with an authenticity that I found absorbing though confirmed mystery addicts may find it just dull. . . . The police have for years been depicted either as utter nincompoops or as Supermen of monstrous brains capable of taking apart four armed thugs single-handed. . . . Trouble is most police work is so methodical it's hard to make it exciting. . . . The alternative is to put crime detection in human terms which "Dragnet" seems to be trying to do.[11]

Val Adams made similar observation in the *New York Times*. Adams wrote, "The listenable quality of 'Dragnet' is rooted in the dramatically simple way in which two detective sergeants methodically track down law-breakers. . . . There is nice work in the way the show is put on the air. . . . [The performers] turn in a commendable job with no false histrionics."[12]

By all accounts, *Dragnet* succeeded in presenting an aural aesthetic that distinguished itself from competing crime dramas that relied on what Crosby described as "screeching sirens, chattering tommyguns [*sic*], teletype noises and filters of all description as to sound no more credible than the 'Adventures of the Falcon.'"[13] Among the shows that claimed to be based on real cases, for listeners in 1949, *Dragnet* was a much simpler and more realistic presentation of a police story.

On radio, the creators of *Dragnet* put into place the core elements of the program, which were later transferred to the audio-visual worlds of television and film. This aural aesthetic painted a sonic portrait of the semi-documentaries' ideal relationship between citizen and state: a professionalized, technologically astute state made possible by responsible, attentive civic participation. These were key concerns of the semi-documentary cycle, in which a nation's wartime experiences were transformed into a postwar confidence in institutional efficacy, expressed through film. In *Dragnet*, we see this same transformation performed via a sophisticated aural aesthetic with distinctive elements: authenticity through framing devices, the creation of space through sound, and the assumption of an attentive auditor. *Dragnet*'s strikingly different sound aesthetic made it more possible for listeners to believe what the announcer claimed at the top of the show: "The story you are about to hear is *true*."

Structure and Framing

Dragnet's episodic structure was a key part of its effectiveness as a realistic procedural drama. Over the years, the structure of a *Dragnet* episode remained stable: in two acts and an epilogue, a crime was investigated and usually solved. The content of the commercials varied, some of the dialogue varied, and sometimes the number of scenes varied; but for the most part, a *Dragnet* listener knew how an episode would proceed, even as the details changed. The clarity of the nearly identical structure of individual episodes reinforced the clarity of the steps of the investigation, creating both a feeling of suspense and a sense of inevitability.

Episode Outline[14]

PROLOGUE

ANNOUNCER: Chesterfield brings you *Dragnet.*

(*Musical cue [DUM-DA-DUM-DUM].*)

ANNOUNCER: Ladies and gentlemen, the story you are about to hear is true. Only the names have been changed, to protect the innocent.

(*Under music*)

You're a detective sergeant. You're assigned to robbery detail. An elderly woman on her way to the bank has been robbed and beaten senseless. The suspects are cruel, ruthless. Your job: Get 'em.

(*Commercial.*)

(*Under the "Dragnet March"*)

ANNOUNCER: *Dragnet*: The documented drama of an actual crime.

For the next thirty minutes, in cooperation with the Los Angeles Police Department, you will travel step-by-step on the side of the law through an actual case transcribed from official police files. From beginning to end, from crime to punishment, *Dragnet* is the story of your police force in action.

ACT 1, SCENE 1 (02:30). **Introduction of the case.** Friday and his partner are assigned the case and collect the first details. At close, Friday and partner depart to the first interview.

FRIDAY [*begins his monologue*]: It was Saturday, August 9th. It was hot in Los Angeles. We were working the day watch out of robbery detail. My partner's Ben Romero. The boss is Ed Walker, Captain of Robbery. My name's Friday. It was 10:14 a.m. when I got to room 27A. Robbery detail.

ACT 1, SCENE 2 (07:30). **Interview.** At the beginning of scenes, Friday's voice-over exposition links the segments of the investigation. Most interviews take place with witnesses, neighbors, suspects, medical personnel, or other citizens. Some interview scenes might more properly be called conversations, as the detectives receive information from police technicians or other officers.

ACT 1, SCENE 3 (10:30). **Interview.** Scene ends with a major turn in the case.

ACT 1, SCENE 4 (14:00). **Office.** The detectives check in at the office, where they receive pertinent information from another police officer or department staff member.

(*Commercial.*)

ACT 2, SCENE 1 (17:30). **Interview.** The detectives close in on the suspect.

ACT 2, SCENE 2 (22:00). **Interview.** The detectives' suspicions are corroborated.

ACT 2, SCENE 3 (23:30). **Arrest.** Detectives conduct the final interview, usually with the suspect, who most often confesses. The detectives make an arrest (or take other final action).

(*Musical cue.*)

EPILOGUE.

ANNOUNCER: The story you have just heard was true. Only the names were changed, to protect the innocent. On March 27th, 1947, trial was held in Superior Court, Department 81, City and County of Los Angeles, State of California. In a moment, the results of that trial.

(*Commercial.*)

(*Musical cue.*)

ANNOUNCER: Both William Marshall and his accomplice were found guilty of armed robbery and grand theft auto and are now serving their terms as proscribed by law.
(*Under the "Dragnet March"*)
ANNOUNCER: You have just heard *Dragnet*, a series of authentic cases from official files. Technical advice comes from the Los Angeles Police Department.

This episode structure evolved from the semi-documentary procedurals from which *Dragnet* directly came while also integrating elements of the radio police dramas with which it shared the airwaves. When listeners tuned into *Dragnet*, they heard a program that was both recognizable within the larger media context and strikingly new within its specific broadcasting context. Scholars have previously pointed out the links between semi-documentary films and *Dragnet*. Jason Mittell and R. Barton Palmer both emphasize the common "claims to authenticity and officialdom," in Mittell's words.[15] *Dragnet* shared several other elements of the semi-documentary cycle as laid out in the previous chapter: the show was based on true stories, was associated with an authorizing agency (the LAPD), was broadcast "on location" in Los Angeles, used actors rather than stars, and incorporated police techniques and technology into its story lines. The semi-documentary film cycle connoted realism immediately by the visual difference between location shots and conventional sets. On radio, documentary realism had to be much more intentionally constructed.

The use of framing devices to declare the program's realist intentions was one recognizable element. Both semi-documentary films and realistic radio crime dramas regularly validated themselves through framing devices, an approach that *Dragnet* adopted. As discussed in the previous chapter, semi-documentaries used title cards to explain their distinctive approach and to affirm the veracity of their narratives. *Border Incident*, a film concerned with the exploitation of Mexican farmworkers in the United States, opens with a voice-over explaining to audiences, "The following composite case is based upon factual information supplied by the Immigration and Naturalization Service of the United States Department of Justice." *Boomerang!*, a fictionalized account of a murder in a small town, announces in is credits, "The story you are about to witness is based on fact. In the interests of authenticity, all scenes, both interior and exterior, have been photographed in the original locale and as many actual characters as possible have been used." The opening titles of *He Walked by Night* read, "THIS IS A TRUE STORY. . . . The record is set down here factually—as it happened. Only the names are changed—to protect the innocent." *Dragnet*'s titles made its intentions immediately clear to listeners. With little variation over the years of its run, *Dragnet* opened with the following announcement, borrowed directly from *He Walked by Night*: "Ladies and gentlemen, the story you are about to hear is true. Only the names have been changed to protect the innocent." The show closed with a parallel reassurance of the episode's basis in a real case.

On radio, this kind of framing was not unique to *Dragnet*; it was a common element of its police-drama predecessors and contemporaries. Communicating through sound alone, radio crime dramas depended even more than film on framing devices to declare their intention and authorize their story. *Calling All Cars* (1933–1939) invited a police official to introduce the episode's crime, his unpracticed radio voice authorizing his nonprofessional status and underlining the speaker's authority in declaring the lesson that often concluded the prologue: "Crime does not pay." *This Is Your FBI* (1945–1953) notified the audience that the show was "an official broadcast from the files of the Federal Bureau of Investigation, presented as a public service by the Equitable Life Assurance Society of the United States." A narrator then guided the listener through the crime and the investigation.

The largest number of listeners would have compared *Dragnet*'s framing to that of the long-running *Gang Busters* (1936–1957), which began with the proud announcement that it was "the only national program that brings you authentic police case histories."[16] That claim was supported by different elements of the show, including the use of a police authority, alongside an announcer, for narrative exposition. The police representatives were sometimes well-known figures, as they were during the late 1930s when Norman Schwarzkopf Sr. lent the show his authority. Schwarzkopf was not only the state superintendent of the New Jersey Police; he was also familiar to many listeners as the lead investigator in the "crime of the century," the kidnapping of Charles and Anne Lindbergh's baby. In subsequent years, *Gang Busters* producers borrowed many other police administrators, each of whom introduced the case at the beginning of the show and reinforced the moral lesson at the end by announcing the criminals' conviction and sentencing.

Listeners comparing *Dragnet* and *Gang Busters* would have noted that *Dragnet* was seeking to move away from the more sensational *Gang Busters*, a difference in tack that could be heard in their different framing. Although *Gang Busters* claimed to be on the side of the law, the producers decided early on that the criminals had the more interesting stories. Indeed, creator Philip Lord, who had worked directly with J. Edgar Hoover on an earlier show [*G-Men* (1935)], intentionally created distance between his new show and the FBI director in order to have the freedom to tell more exciting tales.[17] As the name *Gang Busters* indicates, murders, robberies, and criminal conspiracies were the show's bread and butter, announced by episode titles such as "The Case of Emery 'Killer' Connell" (Mar. 24, 1937), "The Wilkes Barre Murders" (Jan. 27, 1940), and "The Case of the Baby Blanket Burglars" (Dec. 26, 1953). For listeners who did not read the radio guide but simply tuned in, the show's interest in sensational tales was clear from its opening and closing, which featured the whirring of police sirens and the rat-tat-tat of machine guns. As Elena Razlogova has shown, the sound of the show worked against its law-and-order presentation. Razlogova writes, "Reviews and listener interviews showed that details of gangsters' lives and sensational sound effects at the core of the story undermined the official authority affirmed at the beginning and the end"; while "broadcasters aired a 'solid moral lesson'; listeners heard a 'noisy, blood-and-thunder' gangster tale."[18] As listeners drew comparisons between the two shows, they would have noticed similarities in their framing; for example, like *Gang Busters*, *Dragnet* used two voices to frame its stories. Announcers George Fenneman and Hal Gibney were heard during the opening, closing, and interstices. From there, differences would have been apparent: *Dragnet*'s realism was more austere, and more thoroughgoing, carried from the framing devices and into the diegesis.

A Muted Soundscape

Shortly after *Dragnet*'s premiere, the *New York Times* critic Val Adams wrote approvingly of the show and expressed relief that among the spate of crime dramas on the air, "this one, for the most part, is devoid of sensationalism. . . . In general, the sound effects man is called upon for light duty only." This sound aesthetic contributed to Adams's evaluation of *Dragnet* as "one of the few satisfactory radio dramatic shows which has come along this summer."[19] Although he was a professional radio listener, Adams did not hear all of what he heard. In fact, the simplicity of *Dragnet*'s soundscape was produced by a team of "sound men" and a fanatical attention to sound. According to an article in *Time*, "Up to five men [were] needed to handle the 300-odd sound effects on each show."[20] What Adams noticed, rather, was the show's muted soundscape: its minimal music, restrained vocal performance, and deliberate use of effects.

Dragnet's diegesis was distinguished by its quiet, made more noticeable by the sonic contrast between diegetic and nondiegetic elements. The program opened with the bombast of its theme, "Danger Ahead," written by Walter Schumann and Miklós Rósza.[21] It is a dramatic march, dominated

FIGURE 2.2. Beginning in summer 1949, Barton Yarborough (left) and Jack Webb (right) played partners Ben Romero and Joe Friday. After Yarborough's sudden death in December 1951, Webb cast Ben Alexander as Frank Smith, and Friday and Smith remained partners through the end of the series. © NBC/Photofest.

by loud brass and low woodwinds, punctuated by the four notes that have entered our cultural repertoire: "DUM-DA-DUM-DUM." In addition to the theme music's usual place at the beginning and end of the show, variations on the theme marked the end of a scene and played underneath Friday's monologues. Unlike in other programs, the music was restricted to spaces outside of the story; during scenes, there were only voices and effects. The assertiveness of the march, then, stood in strong contrast to the muted tone that characterized the narration. The energetic announcers and assertive march, in the spaces outside the story, lent credibility to the quiet of the narrative world.

The most remarked-upon aspect of *Dragnet*'s muted soundscape was the actors' unusually small range of vocal performance. The word most often associated with this stylistic choice was *monotone*, but Jack Webb did not like that term. Webb preferred the term "underplaying—because underplaying is still acting."[22] Webb and his show broke long-standing conventions of vocal performance on radio by instructing actors to underplay their roles. Kathleen Battles has explained how radio performance conventions arose out of concerns about keeping the listener oriented within the story:

> Standardized performances through voice type, dialect, and patterns of speaking became key to marking the identity of characters that radio listeners could not see. Voice performances were highly varied and offered Depression-era radio listeners a cacophony of difference. . . . These differences represented not just individual differences between characters but the standardization of different character types . . . so that the radio listener, always in danger of distraction and disruption, could easily distinguish each voice from the others.[23]

Battles quotes a guide that insisted that "extreme voice contrast" was necessary for listeners, in both sound and diction. Battles explains that "the burden of producing a weekly program . . . led to the simultaneous impersonalization of the two main characters: the police and the criminal. As recognizable types, criminals and police came to represent broader cultural categories."[24] Indeed, the world of crime and policing on radio in the 1930s and early 1940s was populated by a cast of repeating characters: the high-pitched Brooklyn moll; the uptight, sophisticated society lady; the sneering henchman; the slick crime boss; the stuttering coward. In a world that communicated through sound alone, these types helped listeners distinguish between characters in a radio play.

Dragnet refused all of these types and eschewed their standard characterizations. Instead, Webb directed cast members, again and again, to strip color and emotion from their voices. This performance style was not the result of laziness or lack of talent; it was an intentional move away from what Webb saw as the caricatures of other shows. Webb was very strict with *Dragnet*'s actors, which sometimes fatigued them. Herb Ellis, a busy and talented voice actor, tried to get Webb to let him add some character to his performance. Ellis remembered later, "To my mind, everybody talked robotically. Once I ventured to say, 'Can we just do a . . . ' 'NO! This is the way I want it.' Fine. And he was right."[25]

Of course, *Dragnet*'s monotone was not made up of only one tone. But the actors' underplaying limited the range of emotions that characters were permitted. Sergeant Joe Friday was sometimes pleased but never enthusiastic. His partner, Ben Romero, was often grumpy but never petulant; uneasy, sure, but not panicky; polite, but seldom effusive; anxious, but not overwhelmed; irritated, but not enraged.[26] Actors playing citizens were permitted a broader palette than those playing police officers, but seldom were strong feelings expressed and rarely were voices raised. Series regular Art Gilmore remembered with some bemusement, "We never got to *emote* on Dragnet."[27]

Webb often had to defend his choice. He told one magazine, "We don't do it to be different, as some people think. It's a form of underplaying that's great for a documentary type show. I don't think it would work with fiction. There isn't too much emotion—yet you feel it. It hits you like a blast furnace. . . . It's controversial but people like it."[28] The show's many fans included Joe Beck of *True Detective*, who wrote admiringly of the actors: "Instead of whooping up the characterizations, getting excited about everything and giving the impression that they're playing fictional stuff, they are casual, matter-of-fact, and, consequently, convincing."[29] As Webb predicted, underplaying marked *Dragnet*'s audible difference from other programs and made it an essential marker of the program's authenticity.

Space through Sound

While contemporary crime dramas tended to be vague about their setting or changed cities with every new episode, *Dragnet* was set specifically and explicitly in Los Angeles, and Webb, the writers, and the technical advisors made sure that listeners believed that the "true" stories took place in a real city. Sharing the place-based ethos of *He Walked by Night*, the series offered listening audiences an aural equivalent to semi-documentaries' reliance on location shooting. "Location" on *Dragnet* was achieved by creating space through sound: by the writers' attention to the specific spaces of the city in which the show was set and by the production team's placement of the listener within scenes.

While *Dragnet*'s interest in location derived most directly from *He Walked by Night*, the ways in which the show communicated through sound built on capacities that radio had developed over decades. As Neil Verma writes, broadcast dramas in the 1930s "began wrestling with time and space in every available way."[30] Programs that had started as fifteen-minute shows expanded to thirty; shows hopped more frequently from one location to another; programs such as *The Columbia Workshop* (1936–1943; 1946–1947) experimented with the possibilities of studio sound and location sound. Creators and audiences evolved together. As Verma writes, "1930s radio taught listeners to decode audio in sophisticated ways and generated expectations underlying many future innovations."[31]

This included, Verma notes, innovations in nonfiction radio, which also paid increasingly more attention to space and place. Jack Webb, a fan of news and documentary programming, was likely influenced by programs like those of Edward R. Murrow and producer Norman Corwin.[32] Murrow's famed broadcasts from the London Blitz in 1940 featured the broadcaster standing among the destruction as it happened. American listeners were able to hear the air raid sirens, the firing of anti-aircraft guns, and the explosions. Anyone who has heard those broadcasts has viscerally felt how ambient noise can create a powerful sense of place. After the war, network producers continued to experiment with the ability of broadcast technologies to deliver a sense of place to listeners. All three major networks—NBC, CBS, and the newly established ABC—invested in documentary production, and those programs, too, experimented with sound. Matthew Ehrlich describes the writer and journalist Norman Corwin's *One World* documentary program (1947), in which Corwin took listeners with him on a trip around the world. Ehrlich notes that Corwin wanted to break precedent with his audio documentary "to record the interviews and so-called natural sound from the various locales to use on the air rather than follow the established course of re-creating everything in the studio with actors and sound effects, as, for example, *The March of Time* had done."[33]

Dragnet's ability to create space through sound, then, was motivated by its roots in semi-documentary film and made possible by the developments of radio predecessors. Within its genre context, however, its interest in the specificities of its setting was unusual and was a key part of its realist aesthetic. Scripts were painstakingly precise about the places the detectives visited in the course of their investigation. The distinctive work of realism came from within the diegesis. In an interview later in his career, Jack Webb told a journalist, "I've trained myself to be observant. . . . I don't think you can direct motion pictures or television, I don't think you can become much of a performer unless you're extremely observant."[34] Webb valued an attention to detail that was reflected in the show's scripts. The lead detectives wandered all over Los Angeles, naming and describing the spaces as they went. Joe Friday opened his narration with the day and time, but also with the local weather, as in "The Big Youngster" (August 17, 1950): "It was Tuesday, April 10th. It was cool in Los Angeles. We were working the day watch out of Juvenile Bureau. . . . It was 9:35 a.m. when we got to 1335 Georgia Street—Captain's office." With precision, Friday here invites the listener into the space that he inhabits: spring in Los Angeles *is* generally cool, and the Juvenile Bureau was, in fact, located at the corner of Georgia Street and West Olympic Boulevard in the 1950s.

Throughout episodes, narrator Friday called out the specific geography of Los Angeles. A moment later in "The Big Youngster," the officers travel to the location of a crime and Friday describes the events: "[My partner and I] got in the car and drove south on Figueroa until we got to West 113rd Street. . . . We turned right and went about four miles." Friday describes the view from the street: "a one-story frame residence that had been converted into small business offices. On the right side going in was a neighborhood jeweler's shop; we could see him working in the window. Over the door of the office on the left was a lawyer's shingle. The gold lettering was new." Narrated in the progressive present, this verbal sketch of the drive, the street, and the building allows the viewer to encounter new spaces as Friday encounters them.

Part of the job of the police officers who served as technical advisors was to make sure these details were correct. There are a few stories of flubs, of course. One *New York Times* article tells of Marty Wynn's embarrassment "when he [was] reminded of the time he approved a script which had a police car turn into the Spring Street entrance of the Los Angeles police garage. The day after the broadcast every policeman in the city was asking the sergeant how he survived the crash. It turned out that the only entrance to the garage was on Main Street."[35]

Location itself was important, even beyond accuracy. In "The Mother-in-Law Murder" (Nov. 24, 1949), detectives Friday and Romero canvass near Chavez Road, where a woman has been murdered.[36] They track a door-to-door salesman across the neighborhood, and Friday describes his movements to another officer: "We picked up his tracks down on Floresta Street, sold a couple of subscriptions there; then he headed up Flanders Avenue, went to Chavez Road. The Renards live at 2280 Chavez Road." With no map in front of them, Chavez Road was, to listeners, just another street in Los Angeles; almost no one but those LAPD officers knew about Wynn's oversight in the Spring Street incident. Even when listeners did not know the difference, and even when the details were incorrect, the very specificity of the description remained important to convincing listeners that Friday and his partner were moving through a real city.

Dragnet also displayed the diversity of spaces specific to a boisterous city to invoke realism. Most police dramas took place in a limited set of locations: a bustling police station, the quiet office of the police chief, a noisy nightclub, a busy city street. *Dragnet* had a much wider range of recurring spaces: the detectives' office, the captain's office, interrogation rooms. Other common spaces in *Dragnet* included neighborhood bars, working-class diners, drug stores, and office buildings where they interviewed witnesses and suspects. The show often brought listeners into Georgia Street Receiving Hospital, where the detectives encountered victims, injured suspects, and police officers who had been hurt in the line of duty (including, sometimes, the lead detectives).

The show also brought listeners into more unexpected places, varying the soundscape and connoting the dynamism of the city. For example, "The Big Love" (July 5, 1951) brings listeners into a local baseball stadium. In this episode, the detectives interview the husband of a missing woman. The husband, Gorman, works as the groundskeeper at the stadium, where the detectives go to interview him. We hear the cheers of the crowd as Friday narrates the detectives' arrival. The three men try to speak over the roar of the crowd until Gorman leads them into his shack, quieting the cheers, which we hear in tiny waves under the interview. There is no relationship between the stadium and the case; the purpose of the location is only to bring auditors into the vibrant city.

Once Friday named and described the place, *Dragnet* used sound to place the listener within the space, particularly through the show's attention to ambient noise. Webb is often quoted as saying that he wanted *Dragnet* to be "as real as a guy pouring a cup of coffee," which on his show would include every plop, scrape, tinkle, and sip involved with making, pouring, and drinking coffee.[37] The show would also construct, through sound, the room in which the coffee was being consumed. If in a family kitchen, listeners would hear the electric buzz of the refrigerator, the hum of the fan in the window, and music from the radio leaking in from the next room.

In most radio programs, ambiance is primarily necessary to set a scene (to signal where the event is taking place) and to punctuate a character's movement (footsteps, doors opening and closing). That is, sound is subservient to narrative. *Dragnet* played with these expectations. In the show, ambient noise was often constant throughout a scene, and the noise was often irrelevant to narrative events. In the third scene of "The Big Girl" (Feb. 9, 1950), Friday and Romero visit the "stats office" to request a report. The noise of the room is integrated into the conversation. We hear the whir of the card machine that the staff uses; it is so loud, in fact, that "Ethel" has to complete her run before she can hear the detectives. She says, "Hold on a minute," and we hear the machine slowing to a halt. For *Dragnet*'s realism, it was important to convey the relationship between sounds, between noises and voices, in order to create the spaces in which its characters act.[38]

Dragnet's soundscape was also marked by the intentional inclusion of extraneous sound. In "The Big Hands" (Nov. 11, 1951), Friday and Romero investigate the murder of a woman. In one scene, they question her former landlady. As the detectives ask Mrs. Watson about the victim's life in her boardinghouse, we hear the landlady polishing silver. We hear the clanging of silverware, the plopping of spoons in liquid, and the clinking of utensils, and we hear Mrs. Watson opening and closing doors and cabinets. These sounds are not driven by narrative concerns—the silverware is not important to solving this crime. Rather, these extraneous sounds function to create a sense of the space in which the scene occurs. In "Benny Trounsel" (Aug. 4, 1949), Friday and Romero follow a lead to a doctor's home. Friday tells the listener that a Persian cat has followed the detectives into the house, and in the background of the conversation there is, intermittently, a meow. The cat is not only irrelevant to the case—after its several meows, the cat never again appears—the animal does not even belong to the doctor. In another show, the cat would be a clue, or would inadvertently lead the detectives to a clue, or might even become a victim. In *Dragnet*, a cat was no more likely to be a clue than to be, simply, a cat.

For many of the program's sound effects, "realism" was communicated not only through how the sound was heard but also in how it was recorded. Henry Hewes reported in the *New York Times* that when Webb and his team started to compose the soundscape, "the first thing they threw out was the assortment of filter microphones, echo chambers, and catalogued machine-gun effects" common to crime programs. "Instead," Hewes wrote, they "went after sound in its native state."[39] Webb was an early adopter of new technology like the tape recorder, which allowed the show's "sound men" to pick up sounds "on location." Through their connections with city officials, producers were able to get access to public buildings, including a city jail, and to equipment such as police cars. The professional sound man Bud Tollefson remembered recording sound in every room in Los Angeles City Hall for use on *Dragnet*. Hewes reported, "If the script called for a gun battle on a roof two men with guns would go to the top of Los Angeles' buildings and shoot it out. . . . If a telephone conversation was to be overheard they would plug into an actual telephone circuit set up specially for them."[40] Over the years, the sound men created an entirely new library of sounds for use on the show. To rationalize the expense of this library, *Dragnet*'s sound effects were ostensibly available to other shows, but, as Tollefson explained, "very few times any other show wanted stuff like that, so it was almost a private collection for Jack Webb."[41]

Especially in the early years of the show's run, producers regularly experimented with sound and how it could be used to cue the listener, creating interesting and unusual soundscapes. One such experiment can be heard in "The Big Court" (Jan. 24, 1952), which takes place almost entirely in a courtroom. The episode opens in the usual way, with Friday announcing the time and place as his footsteps walk quickly down a corridor. But he tells us that he is in the Municipal Court rather than police headquarters. The sound that cues his location inside the courtroom is one we recognize as a soft, muffled cough, an unmistakable sound in otherwise silent public spaces. The episode moves back and forth between Friday's monologue and scenes in the courtroom, and the soft coughs help to signal the drama's shift in focus.[42] Although many of the sounds heard on *Dragnet* were uncommon within radio drama, they were not included to draw attention to their use. Both a part of and apart from the story, *Dragnet*'s effects performed the work of realism, creating the space-through-sound that was an essential part of its aesthetic of authenticity.

An Attentive Audience

Dragnet's realistic aesthetic, in addition to intervening into the conventions of radio crime drama, also had phenomenological implications. In a medium that was perpetually concerned about audiences' distractability, *Dragnet* was constructed to require listeners' full attention. The mode of listening solicited by the show's structure and soundscape placed audiences in close proximity to the lead detectives, compelling listeners to experience the world alongside the police.

The conventions of radio drama emerged in the late 1920s and 1930s and prioritized coherence and audibility. This is the same period in which other sonic conventions were being worked out. James Lastra has traced the debate among phonograph industry technicians, who were torn between two models of sound recording: "phonographic" (fidelity, faithful reproduction) and "telephonic" (intelligibility, legibility).[43] Film practitioners, too, were figuring out sound: In the early sound era, film practitioners decided that the "role of speech" in cinema was as "above all, an intelligible conveyor of information."[44] Though some film theorists imagined alternatives to "telephonic" sound in cinema, Hollywood producers understood their job as making sure that the story was communicated above all else, establishing conventions that wove sound seamlessly into the classical Hollywood system.[45]

In the 1920s and 1930s, radio producers developed their own classical system of storytelling. The dominant discourse of producers and technicians made clear that *coherence* and *audibility* were the prevailing values, rather than expression or experimentation. As with classical Hollywood, this change coincided—not accidentally—with the economic stabilization of radio: the commercialization of the airwaves, the consolidation of national networks (NBC and CBS were established in the late 1920s), and the saturation of receivers in American homes. By the mid-1930s the radio landscape looked much like it would for the next twenty years.[46]

The development of radio audiences is more difficult to track than the processes of industrial consolidation. It is not possible to know how all radio audiences listened to programming in the twentieth century. Scholars have suggested that auditors employ different modes of listening for different purposes. Susan Douglas has argued that radio "required—or at least allowed—people to develop a repertoire of listening styles and emotional responses depending on the programming and site of listening." Douglas sketches out three: listening for information ("a relatively flat kind of listening"); "dimensional listening," which asks listeners to be fully immersed in the sound, cocreating the environment through listeners' experience and imagination; and "associational listening," in which listeners connect sounds to memories.[47] As Douglas points out, different programs invoked and shaped different kinds of listening. The very nature of sound meant that radio listening gave audiences freedom and flexibility: auditors could switch between listening modes as they pleased.

Douglas's categories overlap with those of the best-known sound theorist, Michel Chion. In *Audio-Vision*, Chion proposes three different models for listening: causal, reduced, and semantic.[48] To elaborate on one of Chion's examples, if we hear the sound of a voice speaking to us in our native language: in the mode of *causal* listening, we would identify the source of the sound; in the mode of *reduced* listening, we would notice the qualities of the sound, such as its pitch, depth, and volume; and in the mode of *semantic* listening, we would listen to the speaker's words and seek to decipher their message. Chion's focus is on the "added value" that sound provides the image, so his categories do not fully capture the complexity of radio listening, although his modes offer us a way into thinking more carefully about radio sound. At the most basic level, the mode of transmission resolves the mystery of causal listening (the source of the sound is always the radio), and radio most often solicits reduced listening during music broadcasts and semantic listening during spoken broadcasts.

Within the diegesis of a radio play, any of these modes may be manipulated for dramatic effect. An eerie noise within a science fiction program may make "causal listening" the central concern of the play, as the intrepid wanderers seek the source of a peculiar and possibly nonhuman sound. Radio listeners constantly employed reduced listening. Listeners learned to make distinctions between the drama and its commercials by the quality of the speakers' voice; many radio announcers were easily identified by the round tones of their voice, even before they began transmitting the brief messages from the sponsor.[49]

Though they did not use Chion's or Douglas's language, networks and sponsors were attuned to audiences' different modes of listening. Even though radio has been understood theoretically as speaking directly to listeners through a relationship of intimacy, there has always been a practical concern about how carefully the bond of intimacy was upheld on the listeners' side. Producers, assuming the home as the dominant site for listening, understood that it offered many potential distractions, whether from family members or household tasks. This issue came up often in talks with sponsors, who were, of course, concerned about whether listeners were paying attention to their commercials.[50]

Industry representatives had to concede that audiences were, indeed, a wily bunch. The authors of "Radio Audience Measurement," a 1946 report from the National Association of Broadcasters, admitted, "The radio audience to any single program is not static. People are constantly tuning in and out of the programs so that a family who has heard part of a program may be listening to some other program or not listening at all at the time the interviewer calls."[51] In the same report, the authors anticipated the concern of sponsors but could only awkwardly dodge the issue: "A primary question of the advertiser obviously is: Who hears the commercial message?" While listener surveys gave some data, "other questions concerning what the listener really hears and why he or she listens to certain programs" were "beyond the scope" of the NAB report.[52] A study conducted by the Television Research Bureau of Hofstra College confirmed sponsors' worst fears with listeners' confessions. Its 1948 report on audience behavior and attitudes detailed audience members' opinions about the difference between radio and television advertisements: "Another relatively frequent comment was something of a backhanded compliment: 'radio ads are easier to ignore,' 'it takes no effort not to listen.'"[53]

Radio dramas responded to the challenge of distracted listenership through varied means. The best examples of programs that worked with radio's most distractible tendencies were the daytime shows, particularly those of the soap opera genre. Created for radio with intentional redundancy in mind, the soap opera was constructed to allow for the daytime work of a busy housewife, entertainment to be heard over the noise of cooking and cleaning. Soap operas were distinguished not only by their narratives (romance, family drama, and small-town intrigue designed to appeal to the female audience) but also by the structure of the shows themselves. Daily listeners would hear important plot information reinforced throughout the episode: in the opening summary of relevant story lines, in the closing preview of the next episode, and throughout the day's drama, which incorporated intentional repetition of key information within the dialogue. This structure allowed listeners to miss pieces of episodes, even entire episodes, without losing the arc of the story.[54]

Dragnet worked against the distractible tendencies in audiences in a different way: its narration and soundscape required an unusually attentive audience. Narratively, *Dragnet* did not ask the auditor to listen for what happens: very seldom did anything *happen*. Rather, through plotting and pacing, the show asked the auditor to sit in the space that the sound design constructs. *Dragnet* compelled auditors to pay attention by continually prompting them to listen for both literal meaning and implied meaning.

The enjoyment of *Dragnet* was in the suspenseful pedantry of its roundabout investigation, which required the listener to be alert throughout the narrative segments. Storytelling in *Dragnet* was at once linear and indirect. Although events were followed in sequence—"from beginning to end, from crime to punishment"—the events did not lead inevitably to a particular outcome. In its predecessor shows and its contemporaries (*Calling All Cars*, *Gang Busters*, *This Is Your FBI*), the criminals were introduced at the top of the show, and the listener followed the two parallel narratives of cops and criminals, waiting for them to intersect. Labyrinthine plots like *Dragnet*'s were more common in mystery shows. In *Dragnet*, suspects were often wrongly accused; hunches did not pan out; hot trails fizzled out. The show was information based rather than action based, so the narrative turned on small discoveries, which required that the listener pay attention to the dynamics within each scene.

Additionally, within each scene, pertinent information was sprinkled throughout the conversation (as in most real-life conversations) rather than being clearly telegraphed. This was particularly true in Friday's interviews with witnesses, who often talked around the point. Webb referred to this aspect of James Moser's scriptwriting as "writing the dialogue against the situation."[55] Take the following scene from "The Big Parrot" (Nov. 16, 1950). In it, the detectives interview an arson suspect in his apartment. The suspect shows them around the room, and the officers ask him questions as they notice different objects. Friday asks about the electronics and wires; the suspect explains that he tinkers as a hobby. Friday points out a can of kerosene, explaining that it is dangerous to store without a case. Romero pulls out some clothes with some kind of stain on them. Neither detective makes a direct accusation. As the detectives casually survey the room and its contents, the suspect grows defensive, finally insisting that they leave. The last lines in the scene get to the point.

> SUSPECT: This is my apartment, this is my shop. You can get out. You hear me? Both of you, you can get out.
> FRIDAY: What's the matter, Jack?
> SUSPECT: I said, you can get out.
> FRIDAY: All right. You want to tell us before we go?
> SUSPECT: Tell you what?
> FRIDAY: Why you killed the Guthries.
> SUSPECT: What do you mean?
> FRIDAY: Why did you kill Mr. and Mrs. Guthrie?
> SUSPECT. No reason. I just did.

Dragnet applied this same mode of communication throughout the show, not only at points of high drama but also in its intermittent comic exchanges. At the top of "The Big Love" (July 5, 1951), Joe chats with a fellow officer, asking "Mac" about his daughter's upcoming wedding. Mac explains that his daughter Alice is marrying a "real nice fella," though he complains that the wedding is digging deep into his pockets and that his wife may be overly invested in the proceedings. Joe listens indulgently as Mac reflects:

> MAC: Sure is funny.
> FRIDAY: Huh, what's that?
> MAC: Seems for years the wife's been afraid we'd never get Alice married off. Now it's finally in the works, the wife's still unhappy.
> FRIDAY: Oh? Well, how is that?
> MAC: Goes around, moping around the house, wiping at her eyes, keeps muttering something about losing her little girl, her little girl is leaving her. I don't know.
> FRIDAY: Well, how old is your daughter?
> MAC: Thirty-two. Well, I'll be down in the stats office if anybody wants me.

The final lines of scenes were usually dramatic, didactic, ironic, biting, or all at the same time. These were often the lines that twisted the narrative one way or another, and though they were the most important lines in the scene, the auditor could not simply listen for them. Like a punchline, their impact rested on the dialogue that came before.

Dragnet also compelled sustained attention through its incorporation of silence into its storytelling technique. Radio is uncomfortable with quiet; relative silence of more than a split-second on radio usually signals a problem, and there is no other available sense to reassure the listener that all is well. Though usually used very sparingly, silence on radio can also be a powerful tool. In *Dragnet*, silence was most often used to leave space for audiences to hear what was unsaid, giving listeners the opportunity to make their own judgments. For example, in the episode "Claude Jimmerson" (Feb. 2, 1950), the police are invited to coffee at a neighboring house during a tough case involving two missing girls. The wife's weary voice communicates tension between the married couple as she asks each officer whether he wants more coffee, then baits her husband about forgetting to buy sugar. She leaves the scene, and the husband begins to make an excuse: "She's a little upset," he explains. Two seconds of silence elapse after that line—an eternity in radio. During that time, it is easy for the listener to imagine that awkward looks are being exchanged around the kitchen table. In this episode, that moment of uncomfortable silence, in drawing attention to the acute tension between husband and wife, also serves as foreshadowing: it is Jimmerson who is guilty of the kidnapping and murder of the two little girls.

Dragnet also asked audiences to uphold radio's intimate bond by constructing intimacy between the listener and Sergeant Friday. Neil Verma usefully coined the term *audioposition* "to indicate the place for the listener that is created by coding foregrounds and backgrounds."[56] As Verma points out, sound design can place the listener in different places—"toward," "away," or "with" the sonic source.[57] In *Dragnet*, the most appropriate preposition is "alongside": Friday spoke to the listeners as if they were citizens on a ride-along. In dual-narrative police dramas, the listener takes up an objective audioposition, placed by the narrator outside of both the criminal action and the police action. *Dragnet* kept the listener close to the police officer, aurally and affectively. The listener not only moved with the detective through the investigation but also, by following him closely within and across episodes, stayed in a position to observe—intimately yet dispassionately—the effective organization of postwar institutions.

The announcer opened the show by asking listeners to place themselves outside the narrative but also within it. The announcer set the stage with the second person, directly addressing the listener, as in "The Big Cowboy" (June 1, 1954): "You're a detective sergeant. You're assigned to homicide detail. You get a call to investigate unknown trouble. The caller gives no indication of what's wrong. Your job: Check it out." A few moments later, Sergeant Friday begins his narration, and the listener slips into Friday's space. The auditor is led through the case by Friday, who communicates through monologues directed to the audience and through the conversations with witnesses, suspects, and fellow police officers. Although *Dragnet* moved sonically through spaces throughout Los Angeles, the listener's audioposition was possible only through a relationship to Friday. This limited perspective produced listeners who became silent partners in policework, spatially and metaphorically moving alongside the police.

Other elements of *Dragnet*'s narration also produced the sense of being "alongside" the investigators. Particularly through its incorporation of specialized language, the show treated listeners as if they were more inside than outside the force. Police jargon was integral to *Dragnet*'s dialogue style. In "The Big Rip" (Apr. 19, 1953), Friday explains to another officer that his case is stalled, employing a long stretch of jargon: "We've had the stats office make so many runs, they're wearing out the cards. MO isn't new, it's been used before; but all the possibles have been checked out, stuff from Braden up at CII, the other leads from the APBs have all been cleared." *Dragnet* only sometimes explained these terms, though longtime listeners would catch on—the Stats Office is the Office of Statistics; an APB is an "all-points bulletin." Articles about the show sometimes offered translations, such as when the *Saturday Evening Post* pointed out the show's "authentic-sounding, if sometimes puzzling, technical police lingo, salted with such slangy abbreviations as 'R. & I.' (Records and Information), 'the mamma sheet' (index to a criminal's file), 'the moniker file' (list of nicknames), 'stats office' (statistics), and 'MO' (technique, or *modus operandi* of the criminal)."[58] The use of specialized language also placed listeners "alongside" Friday and his partner; they were not a part of the police force, but they were able to listen to the talk between its officers.

Moreover, as they were tagging along with Friday and his partner, listeners began to share aural space with people they came to know. The lead detectives had muted personalities, but they were not fully devoid of them. Joe Friday appeared in every episode, and over time listeners learned things that personalized him. Of course, listeners were impressed by Friday's incorruptible character and his absolute commitment to his job, but they also discovered, over time, humanizing details: he was unmarried and lived with his mother, whom he treated with respect; he was affectionate toward his partners; he had a wry sense of humor. Even such a small collection of details was more information than listeners learned about either of the interchangeable lead detectives of *The FBI in Peace and War*, and listeners certainly knew Friday more intimately than they knew the rotating officers of *Gang Busters*, which changed its location and its cast every episode.

The constituent pieces of *Dragnet*'s aesthetic were intended to connote realism, but not only for its own sake. *Dragnet*'s realist aesthetic was designed to support a new representation of the police in American media. By creating a soundscape that sketched out a real city, and by placing attentive listeners alongside the police as they investigated it, Jack Webb and his team sought to shift audiences' conception of the police officer from the "superman" that Marty Wynn despised to a particularly postwar vision of the police officer as an "organization man." The cultural resonance of this new representation is evidenced by *Dragnet*'s critical and popular success as well as by the imitations that immediately followed.[59]

Influences and Inheritances

As the creators of *Dragnet* enjoyed their radio success, the networks were beginning to disinvest from that medium and invest instead in the promises of television. Even in the sunset of dramatic radio, however, *Dragnet*'s influence on crime storytelling was clear. The show's sounds and silences brought a new form of aural realism to radio, one that was copied by a handful of other programs in the last full decade of radio drama.

The Lineup (1950–1953) and *21st Precinct* (1953–1956) borrowed *Dragnet*'s studied tedium and limited perspective. Both programs showed only the perspective of the police, never the criminals. They both focused on a range of crimes and complaints, broadening their story lines beyond the customary murders and robberies. As the title reflects, *The Lineup* began its narrative with an identity parade conducted in the police headquarters of an anonymous city. Starting with the identification of this first suspect (usually a lead rather than the criminal), listeners followed Lieutenant Ben Guthrie and Sergeant Matt Grebb as they sought an arrest in the week's case.

21st Precinct shared even more elements of *Dragnet*'s aural realism than *The Lineup*. *Variety* introduced the show to readers as "a documentary-style drama . . . [that] obviously is CBS-Radio's answer to NBC's "Dragnet."[60] Like *Dragnet*, *21st Precinct* featured a police officer as its narrator: Frank Kennelly (Everett Sloane) was a stolid, world-weary police captain, as committed to his job as Sergeant Friday. Set in one precinct in New York, the show featured a more restricted geographic view than even *Dragnet*, and the geography of that precinct was equally as important to *21st Precinct*. The announcer reinforced the precision of place at the top of every episode: "21st Precinct. It's just lines on a map of the city of New York. Most of the 173,000 people wedged into the nine-tenths of a square mile between Fifth Avenue and the East River wouldn't know if you asked them that they lived or worked in the 21st. Whether they know it or not, the security of their homes, their persons, and their property is the job of the men of the 21st Precinct." As in *Dragnet*, throughout the episode, street names were called out and important locations were described with care.

The soundscape of producers John Ives (an alumnus of *Gang Busters*) and Stanley Niss pushed *Dragnet*'s "The Big Court" experiment further: *21st Precinct* used no music at all. Instead, the show used sound effects, silence, and vocal differentiation to transition between scenes. Kennelly's monologue was always unadorned—only the voice of Everett Sloane was heard—and the shift into the narrative space was marked by the introduction of ambient sound. A common marker was the sound of footsteps as Kennelly entered a room. Other markers included the scratchy chatter of a police radio, the rumble of a police car engine, and the noisy conversations of a crowded room. The result was a show that, like *Dragnet*, required audiences to lean in to their receivers.

The success of *Dragnet* also inspired aesthetic experimentation on its own network. NBC's short-lived *Confession* (1953) was slotted as a summer replacement for *Dragnet*. *Confession* was a crime drama—though not a procedural. Instead, the show used a police confession as a framing device to tell a story of a criminal trespass. It shared with *Dragnet* an interest in realism supported by a minimalist (or rather, minimalist-sounding) approach to radio sound. As the show began, the announcer intoned, "The confession you are about to hear is an actual tape recording," and few moments later, the listener was informed that these crimes were "a matter of documented record." One heard the beeping of a recording machine, followed immediately by the voice of a police officer prompting the speaker, "Go ahead, please." From there, the criminal narrated his or her misdeeds. During the narration, the recorder beeped intermittently, reminding listeners of the circumstances in which the story was being told. As in *Dragnet*, music was used sparingly, the sparse soundtrack underscoring the seriousness of the endeavor.

Nightwatch (1954–1955) extended *Dragnet*'s experimentation into nonfiction documentary, broadcasting real police work on national radio. In doing so, it created a soundscape located somewhere between an episode of *Dragnet* and a live news broadcast.[61] *Nightwatch* opened with real radio communication between dispatch and a patrol car, confirming the start of the car's "tour of duty" at 6:00 p.m. The show was narrated by a man who introduced himself as "a police recorder." Don Reed directed the audience, "Remember the people you hear are not actors, and all the voices and sounds are authentic. For this is *Nightwatch*." Throughout, Reed performed the same function that Friday did, narrating events and translating where necessary. The brief run of *Nightwatch* is a fascinating set of documents, but there was little suspense in the show's tedium and it lacked the dramatic pull of the scripted "documentary" police shows.

These post-*Dragnet* programs varied in quality, but factors independent of quality influenced the lengths of their runs; the inescapable fact was that the 1950s were the last of the radio days. *Dragnet* continued to air on radio through 1957, but its more profound impact was made on television.[62] The series began its television run in late 1951, and it was soon followed by several of the radio shows it inspired, at the same time that other police dramas were created especially for television. These shows, old and new, shared both *Dragnet*'s realist orientation and its ideology of policing; together, they made the police procedural an anchoring genre of the new medium.

CHAPTER 3

SATURATION AND CITIZENSHIP

Dragnet on Television and in Culture

IN THE *CONGRESSIONAL RECORD* OF July 27, 1954, Representative Sam Yorty (D-CA) devotes more than six hundred words to the commendation of Jack Webb "for his splendid contribution to good citizenship."[1] Writes Yorty, "Today there is not a city or hamlet in the United States, boasting of a radio set or a television receiver, where he is not known to every man, woman, and child. His radio and TV series Dragnet, has become one of the Nation's No. 1 listening and viewing programs. It is soon to take its place as an important motion picture released by Warner Bros."[2] The same lesson was carried across these media, Yorty continues: "It has taught millions of people a better understanding of law enforcement and respect for law enforcement's honest agents." In admiration of the quality of the show's lessons in civic responsibility, Yorty concludes that "Mr. Webb has done more than repay his public for its loyalties and support of him."[3]

Yorty emphasized Webb's commitment to responsible storytelling and linked his show's influence to its success across mediums. In July 1954, *Dragnet* had been a top-rated radio show for several years, it was attaining its peak ratings on television, and it was a few months away from being released as a feature film by Warner Bros. In addition to listening to and viewing the show, audiences encountered *Dragnet* in its other forms, including a newspaper comic strip, licensed games and toys, and hit records. By the mid-1950s, when the commendation was composed, *Dragnet* was an inescapable part of popular culture. The reporter Bob Thomas spoke to the omnipresence of *Dragnet* in everyday life when he wrote that he found himself hounded by the show's theme: "Everywhere you go, it's 'dumm da dum dummm.' It blares from juke boxes and radios. TV comics use it as a punch line. My five-year-old even brought it home from kindergarten the other day."[4] Even when Thomas was not watching *Dragnet* on television, the show followed him around. To understand *Dragnet*'s impact, we must consider the show

FIGURE 3.1. Jack Webb reads his commendation in the *Congressional Record.* Bettmann Archive/Getty Images.

as Thomas and other members of the audience experienced it in the 1950s: as a cultural site spread across multiple mediums and as an inescapable part of postwar US culture. In its ubiquity, *Dragnet* became a text through which audiences developed and expressed their understanding of policing, law, justice, and civic life more broadly.

Scholars of contemporary film and broadcasting have, over the last two decades, sought to understand what happens to texts, audiences, and industries as media cross platforms. Following the work of Henry Jenkins and others, media scholars have become accustomed to thinking of contemporary audiences as fractured and mobile, interacting with transforming mediums on shifting terms.[5] Scholars have also become more used to thinking about the ways in which industries have worked together, creating texts that travel—from Michele Hilmes's early study of radio and television shaking hands during the classical Hollywood period to media franchising that so dominates our contemporary media landscape, as detailed by Derek Johnson and others.[6]

Scholars have spent less time considering the larger cultural consequences of media convergence. As it moved across mediums in the 1950s, *Dragnet* produced a cultural suffusion that shaped civic life. Understanding *Dragnet*'s cultural influence requires a conception of spectatorship that goes beyond individual or group responses to specific texts and considers instead how the circulation of specific texts contributes to larger historical contexts. New research about audiences and texts allows us to think more broadly about those relationships. Particularly useful here is the concept of "engagement" as explored by Annette Hill and others. As Hill writes, engagement "argues for the soft power of audiences who push beyond commercial frames, engaging with culture in ways that complicate, frustrate and outpace traditional media."[7] John Corner emphasizes the productive flexibility of the term and its potential to capture the contemporary media environment, one "in which we live 'within' the media more than live 'with' them."[8] This is not to say that audiences are manipulated, Corner insists: "Living 'within' the media is by no means to assume that the media 'control' us; it is just that older notions of their 'effects' need to be exchanged for a subtler sense of their permeation of the 'everyday' at different levels and from diverse directions."[9] While Hill and Corner are largely thinking about contemporary media, audiences of the past also lived "within" media. In this chapter I consider precisely how this was so by analyzing the permeation of *Dragnet* at different levels and from diverse directions. A unique historical document, *Dragnet* offers evidence of the direct engagement of listening and viewing, as well as the ways in which the show gave form, direction, and language to Americans' engagement with one another.

These expressions, and this permeation, were made possible through the bonds of admiration and affection that *Dragnet* built with audiences through television. In this period, as Michael Newman and Elana Levine write, "the dominant view of television was as a waste of time at best, and possibly also a source of serious and widespread social problems."[10] How did *Dragnet* become understood as a text that *addressed* social problems rather than perpetuated them? Key to the answer were choices made in its adaptation from radio to television, through which *Dragnet* marked itself as a "quality" program. Most critically, Jack Webb's decision to shoot on film permitted a visual aesthetic that set the show apart from its crime-show competition and allowed the show to achieve a broader reach through reruns and syndication. Had *Dragnet* not moved to television, it would likely exist today as an experiment in audio storytelling known almost exclusively to fans and collectors of "old-time radio." Through television, however, *Dragnet* was able to help shape, and simultaneously benefit from, a discourse about quality television that enabled the show's circulation as a text of civic value.

Redefining Quality Television

While the radio program established *Dragnet*'s aesthetic innovations, the television series contributed most directly to the proliferation of *Dragnet* throughout the 1950s. Traditional metrics of audience engagement are the strongest evidence: the show was a hit. It was a hit because it maintained the radio sensibility while creating its own distinctive, influential aesthetic. As an early example of prestige programming, as one of the most watched television shows of the decade, and as the series that created the formula for one of television's most enduring genres, the police procedural, *Dragnet* established itself as one of the most important programs in the medium that was rapidly becoming a major force in American life.

NBC introduced *Dragnet* gingerly. The first television broadcast was a test episode, on December 16, 1951, shown as a special episode on *Chesterfield Sound Off Time*. The first episode, based on a radio script about a bomb scare at Los Angeles City Hall, performed well enough to please the sponsors and the network. At first, *Dragnet* appeared every two weeks, alternating for most of that time with a television adaptation of its radio competitor *Gangbusters*. By late 1952, production had ramped up, *Gang Busters* was canceled, and *Dragnet*'s time slot was its own.

For most of its run, *Dragnet* was unbeatable on Thursday nights. The *Los Angeles Times* critic Cecil Smith declared, "TV shows have no more chance against Sgt. Joe Friday than crooks, thieves and murderers."[11] *Dragnet* was also, for a time, unbeatable among all television programs. A few months before the show was extolled on the floor of the Senate, it had achieved a remarkable feat: it vaulted over *I Love Lucy* in the ratings in the last weeks of 1953.[12] *Dragnet* eventually slid a few spaces from its 1953–1954 peak, but through 1959 it retained a strong audience share and proved to be one of NBC's few reliable hits in the decade.[13]

Dragnet's television success built on its radio success: the television series maintained the style and sensibility of the radio program, and critics responded warmly to the adaptation. *Variety* wrote that "'Dragnet' brings to video the same taut, suspenseful set of proceedings that has made it a radio fave."[14] Jack Gould, writing in the *New York Times*, agreed that the producers had done well making the transition and predicted a positive response from TV audiences, writing that *Dragnet* appeared "destined for success in television." Gould noted the maintenance of the radio show's aesthetic and entertainment value: "The program offered a documentary drama which in its terseness and understatement was an exciting thriller."[15] Just as on radio, critics appreciated the way in which Webb and his team extracted maximum suspense out of a minimalist approach.

Success on television also depended on a series of production choices specific to the newer medium. The most important decision was to shoot on film rather than broadcast live. This decision led to a series of consequences for the show's short-term reception and long-term reputation. Shooting on film resulted in the creation of a distinctive aesthetic, produced critical efficiencies in production and distribution, and opened up new opportunities in syndication. *Dragnet* was not the first filmed program or even the first hit show on film. William Lafferty has argued that the thirty-minute anthology program *Fireside Theater* (1949–1958) "proved the viability of filmed television programming at a point in the medium's evolution when the broadcasting and advertising industries doubted the potential of such programming."[16] However, because *Fireside Theater* was the object of critical scorn even as it did well in the ratings, it contributed to the prevailing association between filmed programming and unambitious, mediocre television.

By producing cost-effective prestige television, Jack Webb helped shift the definition of "quality television" in the 1950s. When critics and scholars reference television's first "Golden Age," the body of referenced texts generally consists of the live anthology series on the major networks, broadcast live from New York.[17] *Kraft Television Theater* (1947–1958), *Philco-Goodyear Television Playhouse* (1948–1955), *Studio One* (1948–1958), *U.S. Steel Hour* (1953–1963), and *Playhouse 90* (1956–1961) have been the darlings of television critics and historians since the 1950s. Critics approved of anthology programs not only because of their high-brow credentials but also because they took advantage of the elements of television's medium-specificity, particularly what were understood to be inherent qualities of "liveness" and "intimacy." As William Boddy writes, "According to many early writers on television, the essential technological feature of television versus the motion picture was the electronic medium's capacity to convey a simultaneous distant performance visually. In this regard, the medium was a unique synthesis of the immediacy of live theatrical performance, the space-conquering powers of radio, and the visual strategies of the motion picture."[18] "Liveness" was integral to broadcasting because it was part of radio and television's common strategy of differentiation. Michele Hilmes explains that the oligopoly of network control was justified by the ideology of liveness: "Only a network, with its real-time connection from station to station across the country, could deliver the simultaneous signal of something happening *right now* to its affiliates and audiences; no other medium could do that."[19]

When NBC entered negotiations to bring *Dragnet* to television, the

FIGURE 3.2. Webb directs Ben Alexander (who played Friday's partner Frank Smith from 1952 to 1959) on set in 1953. John Vachon, *LOOK* Magazine Photograph Collection, Library of Congress, Prints and Photographs Division, LC-DIG-ppmscd-01073.

network wanted the show to be live, like the rest of television's quality programs. Webb, however, wanted film. Webb defended his choice to *Variety* in 1958: "I've got a lot of respect for live television . . . but there are certain limitations I don't like. You can't light live properly; you need floorlamps to get in on a closeup [*sic*], and there's no way to do it in a live show. . . . I just think you can't get the technical perfection we can achieve shooting a film with a live technique."[20] There was, initially, considerable resistance to this preference. *Dragnet*'s success on radio allowed Jack Webb the leverage to insist on shooting on film, but he and his coproducer still had to volunteer to give up their salaries in order to finance the first several episodes.[21]

Dragnet helped illustrate to critics and sponsors that film production could bring a different kind of quality programming to television. *Motion Picture Daily* marked out the difference between *Dragnet* and lower-quality filmed programming, reporting that the show "succeeded in putting on the screen a tense, well-paced show that combined all the advantages of the motion picture and television."[22] The *Los Angeles Times* columnist Hal Humphrey agreed, telling his readers, "Because it is on film, 'Dragnet' is also one of the major arguments against those critics who claim that Hollywood film producers are blanketing TV with mediocrity."[23] Jack Gould wrote in the *New York Times* that *Dragnet* was a sign that "apparently the motion-picture capital is beginning to get the hang of TV."[24] Noticing that in the 1952 season an increasing number of shows were switching from live to film production, *Variety* gave credit to the industry leaders: "Various reasons are given for the surge in celluloid, but two concrete examples are 'I Love Lucy' and 'Dragnet,' success of these toprated [*sic*] telefilm shows accounting for a good deal of sponsor interest in vidpix."[25]

Shooting on film also set up *Dragnet* for early success in the burgeoning realm of television syndication, which increased the size of its audience and expanded its cultural impact. A filmed episode, once produced, could be easily reproduced—and replicated in its original quality, not translated to an inferior kinescope. Older episodes of *Dragnet* were broadcast outside of prime time and across the country, first as *The Cop* and then as *Badge 714*.[26] Affiliates were at first opposed to reruns, but over time it became clear that a sufficient portion of the television audience didn't mind repeats. *Dragnet/The Cop/Badge 714* was a particular favorite among first-time and repeat viewers. According to one Nielsen survey, nearly half of the audience for one rerun episode of *Dragnet* was watching it for the second time. An article in *Variety* celebrated the increased acceptance of reruns in spring 1954. The trade paper credited NBC for proving "that old show business maxim about giving the public a good show above all" by making its best shows available so that "filmbuyers learned that such properties as 'Badge 714' and 'Victory at Sea' can do as good or better a job for them as any firstrun property."[27] Indeed, *Badge 714* continued to do well in syndication both during *Dragnet*'s original run and for years after the final episode was first broadcast.

Dragnet's quality reproductions could not have had their impact, of course, without an impactful aesthetic. The production team created a distinctive style that became immediately iconic. Framing and editing patterns particularly marked *Dragnet*'s visual style and included reliance on close-ups, disregard for eyeline matches, deep focus photography (shooting through things to create depth in the shot), unusual angles for visual interest (particularly high-angle and low-angle shots), visual montages, and the integration of location shooting (including stock footage). The visual style was made to fit the aural style, which was stripped down and heavy on repetition. The look of the show was remarkably consistent throughout its run. As *Newsweek* noted about the show's creator, "In Webb's view, monotony is a definite advantage: 'For a regular half-hour show, stylization and a consistent format are desperately needed. Once you get them they should be treasured.'"[28]

Dragnet's signature was the use of close-ups. Jack Webb did not invent the close-up for television, but television critics have given him credit for using it most effectively.[29] Webb consistently described his cinematographic choices as practical as much as artistic. He explained to one interviewer, "I started singling out faces on television long ago, when I found that three or four just don't show up on the average set."[30] In another interview, he said simply, "Too many people still have 10- and 12-inch screens."[31] The use of close-ups was also derived from the structure of the source material, the original radio scripts. *Dragnet* scripts were made up of a series of interviews connected by monologues, and on television the dialogue scenes most often played out in alternating close-ups of the detectives and the witnesses.

The use of close-ups in *Dragnet* also took advantage of the "intimacy" of television by bringing audiences as close as possible to the performers. An early episode, "The Big Mother" (television: Jan. 31, 1952; radio: Nov. 9, 1950), received positive notices from critics for capturing Peggy Webber's performance as a woman who loses a baby and, in grief, takes another from a hospital. For the majority of the four-minute monologue that serves as the falling action of the episode, the camera is tight on Webber's face. With about a dozen brief cutaways but no change of angle, Webber describes giving birth to a stillborn child while her husband was away, then passing a hospital and feeling compelled to steal one of the babies from the nursery. She asks the officers, quietly, "That's why you want my baby, isn't it? Because I took him? Because my baby died, and I took him?" One critic writing about the episode called Webber's touching performance "real Oscar stuff."[32] The irony of commending the performances of *Dragnet*'s actors, of course, is that actors were permitted only a very limited performance range. It was, then, the effectiveness of the direction as much as the acting that made this scene worthy of critical attention. Over time, the show became so closely associated with the close-up that when other shows tried the technique, they were accused of copying Webb, as when Val Adams wrote about *Mr. District Attorney* (1954–1955): "At times the cameras switch rapidly from one character to another, all in close-up, just like 'Dragnet.'"[33]

In the visual medium, *Dragnet* also retained its underplaying with an assist from a new piece of technology. *Dragnet*'s style of underplaying had been established and maintained by a select group of radio actors reading from scripts since 1949. To recreate this aural performance style on television, Webb brought a new machine to the set: a "TelePrompTer." The incorporation of the machine had the added benefit of cutting production costs by cutting rehearsal time in half.[34]

With its close-ups and underplaying, *Dragnet* was stylized, but it was nevertheless understood to be a "documentary" series, one that was committed

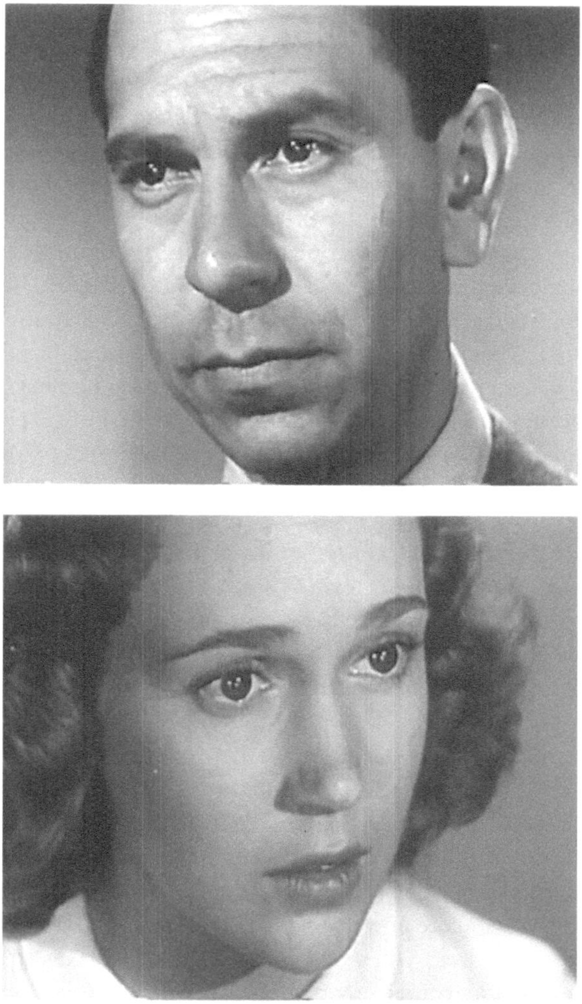

FIGURES 3.3 AND 3.4. Most scenes in *Dragnet* were dialogue scenes, and dialogue scenes were most often conducted via an exchange of close-ups between the detective (top) and the victim/witness/culprit (bottom). In "The Big Seventeen" (Nov. 6, 1952), Friday interviews a teenager on the wrong path (Allene Roberts).

to realistic storytelling based on facts. On both radio and television, *Dragnet* was committed to teaching its audience, and elements of *Dragnet*'s televisual style contributed to a deepening of its pedagogy. One significant change from radio to television was a shift in the narration within the opening sequence. On radio, *Dragnet* opened with a second-person address by the announcer: "You're a detective sergeant. You're assigned to —— detail." Speaking directly to the listener, the show encouraged the listener's identification with the lead officers through words alone.

Dragnet's television opening needed a visual element, and Webb stole it directly from the semi-documentary film that inspired *Dragnet*'s creation, *He Walked by Night*. That film's opening shot is of Los Angeles sprawling into the distance as the narrator speaks: "This is Los Angeles. Our Lady the Queen of the Angels, as the Spaniards named her. The fastest-growing city in the nation. It's been called a bunch of suburbs in search of a city. And it's been called the glamour capital of the world." During this narration, shots overlap and dissolve into one another—from the opening panorama to a Buddhist temple in Chinatown, from a busy intersection to piers jutting into the Pacific Ocean—and end with a shot of City Hall.

On television, *Dragnet* copied this voice-over and gave it to Sergeant Friday rather than an unseen narrator. From the opening of the show, then, Friday took viewers through diverse areas of Los Angeles. For example, in "The Big Crime" (television: Sept. 9, 1954; radio: Feb. 15, 1951), Friday recites his monologue over a slow montage in which the shots change as he speaks.[35] Friday explains to viewers:

> This is the city. One of the biggest in the United States. Spreads out in all four directions like a broadloom rug. To the south and west is the downtown business district. To the east, the industrial area. Los Angeles, California. It's pretty much like your town. This is a Spanish priest, one of the city's founders. . . . It's got high-tension wires, bringing in the power. . . . It's got railroads and freight yards, churches—any kind you want. Public parks and lakes. It's got a police department and a city hall. This is where I work. I'm a cop.

The opening was sometimes long, as in this example. Other times the opening was short (particularly in the later seasons), skipping the details and cutting straight to the investigation. When they were long, Friday's reflections often had explicit pedagogical purpose, teaching facts about Los Angeles and its environs. Several episodes reminded viewers that L.A. is a city made up of two million people. Other episodes gave details about Los Angeles geography, noted historical facts, or showed new buildings and other developments.

The discursive impact of *Dragnet*'s opening is arguable. Ronald Schmidt argues that Friday's "this is the city" is a "statement of total ontological certainty."[36] The montage, jumping from place to place around the city, made clear that the officer's field of vision was broader than the average citizen's—the police were always watching. Though the opening did give an impression of the omnipresence of the police, the ontological certainty was not total. The "this is the city" opening often showed the city as overwhelming, always teetering on the edge between order and chaos. In "The Big Lamp" (television: June 19, 1952; radio: Oct. 20, 1949), Friday tells the audience that in the past year in Los Angeles, there were fifty thousand crimes and fifty thousand criminals, and "every year, they seem to get better at their jobs." Friday knew the city, could point to its nooks and show us its crannies, but he still did not control it. The limits of Friday's abilities and influence were as much a part of *Dragnet*'s televisual realism as they were a part of its aural realism.

Montage sequences were also used to educate audiences. The show incorporated montages primarily because they provided a solution to the practical problem of adapting existing shows: the producers needed to retain the monologues that provided connective tissue of the radio scripts. Indeed, in many episodes, montages simply put relevant images on the screen while Friday spoke. Very common were sequences in which the detectives and witnesses pantomimed conversations while Friday's monologue summarized the false leads and announced the next steps. But in other episodes, these new illustrations were direct and informative, deepening the show's pedagogy, particularly in their display of real-life police artifacts and demonstrations of police procedure. In "The Big Betty" (television: Sept. 24, 1953), as Friday narrates the arrest of the subject, we see actual police forms, one stacked on top of another—first a typed police report, filled in with the details of the case, then two arrest warrants. In "The Big False Make" (television: May 27, 1954), Friday explains that the police "ran the name of the suspect through R&I," and we see a close-up of the Records and Identification Department's machine sorting the records, on cards, into slots.[37] These transitions were also often used to show off the show's library of location footage, whether the detectives were walking up to storefronts to check out a crime scene or officers were pulling out of the police garage and toward a busy intersection on their way to interview a witness.

Through a variety of choices, from the use of film to the use of close-ups, *Dragnet*'s visual style maintained the "authenticity" for which the radio show had been celebrated while creating a distinctly televisual style. Its success, measured by both the approval of critics and the size of its audience, made it one of the most important programs on early television. As the 1950s wore on, its influence spread beyond broadcasting and into other aspects of American cultural life.

DRAGNET ACROSS CULTURE

Dragnet took up more and more cultural space with each passing year. In early 1954, William R. Weaver reflected in the *Motion Picture Herald* on *Dragnet*'s increasing presence, writing, "'Dragnet' is to television at this point what 'Birth of a Nation' was to the silent motion picture for a span of its best years. Its two half-hours on television plus its half hour [on] radio give 'Dragnet' a saturation no other dramatic presentation has matched heretofore or is likely to hereafter."[38] Weaver went on to speculate on the upcoming film adaptation, but he could have also taken into account a number of other ways in which *Dragnet* achieved saturation. In addition to the radio and television series, there were a comic strip, licensed toys and games, and hit records. The release of the feature film in 1954—a hit for Warner Bros.—marked the peak of *Dragnet*'s cultural saturation.

Not long after *Dragnet* premiered on television, local newspapers began to announce that they would be running a new comic strip based on the radio and television series. The *Dragnet* comic (1952–1955) premiered with some fanfare: the *San Antonio Express* carried an announcement of the comic in the news section, in addition to paid advertisements. Indeed, the *Express* thought readers would be interested enough to put the story on the front page. In the print announcement, readers were promised that the comic would be contiguous with the series, featuring stories from "the same expert team, headed by creator Jack Webb."[39] Readers were promised *Dragnet*'s signature authenticity as well: "The Los Angeles Police Department has put complete case files and full access to all its operations to the disposal of the creators of the DRAGNET comic strip, assuring that complete authenticity will be seen by the reader."[40]

The strip used the same major characters as the series, starring Joe Friday and Frank Smith. It featured "realistic" crimes that could have appeared on the broadcast series, as in the fall of 1952, when the comic strip spent three months unspooling the story of a narcotics ring in which most of the users were teenagers. The strip utilized the stylistic tics of the radio and television scripts, such as starting with a written monologue with a precise location and time stamp. For example, a 1952 strip begins, "After booking Rick at Venice Station on suspicion of narcotics violation, Frank and I drove over to meet Brady . . . 8:20 p.m."[41] The dialogue within the strip's frames aped the show's clipped style, as when Friday asks a young man whether he was on drugs when he had a car accident that put his friend in the hospital: "Look, boy, that girl's in bad shape. You were driving the car. . . . The girl's a user.

. . . Your arm looks like a punchboard. Now how 'bout it?" Readers would have been able to hear Jack Webb's delivery in their heads.

The comic strip had many similarities to the radio and television series, but the adaptation to the strip format was not as seamless as the adaptation from radio to television (or, as we will see, from television to film). The comic was not visually consistent, either internally or with the television series. As Michael Hayde details, the artwork was done by different artists over the years, which led to strips of varying styles and varying quality.[42] The comic did not prove to be particularly memorable, though it is remembered with some affection among *Dragnet* fans. Running during *Dragnet*'s height, it contributed to the show's cultural circulation in the middle part of the decade.

As 1953 turned to 1954, *Dragnet* began to appear in an additional section of the newspaper: the "movies" section. In early 1954, the papers began running stories about the start of production on a feature film based on the *Dragnet* series. *Variety* described the production as "the first television show produced intact by a major studio for showing on theatre screens."[43] The careful language seems intended to acknowledge that *Dragnet* was not the very first television series adapted to feature film, but also to distinguish it from lesser adaptations that readers may remember. Before *Dragnet*, very few theatrically released films had been based on television properties. One was the 1950 feature film based on *The Goldbergs*, which did not take the form of the radio and television series. Another was the serial *Captain Video: Master of the Stratosphere*, which was based on the television series *Captain Video and His Video Rangers* (1949–1955) and released in theaters in 1951. In production at the same time as *Dragnet* was *The Long, Long Trailer* (1954), which starred Lucille Ball and Desi Arnaz, but in which the *I Love Lucy* stars played new characters. *Dragnet*'s successful, "intact" translation from broadcast series to feature film did two things at once: it gave audiences a new experience of *Dragnet*, and it gave the industry a model for television-film collaboration.

The *Dragnet* feature gave audiences an experience similar to the one they knew from radio and television, enhanced by several elements of spectacle: a large screen (though not widescreen), glorious WarnerColor, and with its feature length, a bigger story, including the hint of a romance for Sergeant Friday. The film was a coproduction with Webb's company (Mark VII), in which the power was largely Jack Webb's. Though the studio oversaw production and assigned some of its crew and contract players, Webb directed, chose the scriptwriter (Richard L. Breen, with whom he had worked on *Pat Novak for Hire* early in his radio career), and cast most of the roles with actors from his own stock company of radio and television players.

FIGURE 3.5. Warner Bros. placed full-page ads in the trade papers to announce the *Dragnet* feature film, assuring readers that the film would be built on *Dragnet*'s television success. Motion Picture Daily/Media History Digital Library.

All the elements of Dragnetian realism were transferred to the feature film. Webb insisted on, and Warner Bros. made hay out of, the feature film's authenticity. The film, like the radio and television episodes, was based on a real case from the Los Angeles Police Department. In the film, detectives Friday and Smith are assigned to the Intelligence Division and are investigating a murder committed by a crime syndicate. The on-set adviser, Captain James Hamilton of the LAPD, had overseen the real-life investigation; his involvement was a recurring topic in the studio press releases. One release assured audiences that Hamilton "was on the set every moment of shooting and available for answering Webb's many questions." The release continued, "The picture is thus completely accurate where police work is concerned."[44] Another explained that Hamilton, played in the film by Richard Boone, was left-handed: "So Webb had Richard Boone play the role like a lefty, even to wearing a left-handed wrist watch and gun holster."[45] Production design, too, was a topic of interest. One press release reported that Webb had a City Hall office duplicated in its entirety, "down to the last desk ornament and wall decoration." Even the secretaries "were portrayed by two actresses bearing a near resemblance, although the players had no dialogue and showed only in a passing shot."[46] Press materials assured viewers that the assiduous attention to detail was as essential to the film as it was to the series.

The film adaptation also maintained *Dragnet*'s aural and visual style. Reporter Philip K. Scheuer wrote that Webb laughed after Scheuer posed one particular query to him: "Yes, we'll use more big close-ups than some features. . . . Everybody asks us that question."[47] It is clear from the opening of the film that in addition to liberally using close-ups, Webb similarly kept all the elements of his televisual style that violated the classical Hollywood conventions. In the narrative sequence before the credits, we see the murder that Friday and Smith will spend the film investigating.[48] In the sequence, we see unexpected angles, a broken 180-degree rule, and a disregard for eyeline matches, all elements of *Dragnet*'s televisual style. We can also hear an intricately layered soundscape, an inheritance of *Dragnet* on radio. In the sixty seconds of this sequence, there is no dialogue, only selected sounds: high winds across a field mixed with the chirps of different birds, the soft scuffle of shoes against grass as the targeted man tries to run from danger and then the powerful, collective bang of a double-barreled shotgun. It's a standout sequence, a demonstration that televisual aesthetics could adapt to the big screen.

The film was well received by audiences and critics. *Dragnet* opened in first-run houses in New York, Chicago, Boston, and other major cities in late August and early September 1954. Across the country, it was pronounced a success. Some reviewers did not love the film, but of those nearly all agreed with the *Boston Globe* reviewer, who wrote, "If you love Mr. Friday with the devotion of the crowds at the Paramount and Fenway [movie theaters] yesterday, you shouldn't miss this new adventure."[49]

More important to the film studios than critical approbation, *Dragnet* made a considerable return on investment. After its Labor Day weekend opening, the film was held over in each of the 197 theaters in which it was shown over the holiday.[50] In Hartford and Chicago, *Dragnet* broke house records.[51] In all, the *Dragnet* film made nearly $6 million in its first run, which was twelve times its $500,000 budget.[52] In *Dragnet*'s modest but lucrative production, Hedda Hopper saw potential for the whole industry to be enlightened: "The success of 'Dragnet,' Jack Webb's first picture since he became Mr. Television, has made our producers sit up and take notice. At [last] they realize the solid gold value of the little box in the living room and wish they'd gotten in on it long ago."[53] Warner Bros. did indeed begin to move aggressively toward establishing relationships in television, for feature film productions like *Dragnet* and later for its own television productions.

On film, in newspapers, in stores, on the radio, and on television, audiences experienced *Dragnet* in proliferating ways across the 1950s. Another contribution to *Dragnet*'s cultural footprint was the lines of *Dragnet*-associated merchandise that appeared over the years. As Webb remembered, "Toy manufacturers put out a Joe Friday gun, a miniature squad car, a fingerprint kit and a *Dragnet* game, and there was a line of books covering some of the more exciting *Dragnet* cases."[54] Michael Hayde describes a broader set of licensed and unlicensed toys, including target games, puzzles, toy forensics equipment, and several different kinds of water pistols and cap guns. As Hayde writes, "For a time, shelf space for *Dragnet* toys rivaled that for *The Lone Ranger*, *Space Patrol*, and *Howdy Doody*."[55] Jack Webb seems not to have directly participated in the licensing or manufacturing of *Dragnet* toys and games, but his face—in the character of Jack Friday—appears prominently on the packaging.

Finally, *Dragnet* also circulated via a small flurry of records in the middle part of the decade. First among the *Dragnet*-inspired records was a parody by comedian Stan Freburg, who wrote (with Daws Butler) a three-minute skit called "St. George and the Dragonet," in which a knight is sent out to arrest a dragon. Freburg narrates as St. George, underplaying like Webb but within a much sillier situation than *Dragnet* ever offered: "Saturday, July 10th, 8:05 p.m. I was working out of the castle on the night watch when a call came in from the chief. A dragon had been devouring maidens. Homicide. My job: Slay him."[56] *Variety* reported that the record sold more than 1.2 million copies.[57] Also appearing in 1953: a Yiddish parody called "Dregnet" by Happy Lewis, a mambo version of the theme by Machito and His Afro-Cubans, and a comedy record written by comedian and musician Steve Allen called "Dragnet Goes to Kindergarten." None performed as well as Stan Freburg's parody, or as well as the Ray Anthony Orchestra's straight-faced recording of the *Dragnet* theme, released in the late summer of 1953. Both discs ended the year among the top records in retail sales (numbers fifteen and twenty-two, respectively) alongside records from Perry Como, Nat King Cole, Tony Bennett, and Patti Page.[58]

By watching, listening, reading, and buying records, audiences of the 1950s left evidence of their engagement with *Dragnet* across platforms. Audiences also engaged with *Dragnet* in ways that radio and television ratings, newspaper circulation estimates, sales figures, or box office receipts cannot fully capture. Having encountered the show regularly, and in varied ways, audiences brought the consequences of their engagement with *Dragnet* into larger civic life in the 1950s and after.

"INTEGRATED ENLIGHTENMENT": LIVING WITH *DRAGNET*

> Today people are looking for more realism in television. . . . They want to be entertained, but they also want to learn, to benefit and to become better citizens as a result of it."
>
> Jack Webb, qtd. in Walter Ames, "Christmas Rifle Story on Dragnet to Present Dramatic Safety Lesson to Parents," *Los Angeles Times*, December 18, 1952

Direct metrics of listening and viewing tell us that audiences maintained a sustained relationship with *Dragnet* over years. The depth and quality of the relationship between audience members and the program cannot be understood by looking at numbers alone, but *Dragnet* leaves other evidence of depth and quality because the show sought to make itself a part of civic life. The creators of *Dragnet*—and their production partners, most especially the LAPD—wanted listeners and viewers not only to engage with the show and its extensions but also to take those lessons into the wider world, and to use them there. Representative Sam Yorty's citation affirms this impact. As Yorty declared, *Dragnet* "taught millions of people a better understanding of law enforcement and respect for law enforcement's honest agents."[59] Yorty approved not only of the positive representation of police within the show but also of the pedagogical impact on audiences outside of the show.

Dragnet contributed in significant ways to the context in which audiences interacted with the criminal justice system. It even sometimes became a means through which the criminal justice system articulated its expectations of its citizens. Because of *Dragnet*'s commitment to its form of storytelling, if you believed its claims, simply listening or watching the show was an education in the real work of the police. At its height, then, up to forty million Americans took part in thirty minutes of civic education on a weekly basis, learning from *Dragnet* how the criminal justice system worked.[60] In this way, *Dragnet* permeated the everyday of postwar American life (to borrow John Corner's phrasing).

Dragnet was also directly incorporated into the instruments of civic life.

At least once, an episode of *Dragnet* played in a courtroom to illustrate a lesson to a group of defendants. Justice W. C. Ragan of Houston, Texas, had a radio episode broadcast in court as a crime deterrent for a group of thirteen teenagers and their families. The episode, unnamed in the article describing the incident, was likely "The Big Kid" (radio: Nov. 10, 1953; television: Sept. 30, 1954), in which Friday and Smith fail to prevent a gang fight that leads to a boy's death. In that episode, it is clear that absent, uninvolved parents are largely responsible for their children's involvement with gangs. One newspaper reported, "After both parents and their offspring had heard the program, the judge turned to the boys and said, 'I've taken this step because I want to acquaint you boys with the law.'"[61] Ragan's words indicate that, for him and likely for other viewers, the show was what it claimed to be: an accurate representation of the law and its enforcement, accurate enough to be used in the service of the system it represented.

The circulation of other episodes evinces that a range of audience members found *Dragnet* useful, not just entertaining. The producers of the show encouraged its use as direct education; Webb offered episodes for free ("as a public service," Yorty explained) to a variety of groups. Copies of episodes were delivered to the US military, the CIA, the National Safety Council, the Parent-Teacher Association, individual schools, and, of course, the Los Angeles Police Department and other police departments across the country.

Episodes about safe driving particularly highlighted *Dragnet*'s civic influence. Community groups often requested "The Big Trio," a traffic story. Webb told a *TV-Radio Life* columnist that he received four thousand letters after its television airing.[62] Not long after, the same magazine highlighted "The Big Trio" as one of three episodes of *Dragnet* in which Webb "has come out swinging on certain moral issues and against public indifference to the business of saving lives.[63] The episode's potential impact on audience behavior was emphasized by the promotional materials that NBC sent out to affiliates when they reran "The Big Trio" in the summer of 1953. Scheduled to be broadcast on the Thursday before the increased travel around Independence Day weekend, NBC wrote, "This special DRAGNET theme can be instrumental in saving lives in your community, as in other communities wherever DRAGNET is seen."[64]

The director of public relations for the Governor's Highway Safety Committee of Virginia, who was "willing to pay any reasonable price for it," requested a different *Dragnet* episode about responsible driving.[65] The letter did not directly reference the episode title, but it was probably "The Big Run," about a hot rod hit-and-run, which aired March 12, 1953. "The

FIGURE 3.6. In ".22 Rifle for Christmas," a distraught father cries over the body of his son.

Big Run" and "The Big Trio," along with a handful of others, were listed in NBC's internally produced Public Responsibility Reports.[66] The reports identified these episodes (and sometimes the *Dragnet* series as a whole) as "Integrated Enlightenment Material"—examples of NBC programming that served the public interest rather than solely the bottom line.

Dragnet also inspired civic discussion, prompting audiences to respond back to the show as well as to each other. In general, *Dragnet*'s civic education was meant to be uncontroversial. But some episodes took a position on more contentious issues, kicking off public debate rather than inspiring simple admiration. *Dragnet*'s most polarizing episode was probably ".22 Rifle for Christmas," which was broadcast on radio on December 22, 1949, as *Dragnet*'s first holiday program. It is one of *Dragnet*'s most unforgiving episodes. It begins with the disappearance of a child. By the end, the detectives have discovered the boy's body and the circumstances of his death: Stanley, his friend next door, who was going to receive a rifle for Christmas, had found it under the tree a few days early, and as the boys played with it, the gun went off. The episode was performed annually on radio for four consecutive years, from 1949 to 1952, due to the positive reaction from audiences. The only recorded objection to the first radio broadcast, in 1949, came from the National Rifle Association. Their objection made little impact. Indeed, according to *Time*, the LAPD responded to the NRA by "promis[ing] the association ten more shows illustrating the folly of giving rifles to children."[67]

The ".22 Rifle" episode kicked up more public debate when it came to television on Christmas 1952. The increased debate seems to have been in response to visualizing the radio story and particularly the choice to show a child's corpse on-screen. In the television episode, Stanley leads the detectives to where he buried his friend; the film cuts to a close-up as Friday brushes away a layer of leaves, revealing the dead boy's face. A letter in the NBC files responding to a complaint from a viewer replied, "This particular episode is not a pleasant one. However, it is true and its producers endeavor to portray the drama factually, without making it gruesome. . . . Mr. McDade was the first listener, to our knowledge, who has taken exception to the television treatment."[68] (Mr. McDade was not actually the only objector; Michael Hayde quotes a letter in which another viewer objected strenuously to the showing of a dead body.)

Other viewers responded to the politics of the episode. A renewed objection from the National Rifle Association appeared in its periodical, *American Rifleman*, and was reprinted in newspapers.[69] The editorial board wrote that the episode, while "dramatically and effectively presented," got its lesson wrong. The episode ends with two lines of dialogue firmly in the *Dragnet* style. A detective asks Friday, "Well, what's it all prove, Joe?" Friday responds, "You don't give a kid a gun for Christmas." The editorial board of the NRA strongly disagreed, insisting that many young people safely hunt, and many more young people are handed a gun after they are drafted into military service. The show's emphasis, they wrote, should have been on training and education: "Instead of denying his boy the rifle he wants for Christmas, the wise father will give it to him. At the same time he will see to it the boy is properly taught to respect it."[70]

Many other viewers expressed appreciation for the show and its clear lesson. James Abbe, writing in the *Oakland Tribune*, called the episode "truly powerful."[71] The mother of a ten-year-old boy, after seeing ".22 Rifle," wrote to Webb that the show made her son cry: "I put my arms around him and he just kept saying over and over, 'I don't ever want a gun, I don't ever want a gun.' God bless you in your work."[72] One columnist wrote that the episode was "bound to be discussed both pro and con but one cannot deny that it might prove to be the show that saves some youngster's life this Christmas."[73] Every year at Christmastime, viewers wrote in to request a repeat broadcast of the episode. But after a few airings between radio and television, Webb decided to produce a new Christmas episode, "The Big Little Jesus," a gentler story of the recovery of a Baby Jesus statue that had disappeared from a church nativity scene.[74]

Producers positioned *Dragnet* as a direct participant in public life, more often in much less controversial ways. *Dragnet* participated in local and national civic campaigns through on-air advertisement of programs such as National Crime Prevention Week and Fire Prevention Week. This mode of participation sometimes extended into the larger community in ways that overlapped with episodes. In 1951 the *Los Angeles Mirror* covered a former drug addict's visit to a local high school, an event that was part of the city's anti-drug program. Also visiting the school was Jack Webb. *The Mirror* reporter wrote, "The 'Dragnet' Program recently has highlighted the Los Angeles dope problem on three occasions. . . . Coincidentally, the May 5 show included a scene in which Webb, as Det. Sgt. Joe Friday of the Los Angeles Police Department, prepared a speech on narcotics—for delivery before Belmont High School students."[75]

That episode was "The Big Speech," one of a small number of episodes Webb wrote himself. It originally aired on radio on April 19, 1951, and on television on February 11, 1952.[76] In the episode, the detectives try to track down a young addict who has severely beaten a doctor to steal drugs. In the last few minutes of the episode, Friday practices his speech out loud. He begins, "I'd like to tell you about a young boy who started out in high school and ended up on the roof of a downtown hotel, dodging police bullets." The cautionary tale, entwined with Friday's psychological and social analysis of drug addiction, has of course been reinforced by the very case presented in "The Big Speech." Friday explains about the jailed addict and his addicted girlfriend, "Two years ago, they both sat out there in a high school auditorium during an assembly. He went a long way, didn't he, in his two years out of high school?" This episode, and its overlap with Webb's own civic engagement, represented most emphatically how much the show and its creator believed in its own good works. Indeed, Jack Webb had a particular reason for visiting the high school and having Friday deliver the speech: Webb himself was a Belmont High graduate.

As with this visit to Belmont, Jack Webb's circulation marked him as an upright citizen in ways consistent with his show's values. He publicly supported good causes, as in 1953, when he and his on-screen partner, Ben Alexander, hosted a 28½ hour telethon for the Cerebral Palsy Fund.[77] Also in 1953, Webb appeared at the annual Boy Scout Jamboree, starring in a show sponsored by the LAPD. In 1957, the Studio City Chamber of Commerce named Webb the honorary mayor, while Ben Alexander was named the honorary police chief.[78] These were just a few of the many, many instances comprising Webb's public record of good citizenship, instances that tied *Dragnet* to everyday reality.

Webb circulated, too, in ways that highlighted the distance between *Dragnet*'s reality and the lived reality of some of the show's audience.

Especially after the television adaptation added a visual component, it was clear that *Dragnet*'s Los Angeles was nearly exclusively white. (One of the rare exceptions was "The Big Little Jesus," mentioned previously, which is partly set in a Hispanic Catholic church.) Some viewers might have stopped to wonder, then, when the Los Angeles Urban League asked Jack Webb to serve as emcee at its 1954 annual meeting. At that gathering of the prominent civil rights organization, awards were given to groups of citizens recognized for "contributions in the field of human relations," and the main speaker was Lieutenant Commander Dennis Nelson, the highest-ranking African American in the US Navy.[79] Webb's presence suggested that he, too, had made a positive contribution to the field of human relations, but his appearance could also have prompted viewers to notice that *Dragnet* only very rarely gave roles to African Americans or to any other racial or ethnic minority.

Some audience members would have noticed the incomplete representation of public life in *Dragnet* before Webb's appearance at the Urban League event. At least one viewer tried to communicate their concerns about *Dragnet*'s whitewashing of Los Angeles. Around the time of the *Dragnet* feature, former California resident C. A. Simmons wrote to Jack Warner to criticize *Dragnet* for being insufficiently "authentic": "I defy you to get into the [Los Angeles] city hall, the stations in the trouble areas, without seeing persons of color or of minorities working in all sorts of capacities[,] both male and female. It makes you quite proud to see those of all colors and creeds working together, but not as Jack Webb portrays them."[80] The *Baltimore Afro-American* made a similar observation on its entertainment page. As the paper reported one week, "It's really nice to know that the 'Dragnet' world in which Jack Webb travels as 'Sergeant Friday' is entirely free of colored sinners, but it's too bad that his lack of objectivity deprives some tan actors of work."[81] Both writers demonstrate an awareness of the distance between *Dragnet*'s world and the world as they experienced it, suggesting the existence of a larger population of listeners and viewers whose informed skepticism mediated their engagement with the show.

Contemporary ambivalence about the show was not the largest part of its reputation, as *Dragnet* persisted as a cultural touchstone throughout the latter half of the twentieth century. Anticipating the show's last season (1958–1959), an NBC press release summarized *Dragnet*'s reception: "Police departments around the country thundered their approval of the first sincere attempt to show accurately a cop at work. Service clubs applauded the contributions by 'Dragnet' to the reduction of juvenile delinquency. The heap of praise is mountainous and, in fact, continuing—after nearly a decade."[82] *Dragnet*'s high production values, intentional aesthetic, and commitment to civic instruction established its place in the pantheon of quality television. Some instruction was specific: individual episodes were meant to reduce incidences of reckless driving or irresponsible gun ownership. Every episode was instructive in the general principles of the show: the careful presentation of the procedures of law enforcement intended to engender respect for, and cooperation with, the work of the police. Many individuals and institutions benefited from the show's success—its creators, the network, television as a medium—but perhaps none more than the Los Angeles Police Department, which found in *Dragnet* a partner in public relations.

CHAPTER 4

PROFESSIONALIZATION AND PUBLIC RELATIONS

Dragnet and the LAPD

DRAGNET HAD BEEN ON THE air for more than a year when William H. Parker became chief of the Los Angeles Police Department in August 1950. The program had run with the permission of Parker's predecessors, and at first Parker maintained a polite distance from the show, focusing instead on the business of reforming the LAPD. But the man who initially looked upon the show with some suspicion had wholly embraced *Dragnet* by the end of its run. When Sergeant Friday's badge was retired on the show, Parker gave instructions for the badge to "be encased in Lucite and sealed within the cornerstone of one of the new academy classroom buildings."[1] It had not taken long for Parker to notice the stunning overlap between his philosophy of policing and *Dragnet*'s procedural realism, and to appreciate the contribution the show made to improving the reputation of the police department he sought to reform.

In the years after World War II, policing agencies across the country took steps to remake themselves into "professional" departments. This wave of professionalization built on reform movements dating back to the work of August Vollmer, the Progressive reformer who in the early twentieth century transformed the Berkeley, California, police department. His innovations there became part of subsequent professionalization efforts, including improved officer training, new standards for recruitment and hiring, and the development of scientific methods for crime prevention and detection. Following Vollmer, in the 1930s J. Edgar Hoover sought to improve the status of federal agents (and increase his own power) by making large-scale changes in the Federal Bureau of Investigation, including insulating the FBI from political influence, instituting new codes of conduct for officers, and establishing the famed FBI Crime Lab.[2] Over the next decades, "modern" police forces looked like the organizations that Vollmer and Hoover transformed:

centrally organized with minimal political oversight, following modern scientific methods of crime detection and prevention, and populated by formally educated, highly trained officers. In the years after World War II, the LAPD's reforms were so successful that it became the national model of a "professional" police department.

Professionalization reforms were not only designed to make the police more efficient and effective, but also intended to achieve a larger goal: to reshape Americans' relationship to police and policing. This new wave of police reform was an integral part of the transfer of an ideology of bureaucratic competence from wartime to postwar: in the process of demobilization, management by military forces was replaced with management by militarized police. As Christopher Wilson writes, police professionalization was "part of a broader reforming of political consent to police power." Wilson argues that reforms were intended to work "not only through the symbolic power of crime-busting professionalism, but through a more subtle blend of routinized procedures and modern public relations."[3] One critical part of public relations involved departments' efforts to influence the representation of crime and police in the media. No single film or broadcasting program was more effective than *Dragnet* at influencing popular understandings of the police, or corresponded more closely to a policing agency's specific public relations goals.[4]

The alliance between *Dragnet* and the LAPD began even before the series began, when police officer Marty Wynn inspired Webb to create the show. Throughout the run of the show, LAPD officers were directly involved in its production. Each episode was based on story ideas submitted by police officers (for which they were remunerated). A varying crew of police officers provided technical advice on every show on both radio and television.[5] When scripts were read by the public relations division, the show paid the officer twenty-five dollars per script. Interestingly, this relationship was not legally binding on either side. In 1956, when an attorney general looked into the connections between the LAPD and *Dragnet*, "it was noted that there was 'no contract or contractual arrangement' between the producers and the Police Department, as such."[6] In place of a contract was a relationship. Webb's congenial relationship with the LAPD brass got him access: permission to record audio and shoot video in real locations, to base episodes on real cases, and to use the services of officers as technical advisors to ensure realism in the details. The LAPD got a hit show as a publicity vehicle.

Jack Webb did not intend for his show to become part of real-life reforms, and *Dragnet*'s content was not dictated by William H. Parker, as some have suggested. Rather, Webb's and Parker's attitudes were basically similar, and similarly reflected larger cultural shifts. As discussed in previous chapters, there was an increased faith in professionalized knowledge, technology, and procedural justice across postwar US culture. To citizen-audiences, both Webb and Parker offered direct instruction in how average citizens should participate in this newly ordered postwar world. Through the structure of the show as well as the content of individual episodes, *Dragnet* instructed audiences to see police as the LAPD wanted to be seen: as competent, responsible, respectful, self-effacing, imperturbable servants of the public. The direct involvement of LAPD personnel ensured that the work on-air and on-screen plausibly reflected policework off-air and off-screen, earning *Dragnet* the respect of real-life police professionals. This representation resonated with police officers in departments across the country—many undergoing their own professionalization projects—whose public affirmation of the show underscored its status as the true voice of the modern police force.

Dragnet also broadcast the problems of the LAPD's reform movement—though these were detectable only to those who listened and watched against the grain. Abuses of power, racism, and police brutality were, alternately, partly addressed and completely elided by key episodes. Citizens who criticized either the LAPD or *Dragnet* in the late 1940s and 1950s did not get very far. The shared insularity of the professional police department and the genre of the police procedural drew them together in their refusal to take seriously any criticism from the world outside their own systems. Both *Dragnet* and the LAPD, separately and together, helped define the place of the police in postwar culture, a place that was characterized by necessary reforms and impaired by an imperviousness to change that produced devastation in human terms.

PARKER'S LAPD

> We are endeavoring to redeem the police service and to establish a force that is objective, honest, and efficient.
>
> William H. Parker, *Parker on Police*

Legends abound about crime and corruption in the City of Angels in the 1930s and 1940s, and it can be hard to know what to believe. But it seems certain that a significant portion of the police force was either in someone else's pocket (politicians, big-time businessmen, the mob) or had a hand in the pockets of city residents (via payoffs and shakedowns). Mayor Fletcher Bowron was elected on a reform platform after the 1938 recall of the corrupt

Frank Shaw, but his police force was still a work in progress in 1950. That was the year in which the police commission elected William H. Parker, a patrol cop who had worked himself up through the ranks, as chief. On August 9, Parker began his legendary sixteen-year tenure, eventually becoming the first Los Angeles police chief in living memory to survive a change in city administration.

Over the course of more than twenty years as a Los Angeles police officer, Parker built a reputation for being incorruptible, tough, and ambitious—and also difficult, abrasive, and immovable. As chief, Parker successfully initiated or advanced large-scale changes across the department, sometimes because of, and sometimes despite, his personality.[7] Parker campaigned for police job security as well as pensions and benefits for officers, work in which he had been engaged for decades. The campaign worked. Joe Domanick reports that "between 1950 and 1966 the LAPD's budget would quadruple, and by 1956 the LAPD had become the best-paid police department in the nation."[8] Parker also sought to increase and improve the use of scientific knowledge in both crime detection and organizational efficiency. To this end, Parker campaigned for money for capital improvements, including the building of a new central administration building. The Police Administration Building (later renamed the Parker Center) centralized a number of offices and featured an up-to-date technical laboratory, sophisticated enough to rival the FBI's.[9] Alisa Sarah Kramer argues that Parker's most important contribution to policing was his installation of the Planning and Research Division, which increased organizational efficiency and inspired the creation of similar departments in other cities.[10]

Parker was particularly committed to the eradication of corruption. His own reputation as a clean cop and his personal crusade against vice—often fruitless during his early years in the department—made him a familiar figure within the police force long before he became chief. "My attitudes are quite well known," Parker told an interviewer in 1962. "I have never, for example, been offered a bribe; I think that is unusual."[11] As chief, Parker waged a successful war against organized crime in the city, using sophisticated surveillance technologies to track the movements of thousands of known and suspected criminals in order to make Los Angeles an inhospitable place for criminal enterprise.[12] The chief was intolerant, too, of small-time corruption, including theretofore common practices of accepting small gifts or fixing tickets. Officers were subject to stronger punishment for trespasses, and the Internal Affairs Division took on new importance in the new administration.

Many of Parker's changes originated in previous police reform movements: increased training for officers, modernization of communications and technology, increased protections from political influence, and eradication of vice had all been pursued by reformers in previous decades. But some parts of Parker's reforms were either specific to the LAPD or were more strongly emphasized by that department. As sociologist James Lasley writes, "Parker's idea of reform was based on the operational philosophy that police corruption was a product of cops that got too physically, emotionally, and politically close to the community."[13] This attitude was reflected in two intersecting reforms that changed the nature of policing in Los Angeles: the adoption of a paramilitary organizational structure and the insistence on distance between police and citizens.

The hierarchical structure that Parker preferred meant that all decision-making came from above. Writes Lasley, "Chief Parker assumed that the department could not operate as an effective crime-fighting machine without a management style that demanded complete and utter subordination of the officers."[14] Individual officers had little freedom to stray into areas of vice, but also little opportunity to be flexible, resourceful, or accommodating in interactions with citizens. Close relationships between police and members of the community were strongly discouraged. Parker insisted that police were not social workers. The chief often repeated, "We deal with effects, not causes."[15] Lasley writes that "officers were retrained in a community relations style that emphasized a hard-nosed, stoic demeanor in order to create an emotional barrier between themselves and the personalities of ordinary citizens."[16] In part to amplify police presence in a small department in a growing city, and in part to enforce distance between officers and residents, Parker moved from foot patrols to police cruisers.[17] The professional police department of the postwar was, then, an inflexible, detached, roving, paramilitary force.

To educate citizens on their responsibilities in light of the LAPD's reforms, Parker used different forms of media. To facilitate direct communication with the public, Parker created the Public Information Division (PID) within the LAPD. The PID organized and oversaw a number of programs and initiatives, including organizing the community events of "Crime Week," assigning liaisons to community groups, managing press coverage across media platforms, and providing "technical advice" to radio, television, and film. Parker also committed himself to the cause, making myriad public speeches to professional institutions, business associations, and community groups.[18]

As a man who preferred to talk rather than to listen, Parker appreciated the power of the one-way communication of the broadcast media. During 1952 Parker appeared regularly on a panel show called *The Thin Blue Line*, which took its title from the phrase Parker invented to describe the role the

FIGURE 4.1. Jack Webb poses with Chief William H. Parker at his desk in 1953. © Sid Avery/mptvimages.com.

police play as the border between order and chaos. A panel of experts delivered information to the public about the workings of the police each week on the Los Angeles affiliate KNBH.[19] Or, to describe the show less charitably, it provided a space "where [Parker would] answer any stupid, unfounded criticism of himself or the department," as Joe Domanick summarizes the show.[20] This turned out not to be compelling television, and the show was discontinued after five months.

No matter; Parker still had his own megaphone: *Dragnet.*

PUBLIC RELATIONS

> Establishing a base for good public relations is not accomplished by pleasing vocal groups, but rather by being right, staying right, and having faith in the people that they will support right.
>
> William H. Parker, *Parker on Police*

The representation of the police in popular culture was a perennial concern among police leadership. In an essay titled "Police Fact and Fiction in the Entertainment Industry," Parker expressed his belief in the connection between police efficacy and accurate representation. Parker wrote that he believed the negative portrayals of the police "had to be corrected if [they] were to gain public confidence and respect."[21] Parker went on to highlight *Dragnet* as a program that offered a new kind or representation—"clean, wholesome entertainment complete with suspense, humor, tragedy, and public interest"—that made positive contributions to the relationship between the police and the public.[22]

Dragnet's contribution to public relations was in representing the police as thoroughly professionalized. *Dragnet* taught auditors and viewers that police officers were competent public servants who were fully committed to the maintenance of law and order. This representation of the police was built, week by week, by repeating features of the show. Over time, audiences were able to construct a full portrait of police officers as overworked, under stress, and burdened by uncooperative citizens. Audiences also saw that, despite the pressures, the police remained committed to the work of protecting the public.

Even though *Dragnet* began before the major LAPD reforms of the era had been fully implemented, the show captured the distance upon which Parker later insisted. On *Dragnet*, citizens often offered personal details, neighborhood gossip, and general opinions, but the detectives seldom if ever inquired into anything other than information related to the case they were investigating. Friday often reminded interviewees, "We're just trying to get the facts." Later, translated by parodies into "just the facts," those words became the show's tagline. In subsequent popular and scholarly writing, historians have used this line as synecdoche for LAPD conduct in this period.

Dragnet's narrow frame ensured that listeners and viewers understood the daily grind of policing, the strain of professionalism. Friday's narration communicated the relentlessness of the officers' work. For example, Friday famously opened his monologue with date and time stamps. In "The Big Grab" (radio: June 29, 1950), Friday tells the listener, "It was Tuesday, April 4th. It was warm in Los Angeles. . . . It was ten minutes past 6 p.m. when I got to the basement of the City Hall. Carpool." The time stamps continue: 7:30 p.m., the detectives go to the morgue; 11:30, they stop for dinner; 11:50, they return to the office; 2:00 a.m., they return to the victim's home for their watch shift; 5:00, they take a call from their captain. And so it goes, until the case is closed. Throughout this episode, as in every episode, Friday checks in with the audience, marking the extended hours of his workday.

In many episodes, Friday mentions other interruptions: being called in on his day off, being awoken from sleep to respond to an emergency, or arriving for a morning shift after working a late shift. We learn that breaks and vacations for officers are few and far between. In "The Big Present" (radio: Nov. 24, 1953; television: Oct. 21, 1954), Frank Smith teases Joe about taking some of his days off while Smith was still working. Friday responds, "Yeah, I recall. I had a hundred of 'em coming." The precision of Friday's monologue and the passing references to interrupted holidays and delayed vacations made clear to viewers that police officers' work days were long and unpredictable, and that endless, shifting shifts were only part of the sacrifice that officers made on behalf of the public.

Throughout the series, we see the difficult conditions under which officers work. In "Maniac Murder" (radio: Aug. 11, 1949), the detectives are pelted by heavy rain as they seek out leads, marching through every bar, restaurant, and coffee counter in a six-block span. "That killer sure picked fine weather to work in," Friday's partner complains. "Feels like I just been swimming in these clothes." In "The Big Break" (radio: Dec. 14, 1950; television: Mar. 19, 1953), the detectives experience every kind of disappointment. They arrest a robbery suspect, Hoffman, who then escapes from the county jail. The detectives find the apartment in which he had been staying and wait there for hours, only to receive a phone call from their captain letting them know that Hoffman was picked up in Pasadena. Months later, Hoffman visits the cops to let them know that he's been paroled into the army. Friday's partner even lends Hoffman his last two dollars. They find out later in the day that Hoffman had visited them after he escaped from army jail. Eventually, he is rearrested by the lead detectives, a semisatisfying conclusion after an episode full of frustration.

While *Dragnet* featured much less violence than other shows in the cops-and-robbers vein, it nevertheless managed to represent the police officer's job as a dangerous one. The officers intermittently found themselves in physical skirmishes—or even in shoot-outs—while trying to arrest suspects. During the first radio season, the peril inherent to the job was illustrated most forcefully by a closing tribute to real-life police officers killed in the line of duty. At the close of "Helen Corday" (radio: July 7, 1949; television: June 18, 1953), the fifth episode, the "Dragnet March" changes to mournful organ music.[23] An announcer speaks with a serious tone: "Tonight's program is dedicated to police officer Charles A. Brady of the Chicago, Illinois, police department, who on the night of September 2, 1945, gave his life so that yours might be more secure."[24]

The sacrifices made by the police were meant to raise audiences' awareness of their own obligations to the police. Audiences also received instruction in how they should behave by watching their analogues in the diegesis. *Dragnet* presented a range of cooperative and uncooperative citizens and quietly but clearly indicated undesirable behaviors. In *Dragnet*, citizens were grumpy, defensive, or overly suspicious. They were reluctant to talk to the police, slow to get to the point, or afraid of what would happen to them. Sometimes they were just unhelpful. And sometimes, of course, they were guilty. Through these various characterizations, the show illustrated how uncooperative citizens impeded the necessary work of the police.

A grumpy citizen could introduce unnecessary delays into an investigation. In "The Big New Year" (television: Nov. 11, 1954; radio: Mar. 8, 1951) the detectives have to interview a bar owner two separate times because he holds back necessary information about the murder of a police officer outside of his bar. During the second interview, after he tries to brush off the officers again, Friday tells him, "We'd appreciate it if you'd cooperate with us." The man responds with an annoyed sigh: "If you want to know the truth, you're not good for my business here. Cops never are, coming around, asking questions. Customers don't like it. It's no good for business, no good at all." After the officers tell him to get his coat so they can go downtown, the owner gives up the suspect's name and likely place of residence. The bar owner's selfishness in the face of a murder investigation—indeed, the murder of a police officer—is a clear lesson in how *not* to be a good citizen.

Other interactions have different but equally high stakes. "The Big Trio" (radio: July 3, 1952: television: Nov. 20, 1952) includes a conversation with a belligerent father who arrives at the hospital where his son has been admitted after a car accident. Mr. Wheeler bursts into the room and begins yelling. The officers repeatedly ask him to keep his voice down, but he continues to ask whose fault it is that his son is in the hospital. As listeners, we discover that the son had been speeding and driving without a license. The father refuses to listen to sense.

> WHEELER: *You* didn't have to chase him. . . . I taught him how to drive. He drives just like I do. He's a fast driver, but he's a good one. I oughta know.
>
> FRIDAY: Our radio cars had to chase your boy nineteen miles, Mr. Wheeler. Eleven cars chased him. Your boy was endangering the life of everybody on that highway. In a twenty-five-mile-an-hour zone, he was clocked at better than seventy miles an hour. . . . He went through a dozen boulevard stops, barely missed a woman pedestrian—the woman had a baby in her arms. Just before he cracked up, he sideswiped another car, an old couple in it. They're in this hospital, too, and they're hurt—they're hurt bad . . . .
>
> WHEELER: It's not all his fault. He probably wouldn't have done

> it if you didn't chase him. I know my boy can handle a car. . . . Just because you drive fast doesn't make you a bad driver.
>
> FRIDAY: It helps.

As in this episode, these interactions often also highlighted other lessons. Here, listeners and viewers clearly see the dangers of speeding, refusing to be pulled over, willfully disobeying regulations (such as driving tests, which the father says "any moron can pass"), and modeling bad behavior and attitudes for children. In this case, the penalty is death: the son dies of his wounds.

The show presented the relationship between officers and citizens as polite but distant, which aligned with the LAPD reforms. But the show nevertheless made room for audiences to engage with the complexities of human lives. Indeed, police treatment of citizens was one area in which *Dragnet* softened the philosophy and behavior of the newly professional LAPD.

The show asked the audience to empathize with a range of people in different situations, whether through the unspooling of their story or through the patient summary of Friday's monologue. In the television episode "The Big Family" (television: Jan. 13, 1955; radio: Dec. 28, 1950), Friday and Smith interview a wife whose husband is missing. With a decanter of brandy in the foreground of her close-up, it is clear that Mrs. Jarrett has a drinking problem. Although she gives the detectives little usable information, they listen patiently as she explains her family situation. Abandoned by her husband, her children having left home, she explains that she drinks out of boredom and unhappiness. "I drink, sergeant. It's something to do. I drink every day in the week. I drink quite a bit. . . . Jack didn't care. I guess I don't care myself anymore." Though Friday observes that the liquor will not bring her happiness, she replies, "It doesn't matter. . . . I just don't care, that's all." In close-up, Friday's tight face softens with a downward glance. In this scene the audience is encouraged to understand, rather than judge, their fellow citizen.

Scenes like this were one of the show's trademarks. They were often even given over to criminals. In "The Big Honeymoon" (radio: Feb. 7, 1952; television: May 8, 1958), Friday and his partner track down a man named Frank Richland who has been promising to marry women in order to get their money. One of his victims identifies him and explains to the police how the man promised to take her and her brother around the world on a honeymoon but then disappeared. "Why did you want to hurt us?" she asks as she faces him in the interrogation room. After she and her brother leave, Friday asks for Richland's statement:

RICHLAND: All right, I'll tell you. You can't blame me for that one, though. You wouldn't have gone through with that deal yourself. Nobody would've.
JACOBS: What's wrong? A nice-looking girl.
RICHLAND: Sure, I don't mean that.
FRIDAY: What do you mean?
RICHLAND: That big clown, her brother Lars?
FRIDAY: Yeah.
RICHLAND: How'd you like to take that along on a honeymoon?

The second between the last line and the music cue is just long enough for the listener to sympathize with the criminal—for that moment, at least. Richland's reasoning in this instance might have been sound, but his violation of the law was nonetheless unforgivable. Announcer Hal Gibney explains that he was convicted on charges of theft and forgery. In *Dragnet*, the city was filled with people living with all kinds of pain, and sympathy stopped only where trespasses against the law began.

Dragnet painted a picture of a professional police force for postwar audiences, one made up of heroically human public servants who firmly but fairly managed a complex citizenry. The show reflected local reforms being enacted in Los Angeles and broadcast the successes of those reforms from coast to coast. As it did so, the show resonated with police officers around the country, who saw in *Dragnet* the ways in which they themselves wanted to be seen.

Faithful Followers

> Not only do you provide wholesome entertainment, but you are doing more for law enforcement than anyone else in the entertainment field. As a former FBI agent, deputy city attorney and prosecuting attorney, I'm particularly grateful for the public service you are rendering.
>
> Letter to Jack Webb, quoted in *TV Guide*, April 10, 1953, 7

Police officers loved *Dragnet*. No records reveal how much of the show's audience was made up of law enforcement, but it is clear that police officers were a significant and devoted portion of the audience. According to one press account, officers watched regularly enough to be infected by the

Dragnet style: "By a curious twist of American vernacular, many policemen now imitate the crisp speech of Jack 'Dragnet' Webb who, in turn, developed his 'Dragnet' dialogue from listening to cops. . . . It is now a matter of opinion whether police sound like Webb or Webb sounds like the police."[25] The relationship between the two was not one only of linguistic exchange. Contemporary accounts regularly stressed the warm feelings between Webb and the police, and the support of police officers bolstered *Dragnet*'s reputation as an authentic representation. Both on and off the set, Jack Webb cultivated positive relationships not only with members of the LAPD but with police officers everywhere. Collecting accolades locally, nationally, and internationally, *Dragnet* and its police fans created a discursive buffer around the show, which helped to shield both *Dragnet* and the LAPD from criticism.

Law enforcement surrounded *Dragnet* with support because they saw in the show a sympathetic representation of their work. Christopher Wilson writes that an important aspect of professionalization reforms was the effort "to give the cop a human face"—"to stress *both* professional status and the *similarity* of police work to their constituents' labor."[26] Police organizations showed their appreciation to Webb with honors and awards too numerous to count, many of which emphasized the importance of shifting audiences' understanding of the job of the police. At a 1956 luncheon hosted by the LAPD, Webb was "lauded for the great public relations job he'd done, the dignity added to the profession and the clearer understanding of police work engendered on the part of the public."[27] The Los Angeles Board of Police Commissioners awarded a citation to Webb that same year; the citation read that the show "engendered increased respect for law enforcement and greatly enhanced public esteem for the police profession."[28]

While the police brass organized many of the awards (William H. Parker was in attendance at the LAPD luncheon), other awards came from the rank and file. A Warner Bros. press release described one such gift, an engraved plate from the Fraternal Order of Police recognizing Webb for being "one of the best friends the average cop ever had."[29] As Gordon Allison reported in the *Herald Tribune* in advance of *Dragnet*'s television debut, "Cops from Hollywood to Hartford have been some of the program's most faithful followers, owing to the absence of hokum and the presence of realistic police work."[30] Police officers of varying ranks appreciated a representation of police work as *work*, not as the fumbling of a dopey beat cop or as expressions of Holmesian brilliance.

Just as the police publicly celebrated Webb, he in turn carefully tended his relationship with police officers. Webb extended himself to attend police events both large and small, such as when both Webb and his television partner, Ben Alexander, attended an evening dinner and dance in Los Angeles hosted by the Policewomen's Association, or when the partners attended a party for hundreds of Boy Scouts hosted by the LAPD.[31] When Webb went on the road to publicize the *Dragnet* film, he visited thirty major cities and met with law enforcement all along the way. In Chicago, for example, Webb's itinerary included a visit to a crime lab, dinner with the police commissioner, and a photo shoot in a police car. Webb accepted honors even when it was inconvenient, as when in 1955 he traveled to Boston to promote a project unrelated to *Dragnet* and nevertheless made room on his trip to be named "honorary policeman" by the local police chief, an honor bestowed as soon as his plane landed at Logan Airport.[32]

Another means by which Webb maintained a positive relationship with the police was offering special access to *Dragnet*. When the *Dragnet* feature was released, police officers received privileged access through special screenings, such as the one held at the Warner Bros. studio for more than one hundred LAPD officers and their families. Officers were also invited to see Webb and his team live in action: the visitor logs of the film and television productions are dotted with the names and titles of law enforcement agents and their associates. Visitors to the *Dragnet* set included police officers from throughout the LAPD divisions, of course, as well as representatives from other local police (L.A. County Sheriff's Department, Pomona PD) and envoys from areas stretching north, south, and east—Seattle, Denver, Chicago, Midland (TX), Greenville (SC), Kansas City (MO), and Boston.[33] Webb clearly understood his professional duties to include bringing as many police officers as close to the production of his show as was possible.

Webb supported the police privately as well as through his professional activities, and his private interactions with police sometimes became part of *Dragnet*'s public relations. For example, *TV Guide* reported that Webb personally (not the sponsor or the network) "contribute[d] regularly to the Los Angeles Police Department Welfare Fund."[34] The public sometimes learned about personal gifts from law enforcement to Webb as well. One particularly heartfelt offering became public knowledge because the widow of a police officer sent the gift via the *Los Angeles Times* to ensure delivery. The gift was a badge long carried by the woman's late husband, "still in its worn leather case," and it was intended as a contribution to Webb's collection of police badges.[35] Webb, of course, expressed his gratitude for the gift, though he may not have actually actively collected badges. Webb seems to have had more than one collection of police-related objects that were sent to him out of admiration. In one interview, Webb revealed that he came to have a gun collection largely because he received them from fans. Most were Smith &

Wessons and Colts, the types of guns the officers on *Dragnet* used and at least some of which, presumably, were gifts from police officers.[36]

With the genuine appreciation and approbation expressed by police officers in Los Angeles and elsewhere, *Dragnet* was able to authorize itself as a documentary program that authentically represented police and their work. Webb's work to maintain and publicize relationships with real-life officers and police departments sustained his show's reputation during its run and for decades after. The symbiotic relationship between *Dragnet* and law enforcement left little room in public conversation for challenges to the show's status as a reliable representative for the police, and the closeness between the show and the police provided useful protection in the rare moments in which *Dragnet* waded into more controversial territory.

Public Objections

While Webb clearly aligned himself and his show with the police, he also managed to pitch his "documentary" program as an objective representation of their work, a program into which politics did not enter. The show rarely engaged with real-life concerns, debates, and controversies around the LAPD or other policing agencies. Close analysis of these rare instances highlights the moments when the show's "objective" stance revealed the its ideological commitment to the police position. In two instances—in the *Dragnet* film and in the episode "The Big Ruling"—the show took a stance on a public issue. In both cases, *Dragnet* narrated Chief Parker's position. Also in both cases, objections were raised by citizens concerned with civil liberties whose positions were not represented by the show.

In the early 1950s, a series of lawsuits and court cases limited, or threatened to limit, the ability of the police to use certain surveillance technologies on the grounds that they constituted an infringement on civil liberties. Wiretapping had been illegal in California for some time, but the LAPD had dodged this restriction by installing recording devices (Dictaphones) instead. By 1954, Parker saw that this method, too, was coming under threat.[37] Testifying before a House committee that year, Parker delivered a statement titled "Surveillance by Wiretap or Dictograph: Threat or Protection?"[38] The question was strictly rhetorical; Parker vigorously campaigned for the police's right to use surveillance technologies, particularly in the dismantling of organized crime.

As John Buntin points out, the *Dragnet* feature film made Parker's case for him. The film is set in the Intelligence Division, the division tasked with investigating the "gangland killing" at the center of the plot.[39] The focus on organized crime marks a significant departure from the series and functions to legitimate subsequent police actions. Unlike the radio and television episodes that open when the detectives open their investigation, the film begins with a depiction of the crime, the murder of a mobster. After this prologue and the opening credits, Friday's monologue begins, and the film reinstates the familiar limited perspective of the episodes. The film has sharper edges than the series episodes: Friday and Smith are more aggressive than usual, and the dialogue is more cutting. The suspects are treated more harshly, including the use of a "bumper-to-bumper tail," a tactic in which teams of detectives follow the suspects day and night. Friday and Smith go further than required; they pull over their assigned suspect at every opportunity, only to frisk him down and let him go. They follow him into a restaurant and sit on either side of him at a lunch counter, then frisk him again. They follow him to a movie theater, and they frisk him outside. The clear criminality of organized crime—and the brutality of the murder, which the audience witnessed—seems to justify harsher treatment.

For Parker's propagandistic purposes, the key scene in the film is Friday's testimony, in which he speaks directly to a grand jury and helps the jurors and the audience see the utility, even necessity, of wiretapping. To the audience's citizen stand-ins, Friday contextualizes the debate around police methods. Although Friday presents a pattern of telephone calls that suggest a conspiracy to commit murder, the jurors think the pattern is insufficient evidence without knowing the content of the calls. Friday responds, "I'm sorry. To do that, we'd have to be able to wiretap." When a juror objects to the idea of the police having such latitude, Friday responds, "Mrs. Caldwell, as a police officer, I can tell you that none of us would want the responsibility of being able to wiretap at will. It'd have to be by court order." It sounds like a reasonable request, and the prohibition against wiretapping sounds like an unnecessary handicap. Indeed, the audience can see that if the restriction were lifted, then Friday would be able to respond to the citizens' requests for more information.[40] The next scene reveals that the jury refused to indict. The police eventually get the evidence they need by planting a listening device that captures a conversation that leads the detectives to the shotgun used in the murder. Even the detectives' work-around requires them to listen in. The film makes clear that electronic surveillance is a necessary police tool, articulating and defending Parker's position.

Although there was little public opposition to the film, concerns were

FIGURE 4.2. In the 1954 *Dragnet* feature film, Sergeant Friday's grand jury testimony is unconvincing without evidence from a wiretap.

privately expressed. Osmond Fraenkel, staff counsel for the American Civil Liberties Union, wrote about a 1954 meeting:

> At the ACLU meeting the only important discussion was about the movie Dragnet. Herbert Levy suggested that it gave an unfortunate picture of 5th Amendment rights. Some (Ernst, Williams, Thomas) thought that Malin should informally discuss the matter with the Code authorities & the producer. I agreed but to make sure that there would be no "minute" of this had us go into the Committee of the Whole. The proposal passed, but it was rather close. (Huebsch, Frank, Finerty disagreed).[41]

This objection, passed unofficially and recorded only privately, suggests that similar objections, made privately, went unrecorded.

The next year, *Dragnet* served again as Parker's mouthpiece, this time in objection to the "exclusionary evidence rule" decided by *People v. Cahan* (1955). Parker was outspoken in his opposition to this ruling, which determined that evidence acquired through an illegal search could not be used in court. Parker and other police officials complained that the exclusionary evidence rule tied officers' hands. Parker argued, "It is my contention . . . that many searches and seizures branded as 'unreasonable' by the courts are in fact reasonable under attendant circumstances. . . . The true 'unreasonableness' of the situation lies in the insurmountable handicaps placed on police."[42]

Less than six months after *People v. Cahan*, "The Big Ruling" (radio: Sept. 6, 1955; television: Jan. 19, 1956) presented a set of circumstances in which a reasonable search was declared illegal. In the episode, Friday and Smith attempt to prevent the distribution of a shipment of heroin. They get a call from a tipster who lets the police know that someone is planning to sell the drugs to kids. The tipster will not give a name, but he describes the area where the buys take place. Friday and Smith travel there, where they recognize a "known narcotics user and suspected peddler." They find a large amount of heroin on him and stolen goods in his car.

When the detectives meet with the deputy district attorney about the case, the prosecutor hesitates. "Did you place [the suspect] under arrest before you searched him?" he asks Friday and Smith. They did not, but Friday explains, "We knew he was a hype; he knew we were cops. He could have figured that out." The DA explains the exclusionary rule and that they need permission, a warrant, or an arrest for a legal search. Smith comments—and Friday agrees—that with all those requirements, "the only guy who's better off is the criminal." The audience is encouraged to agree by the close of the case: "The Big Ruling" is one of the handful of episodes that does not end in a conviction. The announcer closes the episode with the sober conclusion, "The charges against the suspect were dismissed." The threat could not be clearer: the police are prevented from saving children from a predatory drug dealer, a crime so heinous that a fellow criminal *volunteered* to rat him out. Any reasonable viewer could see that this ruling was on the wrong side of the thin blue line.

And yet some listeners and viewers were unreasonable. Prominent Democrat Paul Ziffren sent a flurry of telegrams to Jack Webb and others, writing, "Although search and seizure law is now settled in California by Supreme Court Decision in Cahan case your program made direct appeal to influence public opinion against such decision in guise of entertainment." Ziffren continued, "Please advise what plans you have for making full and fair presentation of other views on this issue to same audience, according to your responsibility under Federal Communication Law and Regulations."[43] The *New York Post* columnist Jay Nelson Tuck accused NBC of "len[ding] its national facilities to one of its top-rated 'dramatic' programs for an emotion-packed, completely one-sided attack on the U.S. Constitution." He wrote, "If the evidence of the program is to be taken on its face, both [NBC and Webb] believe that it's a pity that American policemen are sometimes restrained from acting like commissars."[44]

NBC, for its part, felt no need to respond publicly. An interoffice memo discussed the charges, and NBC's legal department defended the program.

The attorney Howard Monderer agreed that the show was "somewhat one-sided," but he was "sure that statements by very prominent law enforcement officers . . . could be found which would be much stronger than the statement by Friday."[45] Monderer was clear that the objections by Tuck were out of proportion and ignored the good-faith representation of police on the show. Wrote Monderer, "The policemen on the 'Dragnet' program, in my opinion, are fine examples of the type of policemen which we would like to have in America and I believe the program portrays Friday and his assistant as close to the majority of policemen in the United States as is possible on a dramatic program." In Monderer's view, because *Dragnet* was the true reflection of honest police, the police position the episode took on this issue was not partisan enough to be of concern. The lawyer closed his letter succinctly: "I do not believe the statements by Friday justify the column by Mr. Tuck."[46]

For his part, Jack Webb stayed out of this and any controversy; *Dragnet* and Webb were always publicly on Parker and the LAPD's side. Privately, however, there was more tension. Although Jack Webb's devotion to the LAPD was absolute, his relationship with the chief of police was rockier than he ever publicly admitted. In Webb's FBI file is a missive written by Cartha DeLoach, assistant director of the Crime Records Division, three years after *Dragnet*'s original run ended. Webb had contacted the bureau for permission to use FBI stories for a television program. The letter concluded with the following lines: "I was quite amused over his [Webb's] bitterness toward Chief of Police Parker of Los Angeles. He stated that in the 'Dragnet' series, he had had constant trouble with Parker and often had to refuse filming productions that Parker insisted on Webb producing. He specifically mentioned that Parker had been interested in 'blowing up' his own name. According to Webb, there is little love lost between Webb and Parker."[47]

During the 1950s, however, *Dragnet* fans would have had to look closely for evidence of any friction between Webb and Parker, or between *Dragnet* and the LAPD. A few hints of difficulties appeared in Webb's nonfiction book *The Badge* (1958).[48] The book's subtitle described it as a collection of "True and Terrifying Crime Stories That Could Not Be Presented on TV." It did tell some of these stories, including the story of the Black Dahlia murder. Its main purpose was to inform readers about the LAPD as an organization. Indeed, the book's structure correlates with the structure of the force: chapters are called "The Policeman," "The Sergeant," "The Inspector," "The Commission," and so on. Each chapter includes an explanation of the specific role highlighted and contains stories of heroism from the careers of several police officers. The book was advertised as sensational, but it is mostly educational in an entertaining way—not unlike its author's other productions.

A contemporary reviewer noticed that in the book, Webb "is sympathetic to police problems but he does not lose sight of the areas of controversy."[49] The primary area of controversy was William H. Parker. In the chapter titled "The Chief," Webb's careful language highlights the difficulties in Parker's personality that have become much clearer—and more often admitted publicly—in the decades since. Near the beginning of the chapter, Webb offers his readers a summary of the chief's belief system:

> Parker is an essentially simple man who believes with all his soul that crime and Communism are the twin scourges of America and their suppression, by almost any means, the greatest challenge of our era. Some legal and social philosophers may question his simplifications, but he has built a record that demands from them a simple answer: either accept Parker and the LAPD he has fashioned or make a grave and weakening concession to the hostile elements.[50]

Conspicuously, this sentence is the final one of the section. Like *Dragnet*'s own dialogue tags, it gives readers space to draw their own conclusions—here, specifically as to whether the choice Parker offers is a good one. The author suggests that we might want to support the nuance and contextualization offered by the professional thinkers over the binary thinking of the professional law officer. But *The Badge*, like *Dragnet*, makes no explicit criticism. And like *Dragnet*, it leaves only a little room for readers to make their own criticism, unless, perhaps, that reader was one of the Los Angeles citizens who brought their own knowledge and experiences to the text.

Elisions and Erasures

> If a police service loses the confidence of the people, upheavals will follow that are costly to the community.
>
> William H. Parker, *Parker on Police*

> Despite the depth of the feeling against Chief Parker expressed to us by so many witnesses, he is recognized, even by many of his most vocal critics, as a capable Chief who directs an efficient police force that serves well this entire community.
>
> Governor's Commission on the Los Angeles Riots, "Violence in the City: An End or a Beginning?" (McCone Report), December 2, 1965

Although many Angelenos approved of Parker's implementation of professional policing in Los Angeles, the approval was not universal, and the strengths of the model eventually proved to be the sources of its weaknesses. Most critically, the insularity of the force and its leadership made it unresponsive to the shifting demographics of the city. Los Angeles' mid-century population boom—a consequence of the economic activity provided by wartime industry and the postwar rise of the Sunbelt cities—has been well covered in scholarship. The city's population in 1940 was 1,504,277; in 1960, it was 2,479,015. Just as critically, population changes also altered the makeup of the city and its surrounding areas. Before the war, the Black population was counted at 75,000; between 1940 and 1960, it jumped to over 460,000. Angelenos of Hispanic origin in Los Angeles County were 287,614 in 1950 and 576,716 in 1960. Other sources reveal other diversities: in 1960, an Asian American population of over 100,000 resided within L.A., and Kramer notes that the substantial growth of the Jewish population meant that Los Angeles counted "the third largest Jewish population in the world behind New York and Tel Aviv."[51]

As Kramer points out, despite the changes in the city and its neighbors, there were few changes to the force after the first few years of reforms. The internal cohesion that kept leadership effective and morale high in the LAPD resulted in the department's insulation against larger forces in the city. Minority communities, growing in number, complained regularly of being underprotected and overtargeted by racist police. Parker responded to minority leaders' complaints by explaining that his police simply went where the crimes were. It was a logic that conveniently reinforced itself. Parker's numbers showed that criminal activity was highest in certain neighborhoods; Parker increased patrols in those neighborhoods, leading to more arrests; Parker's numbers continued to show that criminal activity was highest in those neighborhoods. That many of those neighborhoods happened to be composed primarily of minority residents had nothing to do with it, from the chief's perspective. Stuart Hall, Chas Critcher, Tony Jefferson, John Clarke, and Brian Roberts identified a similar "equation of concern" in their study of mugging in 1970s Britain. In *Policing the Crisis*, they describe the cultural phenomenon by which the police and the media interpret crime statistics, so that the only available solution is more and harsher policing.[52] One could expect no other response from Parker, who never strayed from his exclusive commitment to "effects, not causes" and would not investigate the causes of uneven policing.

Although *Dragnet* was more sympathetic in its outlook, the show excluded significant sectors of humanity, replicating the blindnesses of

Parker's administration. In *Dragnet* on radio, the same representational strategies that largely removed markers of ethnicity and race—in order to move away from stereotypes—also rendered certain populations invisible. That is, in creating a social world without difference, *Dragnet* created a social world without distinctions. When *Dragnet* moved to television, the whiteness of the police force and of greater Los Angeles became even more visible. Michael Hayde points out that *Dragnet* could not have authentically integrated its police force. As he explains, "Caucasian and African-American officers were segregated until 1961, which is why no black cops are seen in the 276 *Dragnets* of old."[53] This logic may explain the producers' decisions to restrict the view within the police station, but it does not fully explain why so few minorities (Black or otherwise) appear on the show as a whole. On television, single episodes sometimes took viewers into marked minority communities, but for the most part Webb did not attempt to integrate *Dragnet*'s Los Angeles.

More insidious than enforced invisibility was the show's occlusion of real problems within the LAPD. On the issues of police corruption and police brutality, *Dragnet* either reinforced the department's refusal to face them or wrote over, on the national airwaves, the stories that Angelenos read in their local papers and experienced in their daily lives.

It was not as if the department's problems were not visible to the producers; the hotbed of vice into which *Dragnet* was born can be found hidden in the credits. At the close of the first episodes of *Dragnet*, which aired in June 1949, the announcer informed listeners, "Technical advice for *Dragnet* comes from the office of C. B. Horrall, Chief of Police, Los Angeles Police Department." On July 7, the announcer said simply, "Technical advice for *Dragnet* is furnished by the Los Angeles Police Department." It was not until September 1, 1949, that listeners could be reassured that there was leadership in the department, as it came "from the office of W. A. Worton, Acting Chief of Police, Los Angeles Police Department." Less than a year later, on August 10, 1950, a new name was swapped in—the office now belonged to "Chief of Police W. H. Parker." Attentive audiences, noticing that the LAPD was churning through police chiefs, must have wanted to know: what happened?

Lots. In the summer of 1949, local newspapers broke stories that revealed corruption at the highest levels of the LAPD administration. The major scandal was the revelation that members of the LAPD vice squad were offering protection to—and profiting from—a prostitution ring. One vice officer, Elmer Jackson, was in a relationship with the ringleader, Brenda Allen. Subsequent investigations revealed a cornucopia of illicit activity in the vice squad, including Jackson's inappropriate dealings with gangster Mickey Cohen.[54] In response to the scandals, Mayor Fletcher Bowron forced the chief out, and Horrall stepped down on June 28, 1949. To replace him, Bowron recruited Marine General William A. Worton, who served out his limited term before being replaced by Parker. In 1958, the Brenda Allen story was included in *The Badge* (1958); with several years' distance from the scandal, the successes of the Parker administration overshadowed *Dragnet*'s collaboration with a compromised department. At the time, however, *Dragnet* remained conspicuously silent.

When *Dragnet* did explicitly take on police misconduct, the show would not admit to any systemic problems, forwarding instead the "bad apple" theory of corrupt policing. "The Big Cop" (television: Jan. 1, 1953; radio: Aug. 2, 1951) assured listeners that no one hated a bad cop more than a good cop. In the episode, Friday and his partner investigate a string of burglaries targeting stores and warehouses. In the course of their investigation, they discover that a police officer was at one of the crime scenes—on his day off. They arrest the officer, and, for once, Friday loses his temper with a suspect. He lectures angrily:

> You're a bad cop, Mister. You'll be all over the front pages tonight and tomorrow morning. . . . They're not gonna read about four thousand five hundred other cops, the guys who walked their beats last night, the guys who risked their lives, who did their jobs the way they were trained and the way they're hired to do. They're not gonna read about millions of man-hours turned in by thousands of honest cops, here and all over the country. People ain't gonna read about cops who worked 40 honest years . . . the Donahoe's and the Steed's and the MacCaulley's and the Wisdom's and the Jesse's [*sic*] and all the rest of 'em. The people who read it in the papers, they're gonna overlook the fact that *we* got you, that we washed our own laundry and we cleared this thing up. They're gonna overlook all the good; they'll overlook every last good cop in the country. But they'll remember *you*. Because you're a bad cop.[55]

Friday is clearly lecturing the audience as well as the criminal, instructing the audience to remember when they read their newspapers that "98 percent" of police officers are honest like Friday, and like the list of real-life LAPD officers that he calls out by name in this speech. Law enforcement particularly enjoyed this episode. "The Big Cop" was one of the episodes most often requested by police organizations (including the US Army) and was used for training by departments across the country.[56]

Although "The Big Cop" implicated one police officer in a vice investigation, *Dragnet* would not go anywhere near admitting police brutality and the overlapping problem of police racism. An early reviewer of the radio show predicted this occlusion. After praising the show's realism, John Crosby wrote in the *New York Herald-Tribune*, "There are also, I'm afraid, a great many dodges used to get convictions which are not at all ethical. I don't expect the Los Angeles Police Department to come clean on this score."[57] It would not on that score, and not on others, either. Crosby was correct to predict that *Dragnet* would employ strategic silences, ones only certain segments of Los Angeles could hear.

For years before the Watts riots brought the relationship between Black Angelenos and the LAPD into tragic focus, African Americans and Latinos vocally opposed the aggressive policing of the LAPD. Los Angeles's Black newspapers regularly covered instances of police brutality and regularly reported on efforts to get city authorities to respond to the issue. *Dragnet* did not register these complaints. Instead, it raised the specter of abuse in order to highlight either the absurdity of the claims or the efficacy of the LAPD's procedure. Even before Parker took office, *Dragnet* took the side of the police in accusations. In an early episode, "Tom Laval" (radio: Oct. 1, 1949), a suspect dies in an accident while attempting to escape custody; a witness promises to testify that it was Friday's fault. The show takes us to an inquest where we hear Friday's testimony and those of two witnesses: the first one lies, and the second one tells the truth and corroborates Friday's story.

In "The Big Fake" (radio: June 1, 1950; television: Oct. 22, 1953), *Dragnet* familiarizes audiences with the procedure police follow when a complaint against an officer is made. In this episode, Friday and his partner investigate an accusation of robbery and assault. After the detectives escort the accused officer to meet the captain, the captain explains the process to the accused officer and therefore also to the audience. The captain warns the officer, "If you're innocent, we'll do all we can. If you're guilty, we'll see you get everything that's coming to you." He then lists the next steps: "You're on suspension pending the outcome of the case. After that, if you're cleared, there'll be a hearing before the Board of Rights. . . . You'll be booked for robbery and assault and held in county jail. The case'll be presented to the district attorney tomorrow." The officer is relieved of his badge, gun, and ID card, and Friday escorts him to jail.

The timing of one particular episode suggests that *Dragnet* spoke directly to the first major challenge of Chief Parker's administration, which for a few months raised the possibility that Parker would be forced out of his job. *Dragnet* was on both radio and television during the notorious "Bloody Christmas" incident of 1951 and the high-profile trial in 1952.

In the early hours of December 25, 1951, two police officers got into a fight with a group of young men, mostly Latino, outside a bar. The men were taken to the Central Division jail, where officers were having a boozy Christmas party. A rumor—later proved false—circulated that one of the officers had lost an eye in the original scuffle. In retaliation, the officers at Central took turns beating the prisoners. The stories of the beatings came out during the men's trial. As their testimonies revealed their treatment, the judge called for a grand jury investigation from the courtroom, calling the police officers' behavior "intolerable and reprehensible."[58] Chief Parker insisted that he was investigating the incident internally, and although the police stonewalled the courts as best they could, eventually eight officers were tried and five were convicted.[59]

Coverage in *The Badge* suggests that Webb was well aware of the politics around Bloody Christmas. The book frames the episode as a challenge to institutional cohesion, one that was successfully dealt with. Webb writes, "Parker acted so decisively and IA investigated so thoroughly (making a report of 204 single-spaced typewritten pages) that LAPD survived its ordeal by headlines and politics."[60] Webb was fuzzy on the details—"precisely what did happen has never been fully established"—but he was precise about Parker's response: "In his biggest departmental shake-up, Parker shifted fifty-four men, including two deputy chiefs, two inspectors and four captains."[61] Webb ends the paragraph, however, with a peculiar note about Parker: "But he refused to acknowledge the action was disciplinary, and he went on TV to warn that the underworld was taking advantage of the furore to discredit LAPD."[62] The inclusion of Parker's absurd, paranoid deflection of responsibility suggests that Webb was not entirely comfortable with the incident.

Webb was correct, however, in noting that this was a crisis within the LAPD, and that, through his administrative response and his political sway, Parker was able to protect the autonomy of the force. As Lasley notes, this was possibly "the first time and place the efficacy of [the professional model] as a policing operational style had been called into question."[63] By all accounts Parker won the challenge, and he kept his job until his death in 1966.

In his efforts to show the public that he was leading a fair and effective police department, Parker was assisted by *Dragnet*. *Dragnet* did not stay silent; more insidiously, the show took on the issue of police brutality only to reframe accusations so as to dismiss them. In "The Big Evans" (radio: Mar. 6, 1952; television: Apr. 24, 1958), producers approached this problem by offering a counternarrative that challenged every abuse exposed by coverage of the Bloody Christmas officers' trial.

Stories of the brutality leaked out in the weeks leading up to the young men's trial, and on the day before the first defendant testified to the Christmas Day beatings, NBC broadcast "The Big Evans."[64] In the episode, the lead detectives are assigned to Internal Affairs. They have received a complaint that a police officer beat up the owner of a boarding house. The owner, George Evans, accuses the officer of assaulting him because Evans would not pay him off. The officer says it was actually the other way around, that he refused a bribe from Evans and does not know how the man sustained his injuries. From his entrance, Evans is presented as an unsympathetic character—a flophouse manager and suspected drug user who cries for his lawyer. The officers eventually learn that Evans used an old shoulder injury to trick the investigating officers, and that his other injuries had come from a fight over a card game. To emphasize how unfair false accusations can be, Evans is prosecuted only for filing a false report, a misdemeanor, despite all the trouble he caused the arresting officer and the lead detectives.[65]

A little more than halfway into the episode, Friday grumbles to the listener about the ways the news media exploited the situation and slandered the officer, the department, and the police as a whole: "Saturday, June 15th, 10:00 a.m. The investigation continued. Meantime, the newspapers were still making front-page material out of the story. One of the morning banner lines read, 'Cop Slugs Crippled Citizen to Get Payoff' and another one, 'Police Brutality Rouses Entire City.' Our investigation went on." This comment comes just after Friday and his partner speak to Evans's doctor and learn about his trick shoulder. Within this framing, the newspapers' headlines, in addition to refusing the objective stance toward the incident that the police have taken in their investigation, are now tellingly out of sync with the truth.

The transparency of the investigation in "The Big Evans" stood in stark opposition to the real-life story. Local readers following the trials of the victims and, later, of the police officers saw no clear narrative. Instead, newspaper coverage hinted at stonewalling, perjury, and cover-ups. Critical readers of Los Angeles newspapers were able to speak back, but viewers in other places across the nation were not able to see that *Dragnet* was providing national cover for a local shame.

Some Angelenos publicly called out the abuse perpetrated by the LAPD and the absence of its representation in *Dragnet*. In 1960, Almena Lomax wrote in the *Los Angeles Tribune* about the murder of Danny Thomas King by the LAPD. King was shot multiple times by officers who claimed he was in the middle of an armed robbery of a liquor store.[66] Lomax dismissed the officers' claims, calling the incident one of the LAPD's "'certain death' stake-outs." After seeing the narrative spun around the killing, Lomax concluded that *Dragnet* must have learned its storytelling techniques from the police department. She wrote, "L.A.P.D. absolutely topped itself in the business of dramaturgy, crime prevention, apprehension, and destruction of human life in the recent Danny King case. . . . And then it 'wrapped up' the evidence in as neat and tidy a package as you ever did see." Lomax continued, "Sgt. Friday—who wanted the 'facts, jes' the facts, mam,'—couldn't have done better." For all of *Dragnet*'s effort in authorizing its own stories, Lomax makes clear that audience members who were closest to the LAPD's abuses heard and saw the stories differently. For those audience members, it was the fiction, not the facts, that was assured by the LAPD's involvement in *Dragnet*.

Lomax and journalists for Los Angeles's Black newspapers had long written about the Los Angeles Police Department's abuses of power, but it was not until the 1965 Watts riots that a national audience saw the terrible result of all the anger and frustration among targeted Angelenos that *Dragnet* did not display. When the McCone Commission investigated the riots, they heard testimony after testimony that proved that African American communities had experienced "professional" policing differently than white communities. The McCone Commission, though heavily criticized for misunderstanding the factors that led to the riot, nevertheless could not ignore the antagonism that Black Angelenos felt toward Parker and his police force. Its report states:

> The bitter criticism we have heard evinces a deep and longstanding schism between a substantial portion of the Negro community and the Police Department. "Police brutality" has been the recurring charge. One witness after another has recounted instances in which, in their opinion, the police have used excessive force or have been disrespectful and abusive in their language or manner. . . . Chief of Police Parker appears to be the focal point of the criticism. . . . Many Negroes feel that he carries a deep hatred of the Negro community.[67]

This awareness did not result in any significant changes to the LAPD's model of policing. Parker maintained that model until his death in 1966, and it was continued, with some adjustments, by his immediate successors.

In later decades, problems with the LAPD and its policing methods were more fully revealed to a national audience. In 1991, news outlets broadcast a videotape of a group of police officers savagely beating a prone Rodney King. In expressing their shock, commenters often emphasized the distance between what viewers saw on the tape and what they had been shown for decades on prime time and in syndication. The *Washington Post* captured the distinction succinctly in one 1992 headline: "L.A. Police Dept.: 'Dragnet' It Isn't." In the opening paragraph of the article, reporter Lou Cannon elaborated, "The once-vaunted professional image of the Los Angeles Police Department, celebrated in 'Dragnet' and other television shows, was discredited this week in two Southern California courtrooms where officers were portrayed as vindictive, confused and out of control."[68] When the officers were acquitted, violence broke out, and Los Angeles burned with rage for five days. In the wake of the L.A. Riots, the LAPD was forced to make some changes. Most significant was the resignation of Chief Daryl Gates, who had been a protégé of William H. Parker, and who had led the department with the same iron fist.

Over the next several years, the facade of the LAPD continued to crack. The 1995 trial of O. J. Simpson highlighted that the schisms revealed by the riots were still very present in Los Angeles. While a majority of white Americans thought Simpson was guilty, the majority-Black jury voted for acquittal, an outcome that affirmed Black Angelenos' well-earned distrust of the LAPD.[69] Additionally, the wall-to-wall coverage of the Simpson trial, on broadcast and cable outlets, highlighted the many failures of police procedure committed during the investigation, in both the collection of evidence and in the crime lab's analysis of that evidence. And only a few years after the Simpson trial, between 1998 and 2000, the public began to learn about the crimes committed by officers within and around the anti-gang unit known as CRASH ("Community Response against Street Hoodlums"). The revelations of officer misconduct within the Rampart Division, ranging from planting evidence to dealing drugs, prompted the federal government to intervene. A consent decree between the LAPD and the Department of Justice compelled the police force to undertake serious reforms.

Law professor Laurie Levenson summarized the reputational disturbances of the previous decade in a 2001 AP news article: "Rodney King was about police abuse, O.J. was about police incompetence, and Rampart is about police corruption. That's a pretty grim picture for the LAPD."[70] Though the consent decree has been lifted, the LAPD continues to operate under a reputational cloud of its own making. The 2000s were not the 1940s: when the Rampart wrongdoing began to make news, there was no brand-new, genre-defining broadcast series to step onto a national stage and help paint a different picture of a reforming police department.

During the 1940s and 1950s, *Dragnet*'s national distribution via radio, television, and film supported Chief Parker's assurances that Los Angeles was a model of interethnic and racial harmony, and that "the story of that city's freedom from strife is largely the story of the professionalization of the police department."[71] At that time, one had to be a critical local reader, or a member of a targeted community, to challenge this unified narrative. In the years after 1991, any member of the national audience could challenge official LAPD statements about the state of affairs in Los Angeles, as well as TV shows' claims to be a documentary of that city. In the light of the L.A. Riots, the O. J. Simpson trial, and the Rampart scandal, it was much easier for anyone to see that *Dragnet* had worked to occlude problems within the police department through its representation of an idealized version of the LAPD. The public relations cover provided by the show allowed the department to refuse reflection and change, and to commit to a model of policing that caused considerable harm to Los Angeles citizens and communities. From the 1940s through the 1990s, *Dragnet* gave the LAPD freedom to discard even the possibility that managing a diverse metropolis obligated true dialogue with all of its citizens, permitting the department to instead embrace the indifference encoded in a devotion to just the facts.

EPILOGUE

"One of Us"

THE ENDURING, ENTWINED LEGACIES OF Jack Webb and *Dragnet* were built on the foundation of *Dragnet*'s circulation in the immediate postwar period. In the 1940s and 1950s, *Dragnet* expressed an essential cultural idea—the efficacy of bureaucratic governance—through innovative aural and visual aesthetic choices. Later versions (1967–1970, 1989–1991, 2003–2004) replicated the show's formula but were pale imitations of the original, despite being in color. The wider availability of these less successful productions as well as the simple fact of these series' more recent production have made it harder for today's audiences to recognize *Dragnet* (1949–1959) as the incisive artifact that it was. I have attempted to paint a full picture of one of the most significant programs in American broadcasting, describing how it shaped postwar media in ways that shaped postwar culture.

As the preceding pages have shown, the legacies of Jack Webb and *Dragnet* are also inextricably tied to the history of American policing, specifically to the history of the Los Angeles Police Department. On December 30, 1982, a week after Jack Webb's death, the LAPD honored his life with a memorial service in Elysian Park. The *Los Angeles Times* reported that "several hundred uniformed officers[,] friends of the department, and friends of Webb attended the service—the first of its kind by the department for a civilian." Chief of Police Daryl Gates, who spoke at the service, remembered Webb as "the greatest publicity agent any department could ever have," giving him credit for helping the LAPD "become what we are—a professional law enforcement agency." Webb was, said Gates, "considered by all in the Los Angeles Police Department to be one of us."[1] Today, more than seventy years after *Dragnet*'s premiere, Webb continues to be honored for his contributions to the police. Each year, the Los Angeles Police Historical Society presents the Jack Webb Awards to "honor individuals in the community who have demonstrated outstanding dedication to law enforcement."[2] The proceeds from that dinner support the Historical Society's Los Angeles Police Museum, in which Sergeant Friday's sport coat hangs in a prominent place.

Jack Webb knew that *Dragnet* would always be part of his legacy, but he did not intend for it to be all of it. Even while producing new *Dragnet* episodes, Webb began to pursue other projects. "By 1955 I began to feel *Dragnet* had been on long enough," Webb told *TV Guide*, "but the sponsor kept renewing."[3] In his time away from *Dragnet*, Webb and his production company, Mark VII, developed shows that came and went: *Noah's Ark* (1956–1957), a drama set in a veterinarian's office, and *Pete Kelly's Blues* (1959), a drama set among jazz musicians, which Webb had tried out on radio in 1951 and developed into a feature film in 1955. Webb made other feature films as well, though with less success than he had found on radio and television. In addition to *Pete Kelly's Blues* (1955), Webb directed *The D.I.* (1957), a story of Marine training; *-30-* (1959), a journalism yarn; and *The Last Time I Saw Archie* (1961), an Air Force comedy costarring Robert Mitchum. In the early 1960s, Webb spent a short time—less than a year—as head of television production at Warner Bros., a disastrous period that led to a career slump.

An old friend pulled him out of the downturn: in 1966, Webb brought *Dragnet* back to television. Sergeant Friday first returned to NBC via a made-for-TV movie, with Webb again producing, directing, and starring. Although reboots are a fact of contemporary television, observers at the time expressed surprise that an old show was returning to TV. Jane Ardmore, in a *Los Angeles Times* profile of Webb, expressed incredulity via italics: "Television series don't *come* back. They never *have*."[4] But *Dragnet* did come back, for three seasons from 1967 to 1970. The basic formula of the show remained; 1960s viewers recognized the "this is the city" opening, the interviews in alternating close-ups, and the promise that "only the names have been changed, to protect the innocent."

Some things did change. The show was in color, for one, and Friday had a new partner, Bill Gannon (played by Harry Morgan).[5] Most of all, *Dragnet*'s civic pedagogy took on a new cast. Webb was clear about what he wanted *Dragnet* to stand for within the cultural tumult of the late 1960s. "There's been a breakdown in our mores, a total disregard for constituted authority," he told columnist Hal Humphrey, "and I hope a series like *Dragnet* can do something to help restore respect for the law."[6] Sergeant Friday acquired a new propensity for making moral judgments, whether through pointed, meaningful looks or through speeches that told the offenders exactly what was wrong with them and why it was corrosive for society. The changed attitude was evident in the treatment of crime as well. Jason Mittell noticed that in

FIGURE 5.1. Webb, with actors Harry Morgan (left), cast as Friday's new partner, Bill Gannon, and Michael Burns (right), cast as the drug-addled "Blue Boy" in "The LSD Story," the season opener of *Dragnet 1967*. TV Guide/Courtesy Everett Collection.

the reboot, narcotics cases took on new meaning. Mittell writes that drugs "serve as more than another criminal violation like murder or robbery—they become a metonymic stand-in for the radical changes to the social order that Friday and Gannon combated daily."[7] In the late 1940s, *Dragnet* had been formally distinctive but ideologically unexceptional. In the late 1960s, *Dragnet*'s form was a throwback and its politics reactionary.

The new *Dragnet* might have looked silly to much of the younger generation, but it spoke to a large enough audience to revive Webb's career as a producer. Mark VII followed *Dragnet* with two long-running hits: *Adam-12* (1968–1975), a *Dragnet* for cops on the beat, and *Emergency!* (1972–1979), a fire-and-medical drama. Webb also continued to develop cop shows. At the time of his fatal heart attack in 1982, he had recently pitched a show about police leadership called *The Department*, and there were rumors that he was thinking about bringing *Dragnet* back once again.[8]

A 1980s *Dragnet* would have entered into a television landscape in which the procedural had evolved. Each decade has brought changes to the genre's form and content, often in ways that deviated from *Dragnet*. As early as the late 1950s, *Naked City* (1958–1963) challenged the professional distance between cops and citizens, insisting that police officers needed to use their emotions to do their jobs well.[9] From the first episode, the show introduces a possibility that earlier police procedurals never fully considered: that emotion might be a necessary part of the police officer's job. During the very first conversation between the new partners in the series premiere ("Meridian," Sept. 30, 1958), the elder Lt. Dan Muldoon references the younger Det. Jimmy Halloran's time in the service. The new detective is reluctant to talk about it:

> HALLORAN: Well, sir, Korea seems like a long time ago. A marine, he—he wasn't supposed to have any personal feeling.
> MULDOON: You think a police officer's any different?
> HALLORAN: Yes, sir, I do. I think we've got to have feelings.

This conversation announced *Naked City*'s intention to explore the emotional aspects of policing. It achieved this through its form: a semi-anthology, *Naked City* combined the case-of-the-week structure of the procedural with the dramatic ambitions of anthology storytelling. Its dual-narrative format, which simultaneously followed the police investigators and the criminal (or victim), allowed the series to bring emotional and psychological realism to its characters and resulted in critical acclaim for its complex portraits of contemporary lives.

In the next decade, television viewers saw the police procedural used as a framework to address contemporary social issues in ways that *Dragnet* avoided. In the late 1970s, the writer-producers Barbara Corday and Barbara Avedon wanted to write a script about women and women's issues, but as Corday remembered, "It seemed clear that you couldn't just write a script about two women sitting around talking. . . . No one was going to make it."[10] So Corday and Avedon wrote a script about two female detectives in an otherwise male precinct. The narrative framework allowed officers Christine Cagney and Mary Beth Lacey to explore issues that the feminist movement had brought into public discourse: domestic abuse, date rape, women's health, and, of course, sexism in the workplace. Rather than trying to make an intervention into the form of the genre, *Cagney and Lacey* (1981–1988) used the procedural to make women's perspectives and women's issues part of prime-time television.

The signal police show of the 1980s followed crime writer Joseph Wambaugh's dictum that "the best crime stories are not about how cops work on cases but about how cases work on cops."[11] *Hill Street Blues* (1981–1987) brought the full lives of officers more fully into the frame. The series followed both patrol officers and detectives in an unnamed city, and it showed officers of all kinds: nice cops, racist cops, angry cops, smart cops, and unbalanced cops—often in the same character. Officers had personal problems, professional problems, and family problems, which audiences watched them handle or mishandle, while they buzzed in and around the precinct house. Filmed with a handheld camera to invoke contemporary documentary filmmaking, and featuring a large cast of characters and unprecedented narrative complexity, *Hill Street Blues* redefined realism just as *Dragnet* had done thirty years earlier.

One of the key shows of the "second Golden Age," *The Wire* (2002–2008) became a critical favorite for its rewriting of the procedural. Over five seasons, *The Wire* observed the procedures of not only the police but all the systems shaping civic life in the city of Baltimore: the drug trade, the justice system, the public school system, City Hall, organized labor, newspapers. The show reflected the worldview of its writer and cocreator, David Simon, who said in 2002, "I want [audiences] to think about our institutions and what they've become, and why it is no longer possible for people to believe in them and commit themselves to them."[12] Watching *The Wire*, seeing these systems block and fail one another, reveals a civics lesson both poignant and dire.

Though the form of the television procedural has been stretched over the years, the bulk of today's shows reflect a genre more *Dragnet* than *The Wire*: restricted to the police perspective, starring dull detectives about whose personal lives we know little, and featuring sharp dialogue sprinkled with police jargon. The similarity of many of these shows can be traced to the influence of one man: Dick Wolf. The longtime producer's credits include *Law and Order* (1990–2010), *Chicago P.D.* (2014–present), and *FBI* (2018–present), all of which have become franchises with spin-offs and connected series. *Law and Order* was particularly impactful in the 1990s, reinvigorating the procedural by integrating the legal side of the criminal justice system: the first half of the show is a police investigation, and the second half focuses on the district attorney's prosecution. The show was also aggressively contemporary; episodes were known to be "ripped from the headlines."[13] The original *Law and Order* was followed by a slew of spin-offs, including *Law and Order: Criminal Intent* (2001–2011) and *Law and Order: SVU* (1999–present).[14] Today, the Dick Wolf universe exists alongside other procedural franchises that compose the backbone of network television, including *CSI: Crime Scene Investigation* (2000–present) and its spin-offs, and *NCIS: Naval Criminal Investigative Service* (2003–present) and its spin-offs.

While traditional procedurals continue to offer "aspirational" depictions of the police, other kinds of police shows have reflected the public's awareness of the problems with policing. The strongest direct counterpoint to *Dragnet*'s legacy is *The Shield* (2002–2008), an FX original that was, like *The Wire*, a key series of television's new Golden Age. Like *Dragnet*, *The Shield* was set among the officers of the LAPD. The show's protagonist was an out-of-control police detective, Vic Mackey (Michael Chiklis), who stood at the center of a Rampart-like criminal conspiracy. The series, a narratively complex serial drama, was not a crime-of-the-week procedural, and its hero, who closed the pilot by murdering a fellow officer, was decidedly not Joe Friday. The series, more interested in exploring the complex psychology of its antihero than in presenting a documentary of police work, nevertheless portrayed some truths that *Dragnet* refused: in its representation of a sprawling web of criminality within a police force, *The Shield* incorporated aspects of policing in America that "realistic" procedurals have never fully contended with.[15]

If the revelations of Rampart opened up space for responsive dramas like *The Shield*, we might expect the unchanging police procedural to be challenged by the cascading revelations of police brutality that prompted the Black Lives Matter movement. But as we consider *Dragnet*'s legacy, we can see that the police procedural genre has survived waves of exposés of police misconduct and calls for reform without damage to its core elements. Procedurals treat with hostility any outside forces that threaten their autonomy, whether it's outside investigators, defense lawyers, examining judges, crusading politicians, or resisting citizens. Throughout its history, the genre has managed to maintain its stubborn insularity.

For most contemporary procedurals, challenges to the system in the outside world have resulted in only cosmetic changes within their narrative worlds. For example, decades of protests surrounding police treatment of marginalized citizens have resulted not in changes to the formula but in changes to the cast. Procedural ensembles are now a carefully balanced crew of genders, races, and ethnicities.[16] Though David Simon argued that it is "no longer possible" to have faith in social institutions, the survival of the genre, with only minor adaptations, indicates a persistent cultural investment in the same systems out of which *Dragnet* developed in the postwar period.

At the same time, critiques of the police, and of representations of the police, are far more public and more widespread today than they were in *Dragnet*'s time, in ways that have impacted the cultural conversation about police shows. We can see this change expressed most sharply in the wider adoption of the term *copaganda* within critical discourse. Used to refer to media that promotes—or uncritically occupies—the police perspective, *copaganda* has been used to describe a range of content, from fictional series like *Law and Order*, to reality shows like *Cops*, to viral videos of police officers dancing with children or kneeling with protesters.[17] Not widely used before 2020, one can now regularly read critical pieces that use the term, an indication of a new level of consideration of the cultural stakes of representing the police and policework. In reviews, critics sometimes accuse shows of

Figure 5.2. The officers of *The Shield*, led by Michael Chiklis as Vic Mackey (far left), offered a version of the LAPD that, while heightened, was recognizable to some contemporary viewers. © 20th Century Fox Film Corp. All rights reserved. Courtesy Everett Collection.

Figure 5.3. The most watched police stories on television are procedurals in the mode of the Dick Wolf–produced *Chicago P.D.* Notice the intentionally diverse cast. © NBC/Photofest.

copaganda outright, as when Daniel Feinberg described the Disney+ series reboot of the movie *Turner and Hooch* (2021) as "copaganda just beneath the surface."[18] Even reviews that don't directly label a show evince an awareness of the term, as when a *Slate* sub-headline described CBS's Queen Latifah–led reboot of *The Equalizer* (2021–present) as a series that had been "listening to copaganda's critics."[19] The mainstreaming of copaganda reflects the broader mainstreaming of critiques of police authority. The very word is an indictment; it dismisses the idea that the police perspective is an objective one and suggests that it is perhaps not even a legitimate one.

Across networks and platforms, we see television creators wrestling with the consequences of questioning the legitimacy of police-centered programs. Some showrunners, such as Aaron Rahsaan Thomas of CBS's *S.W.A.T.* (2017–present) and Alexi Hawley of ABC's *The Rookie* (2018–present) have publicly expressed the need for their shows, and the television industry, to respond to the broader awareness of systemic issues within American policing. Reform-minded showrunners promise to deliver police shows that address police brutality and police misconduct, to incorporate conversations about race and racism, and to collaborate more closely with community partners that can guide writers toward more credible representations of police-community relations. They also call on the industry to elevate more diverse voices within writers' rooms and executive offices in order to enable and support new narratives.[20] At the same time, these creator-led conversations also reveal the limits of what is possible from a position inside the industry. When Hawley reflected on the challenge of continuing *The Rookie* in a changed context, he described the thinking of the production team: "Our task was to figure out how we could honor the conversations that were going on about policing within our show, without changing our show."[21] Hawley reveals in a phrase why the procedural survives: within the industry, the goal is to change the police show *without changing the police show*.

More progressive voices would argue that Hawley's project is not only impossible but undesirable. Looking for alternatives rather than adjustments, critic Nina Metz asked explicitly for more ambitious programming in the *Chicago Tribune*: "Where are the TV dramas exploring what our lives could look like *without* police?"[22] Metz's question is aligned with the work of progressive and radical activists who have called for solutions that go beyond police reform. Progressive voices ask us instead to reimagine "public safety" in ways that don't depend on police management: to build systems of mutual aid, to enact forms of restorative justice, to reallocate government funds from police and prisons to health care and housing. These solutions may be more difficult to envisage, but as Metz argues, television has space for the speculative: "If we're struggling to imagine an alternative to our status quo, isn't this where TV and film can—and should—step in?"[23] This imaginative space would need to be filled by genres other than the police procedural: a genre defined by the police perspective can imagine only a world *within* police, not worlds without them.[24] For networks and streaming platforms to commit to envisioning public safety in new ways, they must reallocate their own funds: the best and only solution for television is to defund the police procedural.

But the biggest threat to the future of the police procedural is likely industrial rather than political or cultural. Although police procedurals rank among the top shows on network television, the significance of that achievement has significantly shrunk. Even among Americans watching on television screens (rather than mobile devices), streaming platforms' audience share has surpassed that of the broadcasters.[25] A procedural series, with its standardized format, was a good fit for time-bound network schedules organized around the daily transmission of cognate content. For streaming platforms such as Netflix, however, the priority is the maintenance of the subscriber base via the promise of fresh, new content. The reliable, unsurprising, open-ended form of the procedural is a less attractive model for streamers, which tend toward commissioning shorter seasons and shorter series.

Thinking about his place in the current era, the broadcast super-producer Dick Wolf told a reporter, "We may be an anachronism. I'm not sure. But it sure is fun to be able to do television still on the scale that we do it."[26] Yet even Dick Wolf may not be working on this scale for much longer. Wolf's newest production deal with NBCUniversal promises the delivery of content across the media conglomerate, including the broadcast network, the Peacock streaming service, and other digital extensions yet to be named. Recent and upcoming productions include *Law and Order: Organized Crime* (2021–present), an eight-episode-per-season serialized drama for NBC, and *Law and Order: Hate Crimes*, a procedural set for Peacock. In today's unpredictable media environment, even the contemporary king of the police procedural will be working in more flexible ways.

The procedural endures, though it is not yet clear which genres will persist in an era in which audiences "stream content" rather than "watch TV." Certainly, no series will ever again have the kind of impact that *Dragnet* had. In the 1940s and 1950s, it both captured and promoted a particularly postwar liberal imaginary, and it arrived at exactly the right moment in media history, developing an aural aesthetic that translated to television and then resonated across culture. Millions of listeners and viewers learned about police work from *Dragnet*; its lessons were remarkably incomplete but nevertheless shaped what Americans knew about the police and how they understood their responsibilities as citizens. Today, we continue to not only wrestle with the larger issues with which the show engaged—questions of policing, citizenship, and democracy—but we continue to wrestle with them through the form that *Dragnet* handed down. In many ways, *Dragnet* was a show of its time. But it is also, in its lasting influence, a show of our time.

Notes

Introduction

1. Untitled press release dated May 28, 1954, box 00121, folder 651, Warner Bros. Archives, School of Cinematic Arts, University of Southern California, Los Angeles (hereafter WBA-USC).

2. The last two years of the radio series were rebroadcasts.

3. The police procedural is also a literary genre, though novels are outside of the scope of this study. Readers interested in a critical appraisal of literary police procedurals should seek out George N. Dove, *The Police Procedural* (Bowling Green, OH: Bowling Green University Popular Press, 1982).

4. For some recent work on crime television, see Roger Sabin et al., *Cop Shows: A Critical History of Police Dramas on Television* (Jefferson, NC: McFarland, 2015); Jonathan Nichols-Pethick, *TV Cops: The Contemporary American Television Police Drama* (New York: Routledge, 2012).

5. Haden Guest, "The Police Procedural Film: Law and Order in the American Cinema, 1930–1960" (PhD diss., University of California, Los Angeles, 2005), 3, ProQuest (3218663).

6. Henry A. Giroux, "Public Pedagogy and the Responsibility of Intellectuals: Youth, Littleton, and the Loss of Innocence," *JAC* 20, no. 1 (2000): 10–11.

7. Henry A. Giroux and Grace Pollock, *The Mouse That Roared: Disney and the End of Innocence* (Lanham, MD: Rowman and Littlefield, 2010), 10.

8. See Jeffrey P. Jones, "A Cultural Approach to the Study of Mediated Citizenship," *Social Semiotics* 16, no. 2 (June 1, 2006): 365–383. For a discussion of television specifically, see Anna McCarthy, *The Citizen Machine: Governing by Television in 1950s America* (New York: New Press, 2010). For a consideration of the ways in which sound (including radio) shapes citizenship, see Jennifer Lynn Stoever, *The Sonic Color Line: Race and the Cultural Politics of Listening* (New York: New York University Press, 2016).

9. Lizabeth Cohen, *A Consumer's Republic: The Politics of Mass Consumption in Postwar America* (New York: Knopf, 2003); Sarah Banet-Weiser, *Kids Rule! Nickelodeon and Consumer Citizenship* (Durham, NC: Duke University Press, 2007), 7. See also James Hay and Laurie Ouellette, eds., *Better Living through Reality TV: Television and Post-welfare Citizenship* (Malden, MA: Blackwell, 2008).

10. Elaine Tyler May, *Homeward Bound: American Families in the Cold War Era* (New York: Basic Books, 1988).

11. See M. Keith Booker, *Monsters, Mushroom Clouds, and the Cold War: American Science Fiction and the Roots of Postmodernism, 1946–1964* (Westport, CT: Greenwood, 2001); Thomas Doherty, *Cold War, Cool Medium: Television, McCarthyism, and American Culture* (New York: Columbia University Press, 2003); Michael Kackman, *Citizen Spy: Television, Espionage, and Cold War Culture* (Minneapolis: University of Minnesota Press, 2005).

12. Peter J. Kuznick and James Burkhart Gilbert, eds., *Rethinking Cold War Culture* (Washington, DC: Smithsonian Institution Press, 2001), 2.

13. Kristin L. Matthews, *Reading America: Citizenship, Democracy, and Cold War Literature* (Amherst: University of Massachusetts Press, 2016), 5.

14. Dennis Broe, "Genre Regression and the New Cold War: The Return of the Police Procedural," *Framework: The Journal of Cinema and Media* 45, no. 2 (October 2004): 81–82, 85.

15. Guest, "Police Procedural Film," 157.

16. Guest, "Police Procedural Film," 156.

17. Elia Kazan and Jeff Young, *Kazan: The Master Director Discusses His Films* (New York: Newmarket Press, 1999), 64.

18. This dialogue was transcribed from the broadcast recording. The scene includes overlapping dialogue, which this transcription simplifies for the sake of clarity.

19. Review of *Panic in the Streets*, *Life*, August 21, 1950, *Panic in the Streets* Clipping File, Margaret Herrick Library of the Academy of Motion Picture Arts and Sciences (hereafter AMPAS); Review of *Panic in the Streets*, *L.A. Times*, August 14, 1950, *Panic in the Streets* Clipping File, AMPAS.

20. James Burkhart Gilbert, *Men in the Middle: Searching for Masculinity in the 1950s* (Chicago: University of Chicago Press, 2005), 9.

21. Laura McEnaney, *Civil Defense Begins at Home: Militarization Meets Everyday Life in the Fifties* (Princeton, NJ: Princeton University Press, 2000), 90.

22. Griffin Newman (@GriffLightning), "I'm an out-of-work actor who (improbably) played a detective on two episodes of BLUE BLOODS almost a decade ago. If you currently play a cop? If you make tens or hundreds of thousands of dollars a year in residuals from playing a cop? I'll let you do the math," Twitter, June 2, 2020, https://twitter.com/GriffLightning/status/1267666336731324416?s=20 (tweet removed).

23. Tom Scharpling (@scharpling), Twitter, June 1, 2020, https://twitter.com/scharpling/status/1267576111250075648.

24. "A Conversation about Police and Hollywood with the 'Law and Order: SVU' Showrunner," *TV's Top 5* podcast, *Hollywood Reporter*, June 5, 2020, https://www.hollywoodreporter.com/live-feed/tvs-top-5-a-conversation-police-hollywood-law-order-svu-showrunner-1297222.

25. Alyssa Rosenberg, "Shut Down All Police Movies and TV Shows. Now.," *Washington Post*, June 4, 2020, Opinions, https://www.washingtonpost.com/opinions/2020/06/04/shut-down-all-police-movies-tv-shows-now/.

26. Kathryn VanArendonk, "21 TV Procedurals to Watch That Aren't about

Police," *Vulture*, June 10, 2020, https://www.vulture.com/2020/06/21-crime-procedurals-without-police.html.

Chapter 1: "Our Neo-realism"

1. The exceptionally crabby *New Yorker* reviewer called *Call Northside 777* a "pseudo-documentary." Review of *Call Northside 777*, *New Yorker*, February 28, 1949, *Call Northside 777* Clipping File, AMPAS.

2. See Peter Lev, *Transforming the Screen, 1950–1959*, History of the American Cinema 7 (New York: Scribner's, 2003). For more recent scholarship on the postwar social problem film, see Pearl Latteier, "The Hollywood Social Problem Film, 1946–1959" (PhD diss., University of Wisconsin–Madison, 2010), ProQuest; Chris Cagle, *Sociology on Film: Postwar Hollywood's Prestige Commodity* (New Brunswick, NJ: Rutgers University Press, 2017).

3. The most systematic writing on postwar semi-documentaries has appeared in William Lafferty, "A Reappraisal of the Semi-Documentary in Hollywood, 1945–1948," *Velvet Light Trap: A Critical Journal of Film & Television*, no. 20 (Summer 1983): 22–26; and Will Straw, "Documentary Realism and the Postwar Left," in *"Un-American" Hollywood: Politics and Film in the Blacklist Era*, ed. Frank Krutnik (New Brunswick, NJ: Rutgers University Press, 2007), 130–141. More often, scholars refer to semi-documentaries as part of other cycles, genres, or tendencies (usually film noir), as in Frank Krutnik, *In a Lonely Street: Film Noir, Genre, Masculinity* (New York: Routledge, 1991), 202–208.

4. I use *cycle* to refer to a close relationship between similar films, bounded by time and formula. As Steve Neale summarizes its common use in scholarship, "The term 'cycle' is used as well, usually to refer to groups of films made within a specific and limited time-span, and founded, for the most part, on the characteristics of individual commercial successes: the cycle of historical adventure films made in the wake of *Treasure Island* (1934) and *The Count of Monte Cristo* (1934) . . . or the cycle of 'slasher' or 'stalker' films made in the wake of *The Texas Chainsaw Massacre* (1974) and *Halloween* (1978)." Stephen Neale, *Genre and Hollywood* (New York: Routledge, 2000), 7.

5. Neale, *Genre and Hollywood*, 3.

6. Dove, *Police Procedural*, 2.

7. Rick Altman, *Film/Genre* (London: British Film Institute, 1999), 101.

8. Michel Ciment, ed., *Kazan on Kazan* (New York: Viking, 1974), 56.

9. Ciment, *Kazan on Kazan*, 56.

10. Straw, "Documentary Realism and the Postwar Left," 141.

11. Gary Gerstle, "Race and the Myth of the Liberal Consensus," *Journal of American History* 82, no. 2 (September 1995): 579, https://doi.org/10.2307/2082187. See also Gary Gerstle, "The Reach and Limits of the Liberal Consensus," in *The Liberal Consensus Reconsidered*, ed. Robert Mason and Iwan Morgan (Gainesville: University Press of Florida, 2017), 52–66.

12. Godfrey Hodgson, "Revisiting the Liberal Consensus," in *The Liberal*

Consensus Reconsidered, ed. Robert Mason and Iwan Morgan (Gainesville: University Press of Florida, 2017), 22.

13. Jack C. Ellis, "American Documentary in the 1950s," in *Transforming the Screen, 1950–1959*, ed. Peter Lev, History of the American Cinema 7 (New York: Scribner's, 2003), 257.

14. For more on the participation of these filmmakers, see Mark Harris, *Five Came Back: A Story of Hollywood and the Second World War* (New York: Penguin, 2014).

15. Stephen E. Bowles, "And Time Marched On: The Creation of the March of Time," *Journal of the University Film Association* 29, no. 1 (1977): 7–13; Raymond Fielding, "Time Flickers Out: Notes on the Passing of the March of Time," in *Hollywood Quarterly: Film Culture in Postwar America, 1945–1957*, ed. Eric Smoodin and Ann Martin (Berkeley: University of California Press, 2002), 109–116.

16. The relationship lasted for a few films but eventually broke down; the independent producer found that no Hollywood studio was a perfect match for the kinds of films he wanted to make. According to de Rochemont, both of his studio contracts (he also was affiliated with MGM for a brief time) ended in disputes over the use of stars. He hired the well-known agent Sam Jaffe to help him break his contracts. "I think I'm the only guy in Hollywood who ever hired an agent to make him lose a job," de Rochemont told a reporter. Maurice Zolotow, "Want to Be a Movie Star?," *Saturday Evening Post*, March 29, 1952, 25, 141, box 1, Louis de Rochemont Collection, College Archives and Special Collections, Keene State College, Keene, NH (hereafter CASC-KSC).

17. *The House on 92nd Street*, *13 Rue Madeleine*, and *Boomerang!* were produced by Louis de Rochemont. Otto Lang was credited as producer on *Call Northside 777*, though the look and feel of that film was more likely due to director Henry Hathaway, who directed *House* and *Madeleine*.

18. Guest, "Police Procedural Film," 17–18.

19. Thomas M. Pryor, "Blazing a Trail," *New York Times*, April 1, 1945, X3.

20. "So Near and Yet, Etc.," *New York Times*, August 12, 1945, *The House on 92nd Street* Clipping File, AMPAS.

21. De Rochemont later said that the story wasn't quite true to facts. He told an interviewer in the 1970s that "the spies in real life were Russians, not Germans. In the movie we had to make them Germans because the Russians were still our allies and it wouldn't do to have them as the villains." Charles Jellison, "Lost Dialogue with Filmmaker Louis de Rochemont," *New Hampshire Magazine*, April 2005, 65, box 1, Louis de Rochemont Collection, CASC-KSC. However, other sources say that the film was based on the Duquesne spy ring. See Leon O. Prior, "Nazi Invasion of Florida!," *Florida Historical Quarterly* 49, no. 2 (1970): 129–139; R. Barton Palmer, "Cold War Thrillers," in *The Wiley-Blackwell History of American Film*, ed. Roy Grundmann, Cynthia A. Barto Lucia, and Art Simon (Malden, MA: Wiley Blackwell, 2012), 1–24.

22. Philip Scheuer, "Cameras Use F.B.I. Haunts for Adventure in Reality," *Los Angeles Times*, July 22, 1945, C1.

23. Review of *The House on 92nd Street*, *Time*, October 8, 1945, *The House on 92nd Street* Clipping File, AMPAS.

24. Eugene Lyons, "Louis de Rochemont: Maverick of the Movies," *Reader's Digest*, July 1949, 23, box 2, Louis de Rochemont Collection, CASC-KSC.

25. "Vital Statistics," *The House on 92nd Street* Clipping File, AMPAS.

26. "Vital Statistics."

27. "Vital Statistics."

28. Cinematographer Norbert Brodine "shot hundreds of scenes which would ordinarily have been considered impossible" ("Vital Statistics"). For *Boomerang!*, "it took thirty policemen to keep them [onlookers] out of camera range" (Untitled publicity document, *Boomerang!* Clipping File, AMPAS). Virginia Wright wrote about production coordinators in her column in the *Los Angeles Daily News*: "These indispensables can be spotted by the depth of furrows on their brows" (March 15, 1948, *The Naked City* Clipping File, AMPAS).

29. The remarkable coherence of the classical Hollywood system has been argued by David Bordwell, Janet Staiger, and Kristin Thompson. They identify in Hollywood cinema tendencies toward differentiation and standardization that keep the formal system intact. Their powerful argument helps us explain the coherence of the formal system, but it elides the ways in which audiences experienced these films. David Bordwell, Janet Staiger, and Kristin Thompson, *The Classical Hollywood Cinema: Film Style and Mode of Production to 1960* (New York: Columbia University Press, 1985).

30. "Factual and Forceful," *New York Times*, September 30, 1945, *The House on 92nd Street* Clipping File, AMPAS. Irving Hoffman, "Tales of Hoffman," *Hollywood Reporter*, February 11, 1947, 3.

31. Howard Barnes, "On the Screen," *New York Herald-Tribune*, September 27, 1945, *The House on 92nd Street* Clipping File, AMPAS.

32. Lowell E. Redelings, "The Hollywood Scene," *Hollywood Citizen-News*, November 6, 1945, *The House on 92nd Street* Clipping File, AMPAS.

33. Gerstle, "Race and the Myth of the Liberal Consensus"; George Lewis, "Memories of the Movement: Civil Rights, the Liberal Consensus, and the March on Washington Twenty Years Later," in *The Liberal Consensus Reconsidered: American Politics and Society in the Postwar Era*, ed. Robert Mason and Iwan W. Morgan (Gainesville: University Press of Florida, 2017), 262–282; Helen Laville, "Gender in an Era of Liberal Consensus," in Mason and Morgan, 245–261; Kim Phillips-Fein, "'If Business and the Country Will Be Run Right:' The Business Challenge to the Liberal Consensus, 1945–1964," *International Labor and Working-Class History*, no. 72 (2007): 192–215.

34. Gerstle, "Reach and Limits of the Liberal Consensus," 53.

35. The other major example is Kazan's *Boomerang!* One might also count *Lost Boundaries*, which does not focus on crime but does investigate the injustice of racial segregation.

36. William F. Dermott and Karl Detzer, "Tillie Scrubbed On," *Reader's Digest*, December 1946, 81–84.

37. In the spring of 1950, Teddy Marcinkiewicz, the other man wrongly convicted, was finally released from prison. See "'Northside 777' Case Is Closed," *Life*, March 6, 1950, 39.

38. Review of *Call Northside 777*, *Newsweek*, February 27, 1948, *Call Northside 777* Clipping File, AMPAS.

39. Virginia Wright, review of *Call Northside 777*, *Los Angeles Daily News*, February 27, 1948, *Call Northside 777* Clipping File, AMPAS.

40. "Joe Majczek's Story," *Life*, March 1, 1948, 57–58.

41. Leonarde Keeler is not featured in the credits, but audiences might have guessed that he was a real-life specialist from his delivery, which was slightly awkward compared to the polished intensity of his scene partners. Or they might have read the studio publicity material about Keeler's participation, which explained that "the inventor of the lie-detector" was cast "not only for realistic purposes but also because it would have been rather difficult for an actor to handle the complex machine" (20th Century-Fox news release, January 28, 1948, *Call Northside 777* Clipping File, AMPAS). For more on Keeler and the invention of the lie detector test (he was one of several key figures), see Ken Alder, *The Lie Detectors: The History of an American Obsession* (New York: Free Press, 2007).

42. Review of *The Wrong Man*, *Cue*, December 22, 1956, *The Wrong Man* Clipping File, AMPAS.

43. "Hitchcock 'Wrong Man' Lifelike but Plodding," *Los Angeles Times*, January 24, 1957, *The Wrong Man* Clipping File, AMPAS.

44. Review of *The Wrong Man*, *Time*, January 14, 1957, *The Wrong Man* Clipping File, AMPAS.

Chapter 2: Silence, Not Sirens

1. Jack Webb, "The Facts about Me" (2 of 3), *Saturday Evening Post*, September 12, 1959, 86.

2. *Pat Novak for Hire* was written by Richard L. Breen, who later wrote the *Dragnet* feature. A semiserious, semiparodic private detective program, the show was as aware of its genre play as *Dragnet* was. *Pat Novak* fell apart when Breen moved to Los Angeles for better opportunities (and when Webb followed him there).

3. Webb, "Facts about Me" (2 of 3), 86.

4. Richard Tregaskis, "The Cops' Favorite Make-Believe Cop," *Saturday Evening Post*, September 26, 1953, 25.

5. Tregaskis, "Cops' Favorite Make-Believe Cop," 106. No quotes or italics in original.

6. Joe Beck, "Dragnet," *True Detective*, March 1950, 54, folder 11, Michael Hayde Collection, Library of American Broadcasting, University of Maryland-College Park (hereafter LAB-UMD). Rousseau departed after it had become clear to all that this was Jack Webb's show and an additional producer was a redundancy.

7. Webb, "Facts about Me" (2 of 3), 106.

8. As advisors, their main role was to review radio scripts before airing to correct police procedure and uses of police jargon. For more on the relationship between *Dragnet* and the LAPD, see chapter 4.

9. NBC's affiliates had considerable influence over NBC's decision to continue the program. Michael Hayde notes, "When their affiliates voted it the top sustaining program, the network opted to continue the series into the fall." Michael J. Hayde, *My Name's Friday: The Unauthorized but True Story of* Dragnet *and the Films of Jack Webb* (Nashville, TN: Cumberland House, 2001), 29.

10. "The CBS vs. NBC Summer Story," *Variety*, August 31, 1949, 29. The Hooper ratings (or "Hooperatings") were an audience measurement methodology developed by Claude E. Hooper, and its numbers represent the percentages of total households listening. The main feature of the Hooper system was telephone surveys, in which respondents were called at home and asked about the radio program to which they were currently listening. In 1950, the C. E. Hooper company was acquired by the A. C. Nielsen Company, developer of the Nielsen ratings system. For more, see James G. Webster, *Ratings Analysis: The Theory and Practice of Audience Research*, 2nd ed., LEA's Communication Series (Mahwah, NJ: Lawrence Erlbaum Associates, 2000), 81–98.

11. John Crosby, "Radio in Review," *New York Herald Tribune*, June 13, 1949, Hayde Collection, folder 11, LAB-UMD.

12. Val Adams, "Programs in Review," *New York Times*, August 14, 1949, Hayde Collection, folder 1l, LAB-UMD.

13. Crosby, "Radio in Review."

14. Reference episodes for this composite: "The Big Pug" (May 18, 1950), "The Big Building" (June 14, 1951), "The Big Scrapbook" (Apr. 26, 1953), and "The Big Sisters" (Sept. 13, 1955).

15. Jason Mittell, *Genre and Television: From Cop Shows to Cartoons in American Culture* (New York: Routledge, 2004), 134. R. Barton Palmer, "Dragnet, Film Noir, and Postwar Realism," in *The Philosophy of TV Noir*, ed. Steven M. Sanders and Aeon J. Skoble (Lexington: University Press of Kentucky, 2008), 33–48.

16. *Gang Busters* continued to make this claim even after other shows based on real cases began to air in the mid-1940s. Its boast of national coverage may have been made in response to its predecessor and competitor, *Calling All Cars* (1933–1939), a regional program.

17. Matthew Cecil, "Coming on like *Gang Busters*: J. Edgar Hoover's FBI and the Battle to Control Radio Portrayals of the Bureau, 1936–1958," *Journalism History* 40, no. 4 (January 2015): 254, https://doi.org/10.1080/00947679.2015.12059114.

18. Elena Razlogova, "True Crime Radio and Listener Disenchantment with Network Broadcasting, 1935–1946," *American Quarterly* 58, no. 1 (2006): 141, 144.

19. Adams, "Programs in Review."

20. "Radio & TV," *Time*, May 15, 1950, 60.

21. Walter Schumann was given credit for the score on radio and television. In

1953, Miklós Rósza's publisher filed suit, noting the strong similarities between the *Dragnet* theme and Rósza's theme for *The Killers* (1946). Rósza was eventually acknowledged as co-composer. "Plagiarism Suit on 'Dragnet' Theme," *Variety*, November 15, 1953, 5; Alan Warner, "Dum-Founded," letter to the editor, *Los Angeles Times*, August 1, 1987, SDA2.

22. "Radio & TV," 60.

23. Kathleen Battles, *Calling All Cars: Radio Dragnets and the Technology of Policing* (Minneapolis: University of Minnesota Press, 2010), 77.

24. Battles, *Calling All Cars*, 78, 81.

25. Quoted in Leonard Maltin, *The Great American Broadcast* (New York: NAL Trade, 2000), 85.

26. I use Ben Romero in the example here, but Friday had two long-term partners on the show. Romero, Friday's first partner, was played by Barton Yarborough, who died in December 1951. Several episodes later, the show introduced Frank Smith (played by Ben Alexander), who was Friday's partner on radio and television through 1959. Romero tended toward cranky; Smith tended toward genial.

27. Quoted in *Biography*, "Jack Webb: Just the Facts Ma'am," directed by Sunny Parich, aired on A&E, 2000.

28. Quoted in *Los Angeles Daily News*, November 10, 1953, *Jack Webb* Clipping File, AMPAS.

29. Beck, "Dragnet," 72.

30. Neil Verma, *Theater of the Mind: Imagination, Aesthetics, and American Radio Drama* (Chicago: University of Chicago Press, 2012), 28.

31. Verma, *Theater of the Mind*, 30–31.

32. In a 1960 interview, Webb told Sid Skolsky that he read a lot of "news and news analysis" and watched mostly documentaries on television. Webb expressed particular admiration for the work of Edward R. Murrow. Jack Webb, interview by Sid Skolsky, Sid Skolsky Papers, box 5, folder 95, AMPAS.

33. Matthew C. Ehrlich, *Radio Utopia: Postwar Audio Documentary in the Public Interest* (Urbana: University of Illinois Press, 2011), 30.

34. Jack Webb, interview by Sid Skolsky.

35. Henry Hewes, "Radio: Realistic 'Cops and Robbers' Saga," *New York Times*, June 3, 1951, Hayde Collection, folder 11, LAB-UMD.

36. A note here about titles: early episodes circulated under a description of the crime or the name of the criminal. By episode 20, the titles of episodes were all "The Big ——."

37. "Radio & TV."

38. Michel Chion calls these "materializing sound indices," the noises that make sound concrete. Michel Chion, *Audio-Vision: Sound on Screen*, trans. Claudia Gorbman (New York: Columbia University Press, 1994), 114.

39. Hewes, "Radio," 7.

40. Hewes, "Radio," 7.

41. Maltin, *Great American Broadcast*, 197.

42. While many of the radio scripts were adapted for television, "The Big Court" was not, underscoring that the interest of the show was not in the story but in its aural expression.

43. James Lastra, *Sound Technology and the American Cinema: Perception, Representation, Modernity* (New York: Columbia University Press, 2000), 138–139.

44. Lastra, *Sound Technology and the American Cinema*, 145.

45. Bordwell, Thompson, and Staiger, *Classical Hollywood Cinema*, 298–308.

46. For more on the commercialization of radio, see Susan Smulyan, *Selling Radio: The Commercialization of American Broadcasting 1920–1934* (Washington, DC: Smithsonian Institution Press, 1996); Verma, *Theater of the Mind*, 22–25; Lynn Spigel, *Make Room for TV: Television and the Family Ideal in Postwar America* (Chicago: University of Chicago Press, 1992), 28–29.

47. Susan J. Douglas, *Listening In: Radio and the American Imagination* (Minneapolis: University of Minnesota Press, 2004), 33–34.

48. Chion, *Audio-Vision*, 24–34.

49. Some comedy shows, such as *The Jack Benny Program*, manipulated this expectation by incorporating commercials into the show's diegesis. The sponsor was not sure this was a good idea, but of course audiences loved it—who wouldn't rather hear a joke than a straight commercial? See Milt Josefsberg, *The Jack Benny Show* (New Rochelle, NY: Arlington House, 1977), 321–322.

50. This has been a perpetual concern within the history of commercial broadcasting. The issue has intensified over the last twenty years with the widespread use of DVRs, the popularity of online streaming services, and other alternatives to live broadcasting that put more control in the hands of listeners and viewers.

51. "Radio Audience Measurement" brochure, p. 9, folder P367, History Files, National Broadcasting Company Collection, Recorded Sound Division, Library of Congress, Washington, DC; hereafter NBC-LOC.

52. "Radio Audience Measurement," 14–15.

53. "Television's Effects on the Family's Activities" report, p. 29, folder P565, NBC-LOC. Punctuation as in original.

54. This is not to say that listeners were wholly passive, as previous scholars have argued. Michele Hilmes writes about the ways audiences made soap operas a part of their lives. But this kind of participation was not a result of the aesthetic strategies of the show; rather, it reflects the way listeners took ownership of "their stories." Michele Hilmes, *Radio Voices: American Broadcasting, 1922–1952* (Minneapolis: University of Minnesota Press, 1997), 163. See also Tania Modleski, "The Rhythms of Reception: Daytime Television and Women's Work," in *Regarding Television: Critical Approaches—an Anthology*, ed. E. Ann Kaplan (Frederick, MD: University Publications of America, 1983), 68.

55. Hewes, "Radio," 7.

56. Verma, *Theater of the Mind*, 35.

57. Verma, *Theater of the Mind*, 37.

58. Tregaskis, "Cops' Favorite Make-Believe Cop," 25. An early episode of *TV*

Guide assisted viewers with a feature titled "You Too Can Speak DRAGNET" (July 3–9, 1953, 10).

59. "CBS vs. NBC Summer Story," 29.

60. Review of *21st Precinct*, *Variety*, July 22, 1953, 30.

61. A similar show, *Unit 99*, ran from 1957 to 1958 on ABC. Associated with the Sacramento police, the show is narrated by a sergeant on the force who rides with the unit as it responds to calls. Both *Nightwatch* and *Unit 99* are structured very much like the long-running television reality series *Cops*, which was broadcast in the United States from 1989 to 2020 (and continues to be produced for overseas viewing).

62. Repeat episodes were broadcast as "new" episodes on NBC radio from September 1955 through February 1957. See Hayde, *My Name's Friday*, 263.

Chapter 3: Saturation and Citizenship

1. Rep. Samuel W. Yorty (CA), "Jack Webb Performs Public Service," 100 Cong. Rec. 12316 (daily ed. July 27, 1954).

2. Yorty, "Jack Webb Performs," 12315.

3. Yorty, "Jack Webb Performs," 12315–12316.

4. Bob Thomas, "Four Notes Blare for *Dragnet*," undated, folder 9, Hayde Collection, LAB-UMD.

5. The seminal work here is Henry Jenkins, *Convergence Culture: Where Old and New Media Collide* (New York: New York University Press, 2006). For more on the evolving conversation in this subfield, see "Transmedia Studies: Where Now?," the introduction to Matthew Freeman and Renira Rampazzo Gambarato, *The Routledge Companion to Transmedia Studies* (Milton, UK: Taylor and Francis, 2018).

6. Michele Hilmes, *Hollywood and Broadcasting: From Radio to Cable*, Illinois Studies in Communications (Urbana: University of Illinois Press, 1990); Derek Johnson, *Media Franchising: Creative License and Collaboration in the Culture Industries* (New York: New York University Press, 2013).

7. Annette Hill, *Media Experiences: Engaging with Drama and Reality Television* (London: Routledge, 2018), 7.

8. John Corner, "Afterword: Reflections on Media Engagement," *Media Industries Journal* 4, no. 1 (2017), https://doi.org/10.3998/mij.15031809.0004.109.

9. Corner, "Afterword."

10. Michael Z. Newman and Elana Levine, *Legitimating Television: Media Convergence and Cultural Status* (New York: Routledge, 2012), 3.

11. Cecil Smith, "Bearding the Lion; Ralph Story Takes on Dragnet Tonight," *Los Angeles Times*, July 1, 1954, 30.

12. "Dragnet Rates Over Lucy—ARB," *Broadcasting*, November 9, 1953, 31.

13. As Douglas Gomery recounts, CBS overtook NBC in the ratings in 1952, causing "America's Network" to "enter the 1960s as a perennial second-place network." Douglas Gomery, "'Talent Raids and Package Deals': NBC Loses Its Leadership in the 1950s," in *NBC: America's Network*, ed. Michele Hilmes (Berkeley: University of California Press, 2007), 166.

14. Review of *Dragnet*, *Variety*, December 19, 1951, folder 12, Hayde Collection, LAB-UMD.

15. Jack Gould, "Radio and Television," *New York Times*, December 19, 1951, folder 12, Hayde Collection, LAB-UMD.

16. William Lafferty, "'No Attempt at Artiness, Profundity, or Significance': 'Fireside Theater' and the Rise of Filmed Television Programming," *Cinema Journal* 27, no. 1 (October 1987): 40.

17. As Frank Sturcken asserts, "The biggest and best of that period was all live from New York." Frank Sturcken, *Live Television: The Golden Age of 1946–1958 in New York* (Jefferson, NC: McFarland, 1990), xi. Some critics also include live anarchic comedies, such as *Your Show of Shows* (1950–1954), in their definition.

18. William Boddy, *Fifties Television: The Industry and Its Critics* (Urbana: University of Illinois Press, 1990), 80.

19. Michele Hilmes, *Only Connect: A Cultural History of Broadcasting in the United States*, 2nd ed. (Boston: Wadsworth/Cengage Learning, 2007), 159. Later, "liveness" would be described by Jane Feuer as an "ideology" that hides the many iterations of televisual transmission. Feuer argues, "Network television never truly exploits its capacity for instantaneous and unmediated transmission. Only the ideological connotations of live television are exploited in order to overcome the contradiction between flow and fragmentation in television practice." Jane Feuer, "The Concept of Live Television: Ontology as Ideology," in *Regarding Television: Critical Approaches—An Anthology*, ed. E. Ann Kaplan (Frederick, MD: University Publications of America, 1983), 16.

20. "Jack-in-the-Tape Webb," *Variety*, August 20, 1958, folder 13, Hayde Collection, LAB-UMD. Webb was joined in his insistence on shooting on film by a handful of others, most prominently Lucille Ball and Desi Arnaz. Throughout 1951, the stars of *I Love Lucy* (1951–1957) negotiated with Philip Morris and CBS. The sponsor and the network wanted the show to originate live in New York, but Ball and Arnaz wanted to avoid the degraded quality of kinescope projections and to take advantage of West Coast production capabilities. *I Love Lucy* premiered in October 1951 (a few days after Webb began shooting the first episode of *Dragnet*) and set the standard for the multi-camera sitcom.

21. Hayde, *My Name's Friday*, 41.

22. Fred Hift, "Television-Radio," *Motion Picture Daily*, March 5, 1952, 6.

23. Hal Humphrey column, *Los Angeles Mirror*, November 6, 1952, folder 13, Hayde Collection, LAB-UMD.

24. Gould, "Radio and Television," 48.

25. "Heavy Switch to Film; 46 Shows Now Set for Lensing This Fall," *Variety*, September 17, 1952, 33.

26. Sergeant Friday's badge number was 714. The title was changed after objections by LAPD chief William H. Parker, who disliked the word *cop* as a term for police officers.

27. "TV Film Awards," *Variety*, April 21, 1954, 28.

28. "How to Live on TV," *Newsweek*, May 27, 1957, 100.

29. Some gave Jack Webb sole credit. In the early 1960s, the columnist Sidney Skolsky interviewed Webb and opened a question with, "Jack, you brought a whole new technique to television with the close-up." In his answer, Webb didn't challenge the question's assumption. Jack Webb, interview by Sid Skolsky, Sid Skolsky Papers, box 5, folder 95, AMPAS.

30. Philip Scheuer, "A Town Called Hollywood," *Los Angeles Times*, April 18, 1954, D4.

31. Undated press release, box B00121, folder 651, WBA-USC.

32. Undated Erskine Johnson column sent from Jack Webb to Peggy Webber, folder 12, Hayde Collection, LAB-UMD. There is no question that *Dragnet*'s auteur was Jack Webb, as he was ultimately responsible for almost every aspect of production. But as is true with every auteur, particularly those working within an industrial system, there was no single author for this style. According to Wheeler Winston Dixon, the director Herbert Strock directed the series pilot and contributed the use of tight close-ups. My research hasn't uncovered additional evidence that corroborates Strock's involvement in early episodes, but certainly every iteration of *Dragnet* was the result of a collaborative process (under Webb's authority). For more on Strock, see Wheeler Winston Dixon, *Lost in the Fifties: Recovering Phantom Hollywood* (Carbondale: Southern Illinois University Press, 2005), 106–109; Wheeler Winston Dixon, "Just the Facts, Man: The Complicated Genesis of Television's *Dragnet*," *Film International*, November 25, 2012, http://filmint.nu/just-the-facts-man-the-complicated-genesis-of-televisions-dragnet/.

33. Val Adams, "Video in Review," *New York Times*, August 15, 1954, X9.

34. "TV's Cost-Cutting Gadgets," *Sponsor*, September 22, 1952, 36–37, 60.

35. The episode listed first, whether television or radio, is the version from which the material was transcribed. When a television episode was not adapted from a radio episode (or vice versa), only one broadcast date is noted.

36. Ronald J. Schmidt, *This Is the City: Making Model Citizens in Los Angeles* (Minneapolis: University of Minnesota Press, 2005), xxvi.

37. In at least one radio episode, we hear this machine doing this work; see the description of the soundscape of "The Big Girl" (Feb. 9, 1950) in chapter 2.

38. William R. Weaver, "Hollywood Scene," *Motion Picture Herald*, February 6, 1954, 26.

39. "New Comic Strip to Cover Authentic Police Cases," *San Antonio Express*, June 20, 1952, 1.

40. "New Comic Strip to Cover," 1.

41. Mirror Enterprise Syndicate, *Dragnet 1952: (B&W) Newspaper Comic Strips*, ed. Israel Escamilla (independently published, 2019), 13.

42. Michael J. Hayde, "Just the Funnies, Ma'am," *Better Living through Television* (blog), June 9, 2006, http://betterlivingtv.blogspot.com/2006/06/just-funnies-maam.html. The comic strip artists were Joe Scheiber, Bill Ziegler, and Mel Keefer.

43. "Webb Megs, Stars in Technicolor 'Dragnet' for Warner Release," *Variety*, February 3, 1954, folder 23, Hayde Collection, LAB-UMD.

44. "Production Notes on Dragnet," box 001221, folder 651, WBA-USC.

45. "Production Notes on Dragnet."

46. Undated press release, box 001221, folder 651, WBA-USC. That the secretaries were considered equivalent to ornamentation by the publicity department, I'll leave unexamined.

47. Scheuer, "Town Called Hollywood," D4.

48. This sequence represents the only major difference in narration from *Dragnet* on radio and television, as audiences see the murder and the murderers at the beginning of the film. After the credits, the film restores the restricted perspective of the detectives, and the audience remains with Friday and Smith throughout the rest of the film.

49. Marjory Adams, "Dragnet Attracts Many to Paramount, Fenway," *Boston Globe*, September 3, 1954, 12.

50. Undated press release, box 001221, folder 651, WBA-USC.

51. M. Oakley Stafford, "Informing You," *Hartford Courant*, September 6, 1954, 5. Undated press release, box 001221, folder 651, WBA-USC.

52. Hayde, *My Name's Friday*, 96. Hayde also notes that this was "nearly $2 million more than *The Long, Long Trailer*," Lucy and Desi's film.

53. Hedda Hopper, "Looking at Hollywood," *Chicago Daily Tribune*, August 27, 1954, A6. Webb was not able to replicate *Dragnet*'s success in film; his subsequent Warner Bros. productions—*Pete Kelly's Blues* (1955), *The D.I.* (1957), and *-30-* (1959)—did not perform as well as *Dragnet*.

54. Jack Webb, "The Facts about Me" (3 of 3), *Saturday Evening Post*, September 19, 1959, 144.

55. Hayde, *My Name's Friday*, 104.

56. Stan Freburg, "St. George and the Dragonet," recorded August 26, 1953, track 2 on *The Best of Stan Freburg: The Capitol Years* (1989), streaming audio, accessed December 9, 2021, https://open.spotify.com/track/171irpJ8XAggDKh6Hvq1mr?si=58560161d4c74fb5.

57. "Making His Point," *Variety*, June 9, 1954, 37. Michael Hayde traces *Dragnet*'s tagline ("just the facts," or "just the facts, ma'am") to Freburg's parodies. As Hayde explains, on the B-side of the "St. George" record was another *Dragnet* parody called "Little Blue Riding Hood." That parody included the line "I just want to get the facts, ma'am." "Just the facts" evolved from there. On *Dragnet* proper, Sergeant Friday was much more likely to say, "All we want are the facts." Hayde, *My Name's Friday*, 73.

58. "1953's Top Popular Records," *Billboard*, December 19, 1953, 29.

59. Yorty, "Jack Webb Performs," 12316.

60. Undated press release, box 00121, folder 651, WBA-USC. The publicity material reads in part,

> Jack Webb, an actor who is watched weekly by probably more people than any other performer in previous history, had no desire to be a thespian at the start of his career. He yearned ardently to be a writer. . . . "Unfortunately, I had no talent," he says. "And I'm still a frustrated writer. I don't consider myself

an actor, either. I just have a knack of doing one thing fairly well." . . . That he does it somewhat more than "fairly well" is attested by the fact that his weekly TV program is viewed by 40,000,000 faithful followers.

61. "Judge Uses Dragnet Show as Example," *Los Angeles Sentinel*, November 19, 1953, B7.

62. Evelyn Bigsby, "TV-Radio Lifelines," *TV-Radio Life*, January 30, 1953, p. 20, folder 13, Hayde Collection, LAB-UMD.

63. "Jack Webb's Challenge to You," *TV-Radio Life*, April 24, 1953, folder 13, Hayde Collection, LAB-UMD.

64. Letter from Thaine Engle to affiliates' promotion managers, June 16, 1953, box 137, folder 12, NBC Records, Wisconsin Historical Society, Madison, Wisconsin (hereafter WHS).

65. Letter from Hiram M. Smith Jr. to NBC, September 25, 1953, box 368, folder 52, NBC Records, WHS.

66. NBC Responsibility Reports, 1953 and 1954, folder 426, NBC-LOC.

67. "Radio: Real Thriller," *Time*, May 15, 1950.

68. Letter from Thomas C. McCray to Harold Grams, January 22, 1953, box 368, folder 52, NBC Records, WHS.

69. "Rifle and Dog for American Boy Typical as 'Ham, Eggs,'" *Paris [TX] News*, December 24, 1953, 27.

70. "Rifle and Dog for American Boy."

71. James Abbe, "Abbe Airs It," *Oakland Tribune*, December 21, 1951, 52.

72. Quoted in Hayde, *My Name's Friday*, 52–53.

73. Walter Ames, "Christmas Rifle Story on Dragnet to Present Dramatic Safety Lesson to Parents," *Los Angeles Times*, December 18, 1952, folder 13, Hayde Collection, LAB-UMD.

74. Webb stopped repeating the episode seemingly because he grew tired of it, not because audiences stopped requesting it. John Leter, "Radio and Television," *Elyria [OH] Chronicle-Telegram*, December 24, 1953, 26.

75. "Muir to Tell Drug Perils to Students," *Los Angeles Mirror*, May 17, 1951, Jack Webb Clipping File, AMPAS.

76. The episode's broadcast date reported in the *Mirror* does not match that of other sources, but the reporter may have heard a rebroadcast (or made an error).

77. Walter Ames, "Palsy Show Tops Previous Telethons for Drama; Final Figures Await Mail Count," *Los Angeles Times*, June 9, 1953, 28.

78. "Jack Webb to Be Installed as 'Hizzoner,'" *Los Angeles Times*, February 17, 1957, folder 13, Hayde Collection, LAB-UMD.

79. "Ralph Edwards to Get Urban League Award," *Los Angeles Sentinel*, April 15, 1954, A1.

80. Letter from C. A. Simmons to J. L. Warner, September 29, 1954, box B00121, folder 2954, WBA-USC.

81. Sam Lacy, "Theatrical Whirl," *Baltimore Afro-American*, February 4, 1956, 7.

82. "NBC Feature Story," press release, May 19, 1958, folder 13, Hayde Collection, LAB-UMD.

Chapter 4: Professionalization and Public Relations

1. Hayde, *My Name's Friday*, 141.

2. For more on Vollmer's reforms, see Willard M. Oliver, *August Vollmer: The Father of American Policing* (Durham, NC: Carolina Academic Press, 2017). For more on Hoover's reforms, see chapter 2 of Claire Bond Potter, *War on Crime: Bandits, G-Men, and the Politics of Mass Culture* (New Brunswick, NJ: Rutgers University Press, 1998).

3. Christopher P. Wilson, *Cop Knowledge: Police Power and Cultural Narrative in Twentieth-Century America* (Chicago: University of Chicago Press, 2000), 60–61.

4. The history of the relationship between police agencies and the media industries does not begin with *Dragnet*, of course. For more on the involvement of Vollmer, Hoover, and other police representatives in Hollywood film, see chapter 2 in Guest, "Police Procedural Film." For an in-depth analysis of radio, reform, and public relations in the Depression era, see Battles, *Calling All Cars*.

5. As mentioned in the previous chapter, the technical advisor for the *Dragnet* feature was Captain James Hamilton, who had been the officer in charge of the case dramatized in the film.

6. "Facts, Ma'm: Police Get 'Dragnet' $80,000," unsourced newspaper article dated June 23, 1956, folder 13, Hayde Collection, LAB-UMD. Joe Domanick reports that when *Dragnet* moved to television, Chief Parker used the opportunity to insist on "complete script control," requiring that the scripts be vetted by the Public Information Division, although there isn't much evidence that the scripts ever gave the PID much to object to. The most serious objection seems to have been over *Dragnet*'s television syndication title. Reruns were planned to run as "The Cop," but Parker thought the term *cop* was disrespectful. His preference was accommodated, and "Badge 714" (Friday's number) was used as the syndication title instead. Joe Domanick, *To Protect and to Serve: The LAPD's Century of War in the City of Dreams* (Los Angeles: Figueroa, 2003), 127–129.

7. Although Parker generally receives credit for these reforms, as Alisa Sarah Kramer shows, several were initiated during the tenure of his immediate predecessor, William A. Worton, who served as chief from June 1949 to August 1950. Alisa Sarah Kramer, "William H. Parker and the Thin Blue Line: Politics, Public Relations and Policing in Postwar Los Angeles" (PhD diss., American University, 2007), 33–35, ProQuest (3286654).

8. Domanick, *To Protect and to Serve*, 108.

9. Kramer, "William H. Parker," 149n172. Capital improvements were sorely needed. In a 1954 lecture, Parker asked his audience, "Would you believe me if I told you that the Central Division police station in the City of Los Angeles was condemned in 1913? And that we are still occupying the structure?" William H. Parker, *Parker on Police*, ed. O. W. Wilson (Springfield, IL: Charles C. Thomas, 1957), 93.

The new Police Administration Building was introduced to *Dragnet* viewers on the episode "The Big Tour" (Jan. 5, 1956), which, as the title indicates, took viewers on an extended tour of the structure. The PAB was renamed the Parker Center in 1966. In 2009, a new administration building was completed, and the Parker Center was demolished between 2018 and 2019.

10. Kramer, "William H. Parker," 57–60.

11. Donald McDonald, ed., *The Police: An Interview by Donald McDonald with William H. Parker, Chief of Police of Los Angeles*, Interviews on the American Character (Santa Barbara, CA: Center for the Study of Democratic Institutions, 1962), 5.

12. Kramer, "William H. Parker," 150.

13. James Lasley, *Los Angeles Police Department Meltdown: The Fall of the Professional-Reform Model of Policing* (Boca Raton, FL: CRC, 2012), 4.

14. Lasley, *Los Angeles Police Department Meltdown*, 5.

15. Parker, *Parker on Police*, 12, 161. Parker made an exception to this guiding policy when dealing with arrests related to intoxication. In those cases, police responses did involve some rehabilitation. With a history of alcoholism in his family—including his own struggles—Parker seems to have had uncommon sympathy for this population.

16. Lasley, *Los Angeles Police Department Meltdown*, 4.

17. Lasley also points out that Parker sought a similar distance from political interests that would interrupt police efficacy: "Parker insulated himself from political and other outside influences by breaking ties with governmental entities and affording himself civil service job protection so that he no longer had to serve at the will of the mayor, city council, or external citizen review boards." Parker was able to create a buffer zone that protected himself and his force from outside influence, including critical review. Lasley, *Los Angeles Police Department Meltdown*, 4.

18. For more on Parker's campaign and the work of the PID, see Kramer, "William H. Parker," 62–92.

19. John Buntin, *L.A. Noir: The Struggle for the Soul of America's Most Seductive City* (New York: Three Rivers, 2009), 190–191. KNBH is now KNBC.

20. Domanick, *To Protect and to Serve*, 131.

21. "Police Fact and Fiction in the Entertainment Industry," AMPTP Records, file 282, p. 31, Special Collections, AMPAS.

22. "Police Fact and Fiction."

23. The television episode is called "The Big Barrette." The crime is the same in both episodes, though some of the steps of the investigation differ.

24. The dedication was discontinued after a skirmish among the sponsor, Webb, and NBC. Liggett & Myers wanted to change the tribute—to make it longer and to include FBI personnel—and Webb and the network objected to their meddling. Hayde, *My Name's Friday*, 31–32.

25. Undated press release, box 001221, folder 651, WBA-USC. The press release suggests that Webb himself wrote *Dragnet*'s dialogue, but the scripts that established the *Dragnet* style of dialogue were written by James Moser. Webb only occasionally received writing credit on a radio or television script.

26. Wilson, *Cop Knowledge*, 61. Italics in original.

27. Evelyn Bigsby, "TV Radio Lifelines," *TV Radio Life*, date unclear, p. 8b, folder 13, Hayde Collection, LOC-UMD.

28. "Jack Webb Honored by Police Board," *Los Angeles Times*, June 28, 1956, 37.

29. Untitled press release dated June 17, 1954, box 00121, folder 651, WBA-USC.

30. Gordon Allison, "Television: 'Dragnet' Debut Tonight," *New York Herald Tribune*, December 16, 1951, folder 12, Hayde Collection, LAB-UMD.

31. Dorothy Townsend, "Not So (Dum-De-Dum-Dum): Petticoat Dragnet Nabs Friday, Pal," *Los Angeles Times*, June 4, 1954, B1. "Police Give Party for 800 Boy Scouts," *Los Angeles Times*, December 18, 1955, 20.

32. Marjory Adams, "Jack Webb Breezes into Hub a La President Eisenhower," *Boston Globe*, August 17, 1955, 8. Webb was promoting the film *Pete Kelly's Blues* (1955), which he produced and directed and in which he starred. The film concerns a 1920s jazz musician and contains no police content.

33. *Dragnet* visitors logs, box 6, Jack Webb Collection, UCLA Special Collections, University of California, Los Angeles.

34. "TV's Most Misunderstood Man," *TV Guide*, March 23, 1957, p. 19, folder 13, Hayde Collection, LAB-UMD.

35. "Times Aids Widow in Sgt. Friday Gift," *Los Angeles Times*, June 13, 1960, folder 13, Hayde Collection, LAB-UMD.

36. Jack Webb, interview by Sid Skolsky, undated, Sidney Skolsky papers, Special Collections, AMPAS.

37. For more on these cases, see Buntin, *L.A. Noir*, 208–214.

38. Parker, *Parker on Police*, 99.

39. This was the first time any *Dragnet* story line was set in the Intelligence Division.

40. A juror remarks that even the ability to wiretap wouldn't work and would only push the criminal activities elsewhere: "You'd have them plotting murder on every street corner." Friday gets the last line of the scene: "That's all right. There'd be a cop on it."

41. Entry dated November 22, 1954, Osmond Fraenkel Diaries, Seeley G. Mudd Manuscript Library—Public Policy Papers, Princeton University, Princeton, NJ.

42. Parker, *Parker on Police*, 114.

43. "Ziffren Raps Dragnet Play," unsourced article, ca. 1956, folder 13, Hayde Collection, LAB-UMD.

44. Jay Nelson Tuck, "On the Air," *New York Post*, January 20, 1956, 7.

45. Memorandum from Howard Monderer to Kenneth W. Bilby, January 25, 1956, box 174, folder 28, NBC Records, WHS.

46. Memorandum from Howard Monderer to Kenneth W. Bilby.

47. Memorandum from DeLoach to Mohr, December 31, 1962, Jack Webb FBI file, folder 20, Hayde Collection, LAB-UMD.

48. Another "Jack Webb" wrote a series of pulp crime novels in the 1950s. He likely profited from the confusion.

49. Robert R. Kirsch, "The Book Report," *Los Angeles Times*, October 31, 1958, B5.

50. Jack Webb, *The Badge: True and Terrifying Crime Stories That Could Not Be Presented on TV* (Englewood Cliffs, NJ: Prentice-Hall, 1958), 245.

51. Population estimates are taken from the Los Angeles Almanac (http://www.laalmanac.com/), which compiles statistics from different sources, including the US Census. The Latinx population was not counted by the census during this period; this estimate comes from Frank Sotomayor, "State Shows 69.2% Rise in Latino Population," *Los Angeles Times*, March 28, 1991, http://articles.latimes.com/1991-03-28/news/ti-1095_1_latino-population/2. Kramer, "William H. Parker," 163.

52. Stuart Hall, ed., *Policing the Crisis: Mugging, the State, and Law and Order* (New York: Holmes and Meier, 1978), 9.

53. Hayde, *My Name's Friday*, 192.

54. For more on the scandals, see Buntin, *L.A. Noir*, 123–135.

55. This speech is transcribed from the television script. "The Big Cop," collection number 201, Jack Webb Collection of Scripts for Radio and Television, UCLA Special Collections, University of California, Los Angeles.

56. Webb, "Facts about Me" (3 of 3), 144.

57. John Crosby, "Radio in Review," *New York Herald Tribune*, June 13, 1949, folder 11, Hayde Collection, LAB-UMD.

58. "Judge Urges Jury Inquiry on Brutality," *Los Angeles Times*, March 13, 1952, 1.

59. Kramer, "William H. Parker," 110–115. For more on Bloody Christmas, see Edward J. Escobar, "Bloody Christmas and the Irony of Police Professionalism: The Los Angeles Police Department, Mexican Americans, and Police Reform in the 1950s," *Pacific Historical Review* 72, no. 2 (May 2003): 171–199.

60. Webb, *Badge*, 174.

61. Webb, *Badge*, 174–175.

62. Webb, *Badge*, 175.

63. Lasley, *Los Angeles Police Department Meltdown*, 7. By comparison, later challenges to the professional-reform model were more successful. The challenge of the Rodney King verdict and the subsequent L.A. riots led to the replacement of the professional-reform model (and its Parker-trained leader, Chief Daryl Gates) with a community policing model.

64. "Hit by Officer, Held by Others, Says Ex-Marine," *Los Angeles Times*, March 8, 1952, A5. During these same few weeks, the FBI began its own investigation into the LAPD in response to complaints. "FBI Probing L.A. Police Brutality," *Los Angeles Times*, March 14, 1952, 2.

65. In this episode, the accusation is particularly unjust: in persuading his friends to lie to the police, Evans also organized a criminal conspiracy.

66. Almena Lomax, "Boy, Those L.A. Police . . . They Oughta Be in Pictures, . . . or Making 'Em," April 22, 1960, *Los Angeles Tribune*, 3.

67. Governor's Commission on the Los Angeles Riots [McCone Commission], "Violence in the City—an End or a Beginning?," December 2, 1965, 27–28. Five years later, another tragic incident made clear that Black Angelenos were not the only group

in the Los Angeles area targeted by the police. The 1970 riot in East Los Angeles and the killing of reporter Ruben Salazar (by a projectile from a tear gas gun) brought new visibility to the problem of discrimination against Latinos by police. For more on the killing, the riot, and the militancy it inspired among Latinos, see Edward J. Escobar, "The Dialectics of Repression: The Los Angeles Police Department and the Chicano Movement, 1968–1971," *Journal of American History* 79, no. 4 (March 1993): 1483–1514.

68. Lou Cannon, "L.A. Police Dept.: 'Dragnet' It Isn't: Confusion, Brutality Depicted in Two California Courtrooms," *Washington Post*, March 29, 1992, A3.

69. For more on the raced ways in which Americans interpreted evidence in the Simpson trial, see Darnell M. Hunt, "(Re)Affirming Race: 'Reality,' Negotiation, and the 'Trial of the Century,'" *Sociological Quarterly* 38, no. 3 (1997): 399–422.

70. Associated Press, "Rodney King Was Just the Start," *Cincinnati Post*, March 3, 2001, 2A.

71. Parker, *Parker on Police*, 151.

Epilogue

1. Michael Seiler, "Police Eulogize Jack Webb as One of Their Own," *Los Angeles Times*, December 31, 1982, A3. Webb died of natural causes at age 62.

2. Los Angeles Police Museum, "Jack Webb Awards," Jack Webb Awards, accessed March 31, 2021, http://2019jackwebbawards.laphs.org/.

3. "Jack Webb's Blues," *TV Guide*, May 2–8, 1959, folder 19, Hayde Collection, LAB-UMD.

4. Jane Ardmore, "Jack Webb, Sgt. Friday and the Affluent Society," *Los Angeles Times*, July 2, 1967, 34.

5. Ben Alexander, the actor who played Friday's longtime partner Frank Smith, was working on another television series (also playing a police officer) and wasn't available to reprise his role.

6. Hal Humphrey, "Dragnet Returns to Fill Social Need," *Los Angeles Times*, December 8, 1966, D30.

7. Mittell, *Genre and Television*, 150.

8. Hayde, *My Name's Friday*, 235–236.

9. The series had two connected runs; the first, from 1958–1959, comprised thirty-nine half-hour episodes and used the same lead characters as the film (Detective Jimmy Halloran, played by James Franciscus, and Lieutenant Dan Muldoon, played by John McIntire). Low ratings led to the series' cancellation, but it was revived the next year (1960–1963), this time as an hour-long drama with a different but similar pairing of rookie cop and veteran cop, Detective Adam Flint (Paul Burke) and Lieutenant Mike Parker (Horace McMahon). Some clarification of titles: the film is correctly called *The Naked City*, as are the 1958–1960 television seasons. The 1960–1963 seasons dropped the article, and the show was called *Naked City*. For clarity's sake, and to help distinguish between media, I use *The Naked City* to refer to the film and *Naked City* to refer to the entire 1958–1963 television series.

10. As the producers liked to say, "In a perfect world, Cagney and Lacey would work at the post office." That is, people would be interested in their lives even if they weren't in extraordinary circumstances. Interview with Barbara Corday, "The Interviews," Television Academy Foundation, August 12, 2004, https://interviews.televisionacademy.com/interviews/barbara-corday.

11. Elina Shatkin, "Cop on Crime Writing: Joseph Wambaugh," *Jacket Copy* (blog), *Los Angeles Times*, April 26, 2008, https://latimesblogs.latimes.com/jacketcopy/2008/04/how-do-you-like.html.

12. Hal Hinson, "Revisiting Baltimore's Embattled Streets," *New York Times*, June 2, 2002, http://www.nytimes.com/2002/06/02/arts/television-radio-revisiting-baltimore-s-embattled-streets.html. Simon, a former *Baltimore Sun* reporter, created the show with Ed Burns, a former Baltimore police officer and teacher.

13. The writer David Shore, who went on to create *House* (2004–2012) and *The Good Doctor* (2017–present), remembered his pitches being rejected over and over again until he ripped one from the headlines. Interview with David Shore, "The Interviews," Television Academy Foundation, October 11, 2012, https://interviews.televisionacademy.com/interviews/david-shore.

14. Wolf even picked up Jack Webb's gauntlet by bringing back *Dragnet* (2003–2004), a one-hour experiment that only hung on for two seasons.

15. For a closer analysis of *The Shield*, see chapter 7, "This Cop's for You: The Multiple Logics of the 21st Century Police Drama," in Nichols-Pethick, *TV Cops*.

16. Some shows had to be pushed into diversifying, either by their networks or by vocal, organized viewers. Following its third season, the producers of *Law and Order* were instructed by NBC to add two women to the cast or prepare for cancellation. Creator Dick Wolf added S. Epatha Merkerson as the precinct lieutenant and Jill Hennessy as an assistant district attorney. Bill Carter, "Stars Come and Go, but NBC's 'Law and Order' Plugs Away, Just Getting Stronger," *New York Times*, February 19, 1997, https://www.nytimes.com/1997/02/19/arts/stars-come-and-go-but-nbc-s-law-and-order-plugs-away-just-getting-stronger.html.

17. See, for example, *Copaganda*, YouTube video essay series, posted by Skip Intro, July 2020–present (episode 1, "How Did We Get Copaganda?" at https://youtube.com/watch?v=udhDawfCLHo). For discussions of a wider range of media, see the "Copaganda" Reddit forum: https://www.reddit.com/r/copaganda/.

18. Daniel Fienberg, "Disney+'s 'Turner & Hooch,'" *Hollywood Reporter*, July 20, 2021, https://www.hollywoodreporter.com/tv/tv-reviews/turner-hooch-1234985329/.

19. June Thomas, "Queen Latifah Makes the Impossible: A CBS Cop Show for the Black Lives Matter Era," *Slate*, February 7, 2021, https://slate.com/culture/2021/02/equalizer-queen-latifah-cbs-black-lives-matter-super-bowl.html.

20. Aaron Rahsaan Thomas, "Is TV Finally Done with 'Heroic' Cops? A Black Showrunner Says, 'Hell F*cking No,'" *Vanity Fair*, June 8, 2020, https://www.vanityfair.com/hollywood/2020/06/tv-and-cops; "The Highs ('The Flight Attendant') and Lows (COVID) of 2020," *TV's Top 5* podcast, *Hollywood Reporter*, December 18, 2020, https://www.hollywoodreporter.com/tv/tv-news/tvs-top-5-the-highs-the-flight-attendant-and-lows-covid-of-2020-4107172/.

21. "Highs," *TV's Top 5*.

22. Nina Metz, "A Year after Some of the Most Intense BLM Protests, 'Copaganda' Is Still Alive and Well on TV," *Chicago Tribune*, July 1, 2021,

23. Metz, "Year after Some."

24. Amy Chazkel, Monica Kim, and A. Naomi Paik, "Worlds without Police," *Radical History Review* 2020, no. 137 (May 1, 2020): 1–12.

25. "Tops of 2020: Television," "Insights," Nielsen, December 14, 2020, https://www.nielsen.com/us/en/insights/article/2020/tops-of-2020-television. Brad Adgate, "Nielsen: Streaming Video Audience Share Is Higher than Broadcast TV," *Forbes*, June 17, 2021, https://www.forbes.com/sites/bradadgate/2021/06/17/nielsen-streaming-video-audience-share-is-higher-than-broadcast-tv/.

26. Steve Johnson, "Dick Wolf Talks about His New Series 'Chicago PD,'" *Chicago Tribune*, January 7, 2014, https://www.chicagotribune.com/entertainment/tv/chi-dick-wolf-chicago-pd-20140107-column.html.

Bibliography

Agee, Christopher Lowen. "Crisis and Redemption: The History of American Police Reform since World War II." *Journal of Urban History* 46, no. 5 (September 2020): 951–960.

Alder, Ken. *The Lie Detectors: The History of an American Obsession*. New York: Free Press, 2007.

Altman, Rick. *Film/Genre*. London: British Film Institute, 1999.

Amaya, Hector. *Citizenship Excess: Latino/as, Media, and the Nation*. New York: New York University Press, 2013.

Anderson, Christopher. *Hollywood TV: The Studio System in the Fifties*. Austin: University of Texas Press, 1994.

Arnheim, Rudolf. *Radio*. New York: Arno/New York Times, 1971.

Arntfield, Michael. "TVPD: The Generational Diegetics of the Police Procedural on American Television." *Canadian Review of American Studies* 41, no. 1 (2011): 75–95.

Auerbach, Jonathan. *Dark Borders: Film Noir and American Citizenship*. Durham, NC: Duke University Press, 2011.

———. "Noir Citizenship: Anthony Mann's 'Border Incident.'" *Cinema Journal* 47, no. 4 (July 2008): 102–120.

Avila, Eric. *Popular Culture in the Age of White Flight: Fear and Fantasy in Suburban Los Angeles*. Berkeley: University of California Press, 2004.

Balio, Tino, ed. *Hollywood in the Age of Television*. Boston: Unwin Hyman, 1990.

Banet-Weiser, Sarah. *Kids Rule! Nickelodeon and Consumer Citizenship*. Durham, NC: Duke University Press, 2007.

Battles, Kathleen. *Calling All Cars: Radio Dragnets and the Technology of Policing*. Minneapolis: University of Minnesota Press, 2010.

Baughman, James L. *The Republic of Mass Culture: Journalism, Filmmaking, and Broadcasting in America since 1941*. Baltimore, MD: Johns Hopkins University Press, 2006.

Bazin, André. *What Is Cinema?* Berkeley: University of California Press, 2004.

Beville, Hugh Malcolm. *Audience Ratings: Radio, Television, and Cable*. Rev. ed. Hillsdale, NJ: Lawrence Erlbaum Associates, 1988.

Bird, S. Elizabeth. "Are We All Produsers Now?" *Cultural Studies* 25, no. 4–5 (2011): 502–516.

Boddy, William. "Approaching 'The Untouchables': Social Science and Moral Panics in Early Sixties Television." *Cinema Journal* 35, no. 4 (July 1996): 70–87.

———. *Fifties Television: The Industry and Its Critics*. Urbana: University of Illinois Press, 1990.

———. *New Media and Popular Imagination: Launching Radio, Television, and Digital Media in the United States*. New York: Oxford University Press, 2004.

Bodnar, John. *Blue-Collar Hollywood: Liberalism, Democracy, and Working People in American Film*. Baltimore, MD: Johns Hopkins University Press, 2006.

Booker, M. Keith. *Monsters, Mushroom Clouds, and the Cold War: American Science Fiction and the Roots of Postmodernism, 1946–1964*. Westport, CT: Greenwood, 2001.

Bordwell, David. *The Way Hollywood Tells It: Story and Style in Modern Movies*. Berkeley: University of California Press, 2006.

Bordwell, David, Janet Staiger, and Kristin Thompson. *The Classical Hollywood Cinema: Film Style and Mode of Production to 1960*. New York: Columbia University Press, 1985.

Bowles, Stephen E. "And Time Marched On: The Creation of the March of Time." *Journal of the University Film Association* 29, no. 1 (1977): 7–13.

Broe, Dennis. *Film Noir, American Workers, and Postwar Hollywood*. Gainesville: University Press of Florida, 2009.

———. "Genre Regression and the New Cold War: The Return of the Police Procedural." *Framework: The Journal of Cinema and Media* 45, no. 2 (October 2004): 81–101.

Browne, Nick. "The Political Economy of the Television (Super) Text." *Quarterly Review of Film Studies* 9, no. 3 (1984): 174–182.

Buntin, John. *L.A. Noir: The Struggle for the Soul of America's Most Seductive City*. New York: Three Rivers, 2009.

Byers, Michele, and Val Marie Johnson, eds. *The CSI Effect: Television, Crime, and Governance*. Lanham, MD: Lexington Books, 2009.

Cagle, Chris. *Sociology on Film: Postwar Hollywood's Prestige Commodity*. New Brunswick, NJ: Rutgers University Press, 2017.

Caldwell, John Thornton. *Televisuality: Style, Crisis, and Authority in American Television*. Communication, Media, and Culture. New Brunswick, NJ: Rutgers University Press, 1995.

Cebul, Brent, Lily Geismer, and Mason B. Williams, eds. *Shaped by the State: Toward a New Political History of the Twentieth Century*. Chicago: University of Chicago Press, 2019.

Cecil, Matthew. "Coming on like *Gang Busters*: J. Edgar Hoover's FBI and the Battle to Control Radio Portrayals of the Bureau, 1936–1958." *Journalism History* 40, no. 4 (January 2015): 252–261.

Ceplair, Larry, and Steven Englund. *The Inquisition in Hollywood: Politics in the Film Community, 1930–1960*. Garden City, NY: Anchor/Doubleday, 1980.

Chazkel, Amy, Monica Kim, and A. Naomi Paik. "Worlds without Police." *Radical History Review* 2020, no. 137 (May 1, 2020): 1–12.

Cheyne, Michael. "Sitcom Citizenship: Civic Participation within Postwar Suburban Sitcoms, 1952–1972." PhD diss., University of Minnesota, 2014.

Chion, Michel. *Audio-Vision: Sound on Screen*. Translated by Claudia Gorbman. New York: Columbia University Press, 1994.

Ciment, Michel, ed. *Kazan on Kazan*. New York: Viking, 1974.

Cobb, Sean D. "A Shadow Underneath: The Secret History of Paranoia, Borders and Terrorism in Postwar American Literature and Film." PhD diss., University of Arizona, 2007. ProQuest (3297822).

Cohan, Steven. *Masked Men: Masculinity and the Movies in the Fifties*. Bloomington: Indiana University Press, 1997.

Cohen, Lizabeth. *A Consumer's Republic: The Politics of Mass Consumption in Postwar America*. New York: Knopf, 2003.

Collins, Max Allan, and John Javna. *The Best of Crime and Detective TV:* Perry Mason *to* Hill Street Blues, The Rockford Files *to* Murder She Wrote. New York: Harmony Books, 1988.

Color of Change Hollywood and USC Annenberg Norman Lear Center. *Normalizing Injustice: The Dangerous Misrepresentations that Define Television's Scripted Crime Genre*. Updated complete version. USC Annenberg Norman Lear Center, January 2020. https://hollywood.colorofchange.org//wp-content/uploads/2020/02/Normalizing-Injustice_Complete-Report-2.pdf.

Conroy, Marianne. "Acting Out: Method Acting, the National Culture, and the Middlebrow Disposition in Cold War America." *Criticism* 35, no. 2 (April 1993): 239–263.

Corner, John. "Afterword: Reflections on Media Engagement." *Media Industries Journal* 4, no. 1 (2017). https://doi.org/10.3998/mij.15031809.0004.109.

———. "Performing the Real: Documentary Diversions (with Afterword)." In *Reality TV: Remaking Television Culture*, 2nd ed., edited by Susan Murray and Laurie Ouellette, 44–64. New York: New York University Press, 2009.

———. *Theorising Media: Power, Form and Subjectivity*. Manchester, UK: Manchester University Press, 2011.

Cox, Jim. *Radio Crime Fighters: Over 300 Programs from the Golden Age*. Jefferson, NC: McFarland, 2002.

———. *Say Goodnight, Gracie: The Last Years of Network Radio*. Jefferson, NC: McFarland, 2002.

Crook, Tim. *The Sound Handbook*. New York: Routledge, 2012.

Curtin, Michael. *Redeeming the Wasteland: Television Documentary and Cold War Politics*. New Brunswick, NJ: Rutgers University Press, 1995.

Custen, George Frederick. *Twentieth Century's Fox: Darryl F. Zanuck and the Culture of Hollywood*. New York: Basic Books, 1997.

D'Acci, Julie. *Defining Women: Television and the Case of Cagney and Lacey*. Chapel Hill: University of North Carolina Press, 1994.

Davin, Solange, and Rhona Jackson. *Television and Criticism*. Bristol, UK: Intellect Books, 2008.

Davis, J. Madison. "He Do the Police in Different Voices: The Rise of the Police Procedural." *World Literature Today* 86, no. 1 (January 2012): 9–11.

Deming, Caren. "Locating the Televisual in Golden Age Television." In *A Companion to Television*, edited by Janet Wasko, 126–141. Malden, MA: Blackwell, 2005.

Deutsch, Albert. *The Trouble with Cops*. New York: Crown, 1955.

Dillon, Karen, and Naomi Crummey. *The Wire in the College Classroom: Pedagogical Approaches in the Humanities*. Jefferson, NC: McFarland, 2015.

Dimendberg, Edward. *Film Noir and the Spaces of Modernity*. Cambridge, MA: Harvard University Press, 2004.

Dixon, Wheeler Winston. *Cinema at the Margins*. London: Anthem, 2013.

———. *Film Noir and the Cinema of Paranoia*. New Brunswick, NJ: Rutgers University Press, 2009.

———. "Just the Facts, Man: The Complicated Genesis of Television's *Dragnet*." *Film International*, November 25, 2012. http://filmint.nu/just-the-facts-man-the-complicated-genesis-of-televisions-dragnet/.

———. *Lost in the Fifties: Recovering Phantom Hollywood*. Carbondale: Southern Illinois University Press, 2005.

Doherty, Thomas. *Cold War, Cool Medium: Television, McCarthyism, and American Culture*. New York: Columbia University Press, 2003.

———. "Documenting the 1940s." In *Boom and Bust: The American Cinema in the 1940s*, edited by Thomas Schatz, 397–421. History of the American Cinema 6. New York: Scribner's, 1997.

———. *Projections of War: Hollywood, American Culture, and World War II*. Film and Culture. New York: Columbia University Press, 1999.

Domanick, Joe. *To Protect and to Serve: The LAPD's Century of War in the City of Dreams*. Los Angeles: Figueroa, 2003.

Douglas, Susan J. *Listening In: Radio and the American Imagination*. Minneapolis: University of Minnesota Press, 2004.

Dove, George N. *The Police Procedural*. Bowling Green, OH: Bowling Green University Popular Press, 1982.

Dussere, Erik. *America Is Elsewhere: The Noir Tradition in the Age of Consumer Culture*. New York: Oxford University Press, 2014.

———. "Out of the Past, into the Supermarket." *Film Quarterly* 60, no. 1 (2006): 16–27.

Ehrlich, Matthew C. *Radio Utopia: Postwar Audio Documentary in the Public Interest*. Urbana: University of Illinois Press, 2011.

Ellis, Jack C. "American Documentary in the 1950s." In *Transforming the Screen, 1950–1959*, edited by Peter Lev, 257–277. History of the American Cinema 7. New York: Scribner's, 2003.

Escobar, Edward J. "Bloody Christmas and the Irony of Police Professionalism: The Los Angeles Police Department, Mexican Americans, and Police Reform in the 1950s." *Pacific Historical Review* 72, no. 2 (May 2003): 171–199.

———. "The Dialectics of Repression: The Los Angeles Police Department and the Chicano Movement, 1968–1971." *Journal of American History* 79, no. 4 (March 1993): 1483–1514.

———. *Race, Police, and the Making of a Political Identity: Mexican Americans and the Los Angeles Police Department, 1900–1945*. Latinos in American Society and Culture. Berkeley: University of California Press, 1999.

Evans, Elizabeth. *Transmedia Television: Audiences, New Media, and Daily Life*. London: Routledge, 2011.

Felker-Kantor, Max. "Liberal Law-and-Order: The Politics of Police Reform in Los Angeles." *Journal of Urban History* 46, no. 5 (September 2020): 1026–1049.

———. *Policing Los Angeles: Race, Resistance, and the Rise of the LAPD*. Chapel Hill: University of North Carolina Press, 2018.

Feuer, Jane. "The Concept of Live Television: Ontology as Ideology." In *Regarding Television: Critical Approaches—an Anthology*, edited by E. Ann Kaplan, 12–21. Frederick, MD: University Publications of America, 1983.

Fielding, Raymond. "Time Flickers Out: Notes on the Passing of the March of Time." In *Hollywood Quarterly: Film Culture in Postwar America, 1945–1957*, edited by Eric Smoodin and Ann Martin, 109–116. Berkeley: University of California Press, 2002.

Filene, Peter. "'Cold War Culture' Doesn't Say It All." In *Rethinking Cold War Culture*, edited by Peter J. Kuznick and James Burkhart Gilbert, 124–155. Washington, DC: Smithsonian Institution Press, 2001.

Fogelson, Robert M. "White on Black: A Critique of the McCone Commission Report on the Los Angeles Riots." *Political Science Quarterly* 82, no. 3 (September 1967): 337–367.

Freeman, Matthew, and Renira Rampazzo Gambarato. *The Routledge Companion to Transmedia Studies*. Milton, UK: Taylor and Francis, 2018.

Friedman, Andrea. *Citizenship in Cold War America: The National Security State and the Possibilities of Dissent*. Amherst: University of Massachusetts Press, 2014.

Gerstle, Gary. "Race and the Myth of the Liberal Consensus." *Journal of American History* 82, no. 2 (September 1995): 579–586.

———. "The Reach and Limits of the Liberal Consensus." In *The Liberal Consensus Reconsidered*, edited by Robert Mason and Iwan Morgan, 52–66. Gainesville: University Press of Florida, 2017.

Gilbert, James Burkhart. *Men in the Middle: Searching for Masculinity in the 1950s*. Chicago: University of Chicago Press, 2005.

Giroux, Henry A. "Breaking into the Movies: Pedagogy and the Politics of Film." *JAC: A Journal of Composition Theory* 21, no. 3 (2001): 583–598.

———. *Disturbing Pleasures: Learning Popular Culture*. London: Taylor and Francis, 1994.

———. *Impure Acts: The Practical Politics of Cultural Studies*. New York: Routledge, 2000.

———. "Public Pedagogy and the Responsibility of Intellectuals: Youth, Littleton, and the Loss of Innocence." *JAC: A Journal of Composition Theory* 20, no. 1 (2000): 9–42.

———. "Public Pedagogy as Cultural Politics: Stuart Hall and the 'Crisis' of Culture." *Cultural Studies* 14, no. 2 (April 2000): 341–360.

Giroux, Henry A., and Grace Pollock. *The Mouse That Roared: Disney and the End of Innocence*. Lanham, MD: Rowman and Littlefield, 2010.

Gitre, Edward Joseph Khair. "America Adjusted: Conformity, Boredom, and the Modern Self, c. 1920–1980." PhD diss., Rutgers University, 2008. ProQuest (3359235).

Gomery, Douglas. "'Talent Raids and Package Deals': NBC Loses Its Leadership in the 1950s." In *NBC: America's Network*, edited by Michele Hilmes, 153–168. Berkeley: University of California Press, 2007.

Gould, Jack. *Watching Television Come of Age:* The New York Times *Reviews by Jack Gould*. Edited by Lewis L. Gould. Focus on American History. Austin: University of Texas Press, 2003.

Governor's Commission on the Los Angeles Riots [McCone Commission]. "Violence in the City--an End or a Beginning?" December 2, 1965.

Grainge, Paul. *Brand Hollywood: Selling Entertainment in a Global Media Age*. New York: Routledge, 2008.

Grams, Martin. *Gang Busters: The Crime Fighters of American Broadcasting*. Forest Hill, MD: OTR Publishing, 2004.

Gray, Jonathan. *Watching with The Simpsons: Television, Parody, and Intertextuality*. New York: Routledge, 2006.

Guest, Haden. "The Police Procedural Film: Law and Order in the American Cinema, 1930–1960." PhD diss., University of California, Los Angeles, 2005. ProQuest (3218663).

Hall, Stuart, ed. *Policing the Crisis: Mugging, the State, and Law and Order*. New York: Holmes and Meier, 1978.

Harris, Mark. *Five Came Back: A Story of Hollywood and the Second World War*. New York: Penguin, 2014.

Hawes, William. *Filmed Television Drama, 1952–1958*. Jefferson, NC: McFarland, 2002.

———. *Live Television Drama, 1946–1951*. Jefferson, NC: McFarland, 2001.

Hay, James, and Laurie Ouellette, eds. *Better Living through Reality TV: Television and Post-welfare Citizenship*. Malden, MA: Blackwell, 2008.

Hayde, Michael J. "Just the Funnies, Ma'am." *Better Living through Television* (blog), June 9, 2006. http://betterlivingtv.blogspot.com/2006/06/just-funnies-maam.html.

———. *My Name's Friday: The Unauthorized but True Story of* Dragnet *and the Films of Jack Webb*. Nashville, TN: Cumberland House, 2001.

Herman, Ellen. *The Romance of American Psychology: Political Culture in the Age of Experts*. Berkeley: University of California Press, 1995.

Hill, Annette. *Media Experiences: Engaging with Drama and Reality Television*. London: Routledge, 2018.

Hill, Annette, and Jeanette Steemers. "Media Industries and Engagement." *Media Industries Journal* 4, no. 1 (2017). http://dx.doi.org/10.3998/mij.15031809.0004.105.

Hilmes, Michele. *Hollywood and Broadcasting: From Radio to Cable*. Urbana: University of Illinois Press, 1990.

———. "Is There a Field Called Sound Culture Studies? And Does It Matter?" *American Quarterly* 57, no. 1 (2005): 249–259.

———, ed. *NBC: America's Network*. Berkeley: University of California Press, 2007.

———. *Only Connect: A Cultural History of Broadcasting in the United States*. 2nd ed. Boston: Wadsworth/Cengage Learning, 2007.

———. *Radio Voices: American Broadcasting, 1922–1952*. Minneapolis: University of Minnesota Press, 1997.

Hoberek, Andrew. *The Twilight of the Middle Class: Post–World War II American Fiction and White-Collar Work*. Princeton, NJ: Princeton University Press, 2005.

Hodgson, Godfrey. "Revisiting the Liberal Consensus." In *The Liberal Consensus Reconsidered*, edited by Robert Mason and Iwan Morgan, 12–28. Gainesville: University Press of Florida, 2017.

Horwitz, Jonah. "Visual Style in the 'Golden Age' Anthology Drama: The Case of CBS." *Cinémas: Journal of Film Studies* 23, no. 2–3 (2013): 39–68.

Hunt, Darnell M. "(Re)Affirming Race: 'Reality,' Negotiation, and the 'Trial of the Century.'" *Sociological Quarterly* 38, no. 3 (1997): 399–422.

Igo, Sarah E. *The Averaged American: Surveys, Citizens, and the Making of a Mass Public*. Cambridge, MA: Harvard University Press, 2008.

Jenkins, Henry. *Convergence Culture: Where Old and New Media Collide*. New York: New York University Press, 2006.

———. *Textual Poachers: Television Fans and Participatory Culture*. New York: Routledge, 2012.

———. "Transmedia Storytelling and Entertainment: An Annotated Syllabus." *Continuum* 24, no. 6 (2010): 943–958.

Johnson, Derek. *Media Franchising: Creative License and Collaboration in the Culture Industries*. New York: New York University Press, 2013.

Jones, Jeffrey P. "A Cultural Approach to the Study of Mediated Citizenship." *Social Semiotics* 16, no. 2 (June 1, 2006): 365–383.

Jorgensen, Paul A. "The Permanence of *Dragnet*." *Film Quarterly* 12, no. 1 (October 1958): 35–40.

Josefsberg, Milt. *The Jack Benny Show*. New Rochelle, NY: Arlington House, 1977.

Kackman, Michael. *Citizen Spy: Television, Espionage, and Cold War Culture*. Minneapolis, MN: University of Minnesota Press, 2005.

———. "Nothing On but Hoppy Badges: Hopalong Cassidy, William Boyd Enterprises, and Emergent Media Globalization." *Cinema Journal* 47, no. 4 (August 14, 2008): 76–101.

Kaplan, E. Ann, ed. *Regarding Television: Critical Approaches—an Anthology*. Frederick, MD: University Publications of America, 1983.

———. *Women in Film Noir*. London: British Film Institute, 1998.

Kazan, Elia. *Elia Kazan: A Life*. New York: Knopf, 1988.

Kazan, Elia, and Jeff Young. *Kazan: The Master Director Discusses His Films*. New York: Newmarket, 1999.

Keeler, Amanda. "'A Certain Stigma' of Educational Radio: Judith Waller and 'Public Service' Broadcasting." *Critical Studies in Media Communication* 34, no. 5 (November 2017): 495–508.

Kempner, Aviva, dir. *Yoo-Hoo, Mrs. Goldberg*. Docurama Films, 2010.

Kepley, Vance, Jr. "From 'Frontal Lobes' to the 'Bob-and-Bob' Show: NBC Management and Programming Strategies, 1949–65." In *Hollywood in the Age of Television*, edited by Tino Balio, 41–61. Boston: Unwin Hyman, 1990.

Kindem, Gorham Anders. *The Live Television Generation of Hollywood Film Directors: Interviews with Seven Directors*. Jefferson, NC: McFarland, 1994.

Kisseloff, Jeff. *The Box: An Oral History of Television, 1929–1961*. New York: Viking, 1995.

Klaus, Elisabeth, and Margreth Lünenborg. "Cultural Citizenship: Participation by and through Media." In *Feminist Media: Participatory Spaces, Networks and Cultural Citizenship*, edited by Elke Zobl and Ricarda Drüeke, 197–212. Bielefeld, Germany: Transcript Verlag, 2012.

Klein, Amanda Ann, and R. Barton Palmer, eds. *Cycles, Sequels, Spin-Offs, Remakes, and Reboots: Multiplicities in Film and Television*. Austin: University of Texas Press, 2016.

Klein, Christina. *Cold War Orientalism: Asia in the Middlebrow Imagination, 1945–1961*. Berkeley: University of California Press, 2003.

Kozloff, Sarah. "Humanizing 'The Voice of God': Narration in 'The Naked City.'" *Cinema Journal* 23, no. 4 (July 1984): 41–53.

Kracauer, Siegfried. *Siegfried Kracauer's American Writings: Essays on Film and Popular Culture*. Edited by Johannes Von Moltke and Kristy Rawson. Berkeley: University of California Press, 2012.

Kramer, Alisa Sarah. "William H. Parker and the Thin Blue Line: Politics, Public Relations and Policing in Postwar Los Angeles." PhD diss., American University, 2007. ProQuest.

Krampner, Jon. *The Man in the Shadows: Fred Coe and the Golden Age of Television*. New Brunswick, NJ: Rutgers University Press, 1997.

Krutnik, Frank. *In a Lonely Street: Film Noir, Genre, Masculinity*. New York: Routledge, 1991.

———, ed. *"Un-American" Hollywood Politics and Film in the Blacklist Era*. New Brunswick, NJ: Rutgers University Press, 2007.

Kuznick, Peter J., and James Burkhart Gilbert, eds. *Rethinking Cold War Culture*. Washington, DC: Smithsonian Institution Press, 2001.

Lafferty, William. "'No Attempt at Artiness, Profundity, or Significance': 'Fireside Theater' and the Rise of Filmed Television Programming." *Cinema Journal* 27, no. 1 (October 1987): 23–46.

———. "A Reappraisal of the Semi-Documentary in Hollywood, 1945–1948." *Velvet Light Trap*, no. 20 (Summer 1983): 22–26.

Langford, Barry. *Post-classical Hollywood: Film Industry, Style and Ideology since 1945*. Edinburgh: Edinburgh University Press, 2010.

Lasley, James. *Los Angeles Police Department Meltdown: The Fall of the Professional-Reform Model of Policing*. Boca Raton, FL: CRC, 2012.

Lastra, James. *Sound Technology and the American Cinema: Perception, Representation, Modernity*. New York: Columbia University Press, 2000.

Latteier, Pearl. "The Hollywood Social Problem Film, 1946–1959." PhD diss., University of Wisconsin–Madison, 2010. ProQuest.

Laville, Helen. "Gender in an Era of Liberal Consensus." In *The Liberal Consensus*

Reconsidered: American Politics and Society in the Postwar Era, edited by Robert Mason and Iwan W. Morgan, 245–261. Gainesville: University Press of Florida, 2017.

Leishman, Frank. *Policing and the Media: Facts, Fictions and Factions*. Devon, UK: Willan, 2003.

Lev, Peter. *Transforming the Screen, 1950–1959*. History of the American Cinema 7. New York: Scribner's, 2003.

Lewis, George. "Memories of the Movement: Civil Rights, the Liberal Consensus, and the March on Washington Twenty Years Later." In *The Liberal Consensus Reconsidered: American Politics and Society in the Postwar Era*, edited by Robert Mason and Iwan W. Morgan, 262–281. Gainesville: University Press of Florida, 2017.

Loader, Ian. "Policing and the Social: Questions of Symbolic Power." *British Journal of Sociology* 48, no. 1 (March 1997): 1–18.

Loviglio, Jason. *Radio's Intimate Public: Network Broadcasting and Mass-Mediated Democracy*. Minneapolis: University of Minnesota Press, 2005.

Luciano, Patrick, and Gary Coville. "'Behind Badge 714': The Story of Jack Webb and *Dragnet*." *Filmfax*, August–September 1993.

MacDonald, J. Fred. *Don't Touch That Dial! Radio Programming in American Life, 1920–1960*. Chicago: Nelson-Hall, 1979.

Maltby, Richard. "'Film Noir': The Politics of the Maladjusted Text." *Journal of American Studies* 18, no. 1 (April 1984): 49–71.

Maltin, Leonard. *The Great American Broadcast*. New York: NAL Trade, 2000.

Marc, David, and Horace Newcomb. *Demographic Vistas: Television in American Culture*. Philadelphia: University of Pennsylvania Press, 1996.

Marling, Karal Ann. *As Seen on TV: The Visual Culture of Everyday Life in the 1950s*. Cambridge, MA: Harvard University Press, 1994.

Martin, Catherine. "Adventure's Fun, but Wouldn't You Rather Get Married? Gender Roles and the Office Wife in Radio Detective Dramas." *Velvet Light Trap* 74, no. 1 (2014): 16–26.

Mason, Robert, and Iwan W. Morgan, eds. *The Liberal Consensus Reconsidered: American Politics and Society in the Postwar Era*. Gainesville: University Press of Florida, 2017.

Matthews, Kristin L. *Reading America: Citizenship, Democracy, and Cold War Literature*. Amherst: University of Massachusetts Press, 2016.

May, Elaine Tyler. *Homeward Bound: American Families in the Cold War Era*. New York: Basic Books, 1988.

May, Lary, ed. *The Big Tomorrow: Hollywood and the Politics of the American Way*. Chicago: University of Chicago Press, 2002.

———. *Recasting America: Culture and Politics in the Age of Cold War*. Chicago: University of Chicago Press, 1989.

McCarthy, Anna. *The Citizen Machine: Governing by Television in 1950s America*. New York: New Press, 2010.

McCracken, Allison. "Scary Women and Scarred Men: Suspense, Gender Trouble, and Postwar Change, 1942–1950." In *Radio Reader: Essays in the Cultural History of Radio*, edited by Michele Hilmes and Jason Loviglio, 183–208. New York: Routledge, 2002.

McDonald, Donald, ed. *The Police: An Interview by Donald McDonald with William H. Parker, Chief of Police of Los Angeles*. Interviews on the American Character. Santa Barbara, CA: Center for the Study of Democratic Institutions, 1962.

McEnaney, Laura. *Civil Defense Begins at Home: Militarization Meets Everyday Life in the Fifties*. Princeton, NJ: Princeton University Press, 2000.

McLane, Betsy A. *A New History of Documentary Film*. 2nd ed. London: Bloomsbury, 2018.

Miklitsch, Robert William. "Fear of a Red Planet: *I Was a Communist for the F.B.I.* and 'Black Film.'" *Journal of Popular Film and Television* 41, no. 1 (2013): 43–54.

Miller, Toby. *Cultural Citizenship: Cosmopolitanism, Consumerism, and Television in a Neoliberal Age*. Philadelphia: Temple University Press, 2007.

———. *Technologies of Truth: Cultural Citizenship and the Popular Media*. Minneapolis: University of Minnesota Press, 1998.

Minnow, Newton N. "Television and the Public Interest." *Federal Communications Law Journal* 55, no. 3, article 4 (2003): 396–406.

Mittell, Jason. *Genre and Television: From Cop Shows to Cartoons in American Culture*. New York: Routledge, 2004.

Modleski, Tania. "The Rhythms of Reception: Daytime Television and Women's Work." In *Regarding Television: Critical Approaches—an Anthology*, edited by E. Ann Kaplan, 67–74. Frederick, MD: University Publications of America, 1983.

Moores, Shaun. "'The Box on the Dresser': Memories of Early Radio and Everyday Life." *Media, Culture and Society* 10, no. 1 (1988): 23–40.

Moyer, Daniel. *Just the Facts, Ma'am: The Authorized Biography of Jack Webb*. Santa Ana, CA: Seven Locks, 2001.

Munich, Adrienne. "In the Radio Way." In *Communities of the Air: Radio Century, Radio Culture*, edited by Susan Merrill Squier, 217–236. Durham, NC: Duke University Press, 2003.

Murray, Susan, and Laurie Ouellette, eds. *Reality TV: Remaking Television Culture*. 2nd ed. New York: New York University Press, 2009.

Nadel, Alan. *Containment Culture: American Narrative, Postmodernism, and the Atomic Age*. Durham, NC: Duke University Press, 1995.

———. *Television in Black-and-White America: Race and National Identity*. Lawrence: University Press of Kansas, 2005.

Napoli, Philip M. *Audience Evolution: New Technologies and the Transformation of Media Audiences*. New York: Columbia University Press, 2011.

Naremore, James. "American Film Noir: The History of an Idea." *Film Quarterly* 49, no. 2 (December 1995): 12–28.

———. *More than Night: Film Noir in Its Contexts*. Berkeley: University of California Press, 2008.

Neale, Stephen. *Genre and Hollywood*. New York: Routledge, 2000.

Newcomb, Horace, ed. *Encyclopedia of Television*. New York: Fitzroy Dearborn, 2004.

———, ed. *Television: The Critical View*. 3rd ed. Oxford: Oxford University Press, 1982.

Newman, Michael Z., and Elana Levine. *Legitimating Television: Media Convergence and Cultural Status*. New York: Routledge, 2012.

Nichols-Pethick, Jonathan. *TV Cops: The Contemporary American Television Police Drama*. New York: Routledge, 2012.

Nicosia, Laura M., and Rebecca A. Goldstein. *Through a Distorted Lens: Media as Curricula and Pedagogy in the 21st Century*. Rotterdam: Brill, 2017.

Oliver, Willard M. *August Vollmer: The Father of American Policing*. Durham, NC: Carolina Academic Press, 2017.

Orgeron, Devin, Marsha Orgeron, and Dan Streible, eds. *Learning with the Lights Off: Educational Film in the United States*. Oxford: Oxford University Press, 2012.

Palmer, Landon. "'And Introducing Elvis Presley': Industrial Convergence and Transmedia Stardom in the Rock 'n' Roll Movie." *Music, Sound, and the Moving Image* 9, no. 2 (January 31, 2016): 177–190.

Palmer, R. Barton. "Cold War Thrillers." In *The Wiley-Blackwell History of American Film*, edited by Roy Grundmann, Cynthia A. Barto Lucia, and Art Simon, 1–24. Malden, MA: Wiley Blackwell, 2012.

———. "*Dragnet*, Film Noir, and Postwar Realism." In *The Philosophy of TV Noir*, edited by Steven M. Sanders and Aeon J. Skoble, 33–48. Lexington: University Press of Kentucky, 2008.

Parker, William H. *Parker on Police*. Edited by O. W. Wilson. Springfield, IL: Charles C. Thomas, 1957.

Patton, Cindy. *Cinematic Identity: Anatomy of a Problem Film*. Theory out of Bounds, vol. 29. Minneapolis: University of Minnesota Press, 2007.

Perlmutter, David D. *Policing the Media: Street Cops and Public Perceptions of Law Enforcement*. Thousand Oaks, CA: Sage, 2000.

Phillips-Fein, Kim. "'If Business and the Country Will Be Run Right': The Business Challenge to the Liberal Consensus, 1945–1964." *International Labor and Working-Class History*, no. 72 (2007): 192–215.

Porter, Jeff. *Lost Sound: The Forgotten Art of Radio Storytelling*. Chapel Hill: University of North Carolina Press, 2016.

Potter, Claire Bond. *War on Crime: Bandits, G-Men, and the Politics of Mass Culture*. New Brunswick, NJ: Rutgers University Press, 1998.

Prior, Leon O. "Nazi Invasion of Florida!" *Florida Historical Quarterly* 49, no. 2 (1970): 129–139.

Razlogova, Elena. *The Listener's Voice: Early Radio and the American Public*. Philadelphia: University of Pennsylvania Press, 2011.

———. "True Crime Radio and Listener Disenchantment with Network Broadcasting, 1935–1946." *American Quarterly* 58, no. 1 (2006): 137–158.

Richardson, Carl. *Autopsy: An Element of Realism in Film Noir*. Metuchen, NJ: Scarecrow, 1992.

Robards, Brooks. "The Police Show." In *TV Genres: A Handbook and Reference Guide*, edited by Brian Geoffrey Rose, 11–32. Westport, CT: Greenwood, 1985.

Roffman, Peter, and Jim Purdy. *Hollywood Social Problem Film: Madness, Despair, and Politics from the Depression to the Fifties*. Bloomington: Indiana University Press, 1981.

Russo, Alexander. *Points on the Dial: Golden Age Radio beyond the Networks*. Durham, NC: Duke University Press, 2010.

Sabin, Roger, Ben Bethell, Brian Faucette, Linda Speidel, and Ronald Wilson. *Cop Shows: A Critical History of Police Dramas on Television*. Jefferson, NC: McFarland, 2015.

Sanders, Steven, and Aeon J. Skoble, eds. *The Philosophy of TV Noir*. Lexington: University Press of Kentucky, 2015.

Sandlin, Jennifer A., Michael P. O'Malley, and Jake Burdick. "Mapping the Complexity of Public Pedagogy Scholarship: 1894–2010." *Review of Educational Research* 81, no. 3 (September 1, 2011): 338–375.

Sandlin, Jennifer A., Brian D. Schultz, and Jake Burdick. *Handbook of Public Pedagogy: Education and Learning beyond Schooling*. New York: Routledge, 2010.

Santo, Avi. *Selling the Silver Bullet: The Lone Ranger and Transmedia Brand Licensing*. Austin: University of Texas Press, 2015.

Schatz, Thomas. *Boom and Bust: The American Cinema in the 1940s*. History of the American Cinema 6. New York: Scribner's, 1997.

Schmidt, Ronald J. *This Is the City: Making Model Citizens in Los Angeles*. Minneapolis: University of Minnesota Press, 2005.

Schrader, Stuart. *Badges without Borders: How Global Counterinsurgency Transformed American Policing*. Berkeley: University of California Press, 2019.

Seo, Sarah A. *Policing the Open Road: How Cars Transformed American Freedom*. Cambridge, MA: Harvard University Press, 2019.

Shagawat, Robert. "Early Electronic Television." Early Television Foundation and Museum, 2011. Accessed June 11, 2014. http://www.earlytelevision.org/tv_recordings_the_origins.html.

Sharrett, Christopher. "Jack Webb and the Vagaries of Right-Wing TV Entertainment." *Cinema Journal* 51, no. 4 (2012): 165–171.

Skutch, Ira, ed. *The Days of Live: Television's Golden Age as Seen by 21 Directors Guild of America Members*. Lanham, MD: Scarecrow, 1998.

Smith, Judith E. *Visions of Belonging: Family Stories, Popular Culture, and Postwar Democracy, 1940–1960*. New York: Columbia University Press, 2004.

Smulyan, Susan. *Selling Radio: The Commercialization of American Broadcasting 1920–1934*. Washington, DC: Smithsonian Institution Press, 1996.

Spelling, Aaron, and Jefferson Graham. *Aaron Spelling: A Prime-Time Life*. New York: St. Martin's Press, 2002.

Spigel, Lynn. *Make Room for TV: Television and the Family Ideal in Postwar America*. Chicago: University of Chicago Press, 1992.

Staiger, Janet, and Sabine Hake, eds. *Convergence, Media, History*. New York: Routledge, 2009.

Steenberg, Lindsay, and Yvonne Tasker. "'Pledge Allegiance': Gendered Surveillance, Crime Television, and 'Homeland.'" *Cinema Journal* 54, no. 4 (2015): 132–138.

Sterne, Jonathan. *The Audible Past: Cultural Origins of Sound Reproduction*. Durham, NC: Duke University Press, 2003.

Stoever, Jennifer Lynn. *The Sonic Color Line: Race and the Cultural Politics of Listening*. New York: New York University Press, 2016.

Straw, Will. "Documentary Realism and the Postwar Left." In *"Un-American" Hollywood: Politics and Film in the Blacklist Era*, edited by Frank Krutnik, 130–141. New Brunswick, NJ: Rutgers University Press, 2007.

Strock, Herbert L. *Picture Perfect*. Filmmakers Series 80. Lanham, MD: Scarecrow, 2000.

Sturcken, Frank. *Live Television: The Golden Age of 1946–1958 in New York*. Jefferson, NC: McFarland, 1990.

Tasker, Yvonne. "Television Crime Drama and Homeland Security: From 'Law & Order' to 'Terror TV.'" *Cinema Journal* 51, no. 4 (2012): 44–65.

Torres, Sasha. *Black, White, and in Color: Television and Black Civil Rights*. Princeton, NJ: Princeton University Press, 2003.

Turner, Fred. "The Family of Man and the Politics of Attention in Cold War America." *Public Culture* 24, no. 1 (January 2012): 55–84.

Varni, Charles Anthony. "Images of Police Work and Mass Media Propaganda: The Case of 'Dragnet.'" PhD diss., Washington State University, 1974. ProQuest.

Verma, Neil. *Theater of the Mind: Imagination, Aesthetics, and American Radio Drama*. Chicago: University of Chicago Press, 2012.

Webb, Jack. *The Badge: True and Terrifying Crime Stories That Could Not Be Presented on TV*. Englewood Cliffs, NJ: Prentice-Hall, 1958.

Webster, James G. *Ratings Analysis: The Theory and Practice of Audience Research*. 2nd ed. LEA's Communication Series. Mahwah, NJ: Lawrence Erlbaum, 2000.

Westbrook, Robert. *Why We Fought: Forging American Obligations in World War II*. Washington, DC: Smithsonian Institution Press, 2004.

Whitfield, Stephen J. *The Culture of the Cold War*. 2nd ed. Baltimore, MD: Johns Hopkins University Press, 1996.

Williams, Linda. *On The Wire*. Durham, NC: Duke University Press, 2014.

Wilson, Christopher P. *Cop Knowledge: Police Power and Cultural Narrative in Twentieth-Century America*. Chicago: University of Chicago Press, 2000.

Worden, Robert E., and Sarah J. McLean. *Mirage of Police Reform: Procedural Justice and Police Legitimacy*. Oakland: University of California Press, 2017.

Index

A page number followed by f denotes an illustration.

www.ingramcontent.com/pod-product-compliance
Lightning Source LLC
LaVergne TN
LVHW100155011026
848888LV00016B/74
* 9 7 8 1 4 7 7 3 2 5 3 9 1 *